Critical Essays on Hawthorne's Short Stories

Critical Essays on Hawthorne's Short Stories

Albert J. von Frank

G. K. Hall & Co. • Boston, Massachusetts

PS
1888
V65
1991

Copyright 1991 by Albert J. von Frank
All rights reserved.

First published 1990.
10 9 8 7 6 5 4 3 2 1

Library of Congress Cataloging-in-Publication Data

von Frank, Albert J.
   Critical essays on Hawthorne's short stories / Albert J. von
Frank.
      p.   cm.—(Critical essays on American literature)
   Includes bibliographical references.
   ISBN 0-8161-1843-4
   1. Hawthorne, Nathaniel, 1804–1864—Criticism and inter-
pretation.
   2. Short story.   I. Title.   II. Series.
   PS1888.V65 1991
   813'.3—dc20   90-39088
                                                 CIP

The paper used in this publication meets the minimum requirements of American National Standard for Information Sciences—
Permanence of Paper for Printed Library Materials, ANSI Z39.48-
1984. ∞ ™

Printed and bound in the United States of America

CRITICAL ESSAYS ON AMERICAN LITERATURE

This series seeks to anthologize the most important criticism on a wide variety of topics and writers in American literature. Our readers will find in various volumes not only a generous selection of reprinted articles and reviews but also original essays, bibliographies, manuscript sections, and other materials brought to public attention for the first time. *Critical Essays on Hawthorne's Short Stories* provides a valuable new resource for the study of one of the most important American authors. It contains both a sizable gathering of early reviews and a broad selection of more modern scholarship as well. Among the authors of reprinted reviews are a number of Hawthorne's contemporaries, including Henry Wadsworth Longfellow, Edgar Allan Poe, Margaret Fuller, Herman Melville, and Henry James. There are articles by Q. D. Leavis, Frederick Crews, John F. Sears, Judith Fetterley, and Sharon Cameron. In addition to a substantial introduction by Albert von Frank, there are also three original essays commissioned specifically for publication in this volume—new studies by Teresa Toulouse, Jerome Loving, and Allan Lloyd-Smith. We are confident that this book will make a permanent and significant contribution to the study of American literature.

James Nagel, GENERAL EDITOR

Northeastern University

For my wife, Jane

CONTENTS

INTRODUCTION

The career of Nathaniel Hawthorne divides neatly at 1850 when he turned abruptly from the writing of short fiction to the composition of book-length romances, beginning with his masterpiece, *The Scarlet Letter*. Apart from the early *Fanshawe*, which Hawthorne came to regard as a failure, his work for a quarter of a century was exclusively in the forms of the short story and the sketch. His production during this period was by no means the work of an apprentice preparing for greater things to come; had the late romances never appeared, the tales and sketches he wrote between 1825 and 1850 would by themselves have secured a lasting reputation for their author. Finished and autonomous works of art, they include some of the very finest examples of the genre ever composed.

Hawthorne was born in Salem, Massachusetts, on the fourth of July, 1804, into the sixth generation of his family in America.[1] His earliest New England ancestors lived, to the writer's well-informed imagination, as persecuting Puritans, pious, strong-willed, larger-than-life figures of overbearing cruelty and superstitious intolerance. William Hathorne, scourge of the early Quakers, and his son John, judge of the Salem witchcraft trials, implicated the family in the moral history of New England. Later generations took to the sea and played smaller roles in the affairs of Massachusetts, giving rise to Hawthorne's private myth of familial decline: his grandfather was a privateer during the Revolution, his father the captain of a merchant ship. The death of Hawthorne's father in 1808 left the family financially and emotionally dependent on the Mannings, the family of Hawthorne's mother, Elizabeth.

Much of Hawthorne's boyhood was spent in the company of the Manning aunts and uncles, who supervised his summer recreation at Sebago Lake near Raymond, Maine, gave him part-time employment in the family-owned stagecoach line, and paid for his education at Bowdoin College. His years at college (1821–25) would have prepared him about equally well for any of the standard professions—the ministry, medicine, or the law—and Hawthorne considered each

1

carefully before rejecting it. Since the age of twelve, when an injury to his foot curtailed his physical activities, he had been an avid reader of imaginative literature.[2] Thus as a youth he discovered the attractions of allegory in Spenser and Bunyan, of historical fiction in Scott's Waverley novels, and of urbane and witty observation in the essays of Addison, Steele, and Johnson.[3] Knowing full well that authorship would scarcely provide a means of support, but lacking interest in any other way of life, Hawthorne, after graduating from college, returned to his mother's house in Salem and began to write.

His short novel *Fanshawe*, published at his own expense in 1828, drew on his experience at Bowdoin; sentimental and humorous by turns, the work was trivial and unsophisticated. In later years, Hawthorne was glad that it had been published anonymously. Much of the short fiction that he wrote during these first years after college has not survived; he seems to have burned a good bit of it, either because he was dissatisfied with its quality, or because he failed to interest a publisher in bringing it out. "The Devil in Manuscript," which depicts a similar situation, is generally held to be autobiographical.

Much of Hawthorne's difficulty at this time was the result of a lack of publishing outlets. In these preindustrial days before large publishing houses commanded efficient systems of printing and distributing books, established genres such as novels and poetry might, with luck, encounter a small but respectable commercial success; no one, however, seemed willing to risk money on collections of short stories. Washington Irving, whose thematically organized collection of tales and familiar essays, *The Sketch-Book* (1818–19), proved popular on both sides of the Atlantic, was no doubt an inspiration to Hawthorne, who planned—and was forced to abandon—several such collections of his own. *Seven Tales of My Native Land*, *Provincial Tales*, and *The Story-Teller* were successively disintegrated, their contents destroyed or published piecemeal.[4] During the early years of Hawthorne's career, the few literary magazines that carried fiction tended to reprint the work of British writers, since in the absence of an international copyright, American editors could take what they wanted without paying royalties to the authors. Hawthorne was left, at first, to publish his work in newspapers of very modest circulation; indeed, his first published story, "The Battle Omen," appeared— anonymously—in his home town Salem *Gazette*.

In the late 1820s, gift books, or annuals, took root in America after first proving successful in England. These were books, brought out each October for the Christmas trade, made up of poems, short stories, essays, and—a main point with purchasers—several elegant steel engravings, all handsomely bound in gilt-decorated imitation leather. In America the great purveyor of these very popular items was Samuel G. Goodrich, whose *Token* was unquestionably the most successful. Throughout the decade of the thirties—the high-water mark of the vogue of the gift book—Hawthorne was the most prolific contributor of short fiction to the *Token*. "Sights from a Steeple" and "The Haunted Quack" were his first contributions, followed by such well-known works as "My Kinsman, Major Molineux," "Roger Malvin's Burial," "The Gentle Boy," "Alice Doane's Appeal," "The May-Pole of Merry Mount," "The Minister's Black Veil," "The Great Carbuncle," and "Endicott and the Red Cross." Probably at Hawthorne's own insistence, these contributions did not carry his name. Instead, they were sometimes listed in the table of contents as "by the Author of 'The Gentle Boy,' " or "by the Author of 'Sights from a Steeple' "; more commonly, no indication of authorship was given at all. Since the *Token* might carry as many as eight contributions from Hawthorne, it was undoubtedly convenient to Goodrich that their authorship be concealed.

Hawthorne's connection with the *Token* brought him little money and, of course, no reputation.[5] Magazine reviews of the successive volumes did, however, contain some heartening praise for his stories, which perhaps emboldened him to consider a plan, finally, to collect—and acknowledge—his fugitive work.[6] *Twice-told Tales*, consisting of eighteen previously published tales and sketches, appeared in 1837—but only after Horatio Bridge, a friend and college classmate, agreed to indemnify the publisher against any potential losses. This agreement, which the publisher required, was entered into without Hawthorne's knowledge.

Twice-told Tales, the work after all of an unknown writer, did not sell particularly well at first,[7] but it brought Hawthorne's name before the public—mainly by means of a few encouraging reviews. Perhaps the most important of these was one that Hawthorne himself solicited from another Bowdoin acquaintance, Henry Wadsworth Longfellow, by then a Harvard professor and an established poet. Longfellow's essay, published in the influential *North American Review*, largely set the terms and tone of future discussion of Hawthorne's work.[8] To Longfellow, Hawthorne's writing seemed proof that even in this dull and prosaic nineteenth-century America, "the heaven of poetry and romance still lies around us and within us." He remarks, as others would, on the beauty and crystal clarity of Hawthorne's prose style and on its tones of "quiet humor," crossed now and then by "a shade of sadness." Pleased that the work bore the stamp of a national (that is to say, a New England) character, Longfellow would conclude that it was the product of a man of genius. Such a review at any later date might well have been the making of Hawthorne's career; however, coming as it did in 1837, the year of an unprecedentedly severe financial panic that depressed the book market and hurt all American authors, it served at best to make him, as Poe would shortly point out, a well-thought-of, though still largely unread, writer of fiction.

Poe's commentary on the expanded edition of 1842 was equally cordial, connecting Hawthorne's work with Irving's through the shared qualities of "repose" and purity of prose style, but insisting that Hawthorne was a writer of marked originality and force, the possessor of a "truly imaginative intellect."[9] Poe's misgivings surfaced only later, in his influential review of *Mosses from an Old Manse*, in which he laid out his objections to Hawthorne's allegories and his Transcendentalism, and ended by denying that Hawthorne was original at all.[10] He implied that the German romantic writer Tieck was a source for much in Hawthorne.[11]

Toward the end of the decade, with the *Token* in eclipse and relations with Goodrich strained, Hawthorne turned by invitation to the recently established *Democratic Review* as an outlet for his work. *The United States Magazine and Democratic Review*, as it was formally entitled, was the brainchild of the young, energetic John L. O'Sullivan, a devoted Democrat and staunch literary nationalist now mainly known as the author of the phrase "manifest destiny." The journal's advertised rates of pay—three to five dollars a page—attracted contributions from nearly all the best known writers of the day, including the New Yorkers William Cullen Bryant, James Kirke Paulding, and the young Walter Whitman, as well as the Massachusetts poets Longfellow, Lowell, and Whittier. Payments for contributions to the *Democratic Review* were long in coming to all these writers; nevertheless, other advantages of publication accrued to Hawthorne, who had not before had much to do with the New York literary scene. He became, for example, a prime beneficiary in the literary nationalist crusade centering in O'Sullivan and Evert Duyckinck, both of whom were later to render the author a variety of literary and political favors.

Hawthorne's standing with the Democratic party was strengthened by his connection with O'Sullivan, and particularly by his contribution to the *Democratic Review* of a memorial essay on Congressman Jonathan Cilley, a Democratic hero and personal friend of Hawthorne's who had recently been killed in a duel. Hawthorne had been an enthusiastic supporter of Andrew Jackson, but his political involvements were superficial, traceable in virtually every instance to personal friendships; still, these friendships resulted in various government jobs when he most needed a steady income.

The need for such an income was evident by the fall of 1838, when Hawthorne met and fell in love with Sophia Peabody. By the following January he was employed, at an annual salary of $1,500, as measurer of coal and salt at the Boston Custom House. Having just completed the four connected "Legends of the Province House,"

published in the *Democratic Review*,[12] his literary productivity during
this period fell off, as it would later when he worked at the Custom
House in Salem. Hawthorne labored for two years on the wharves
of Boston, hoping to save enough money to support a wife. In 1841,
when he quit, he invested $1,000 in the transcendentalist commune,
Brook Farm, where he hoped to make a home for himself and Sophia.
But Hawthorne, no transcendentalist, found farming and philosophy
equally uncongenial; he first shifted his status from worker to boarder,
and ended by suing for the return of his money.

He and Sophia were married on 9 July 1842 and immediately
moved into the "Old Manse," the house of the recently deceased
Ezra Ripley of Concord, the very house in which Emerson had shortly
before written *Nature*. Margaret Fuller wrote to Sophia: "If ever I
saw a man who combined delicate tenderness to understand the heart
of a woman, with quiet depth and manliness enough to satisfy her,
it is Mr. Hawthorne."[13] The life they lived there, hard by the Concord
River and the battle bridge, was quiet and extremely happy. Never
very sociable or outgoing, Hawthorne got to know Emerson and
Thoreau and Alcott and Channing,[14] but still preferred the society
of his wife, the quiet of the study, and a renewed round of writing.
Dependent now on his pen for a living, Hawthorne wrote prolifically.
From January 1839 to December 1842—while making the acquaintance of coal and salt in Boston and manure in West Roxbury—
Hawthorne had written only a slim volume of historical essays for
children, *Grandfather's Chair* (1841), and two meager sketches, "John
Inglefield's Thanksgiving" and "A Virtuoso's Collection," both of
which were included in the expanded two-volume edition of *Twice-
told Tales* in 1842. In 1843 and 1844, however (during which time
his daughter Una was born), he wrote and published twenty pieces,
twelve of which appeared in the *Democratic Review*. This was to be
Hawthorne's last sustained burst of creativity as a writer of short
fiction.

In *Mosses from an Old Manse* (1846), he gathered seventeen of
these tales and sketches,[15] and added five earlier ones, including
"Roger Malvin's Burial" and "Young Goodman Brown," which had
been previously overlooked in old issues of the *Token*. It is curious
and fascinating that for each of his collections after the first—that
is, those published in 1842, 1846, and 1851—he could find, and
almost grudgingly insert, some neglected masterpiece, as if he had
been holding it in reserve—or, perhaps, as if he could not discriminate
his excellent work from his writings of average quality.

Hawthorne's preface to *Mosses* was a subtle, pastoral retrospective
survey of life at the Old Manse, for by the time the book was
published, Hawthorne was again living in his mother's house in Salem,
trying, as ever, to economize.[16] His job at the Custom House—a

political appointment, the fruit of elaborate interventions—began that April, just two months before the birth of his second child, Julian. The "Custom-House" preface to *The Scarlet Letter* indicates how preoccupying his routine work as Surveyor was, and how difficult it had become to write. In fact, Hawthorne was to compose only five more short stories, beginning with "Ethan Brand" (possibly the remnant of a longer work) and "Main Street" (actually a sketch)—the first rejected, the second accepted, by Elizabeth Peabody, Hawthorne's sister-in-law, for her distinguished but short-lived periodical, *Aesthetic Papers* (1849).[17]

Hawthorne's abandonment of the short form in favor of booklength romances was the effect of various circumstances, extending even to the election of President Zachary Taylor. Taylor's Whig administration had no room for a Democratic Surveyor in Salem, and protests—of which there were many—were ineffectual in saving Hawthorne's job. Then, just two months after being ousted from the Custom House, his mother died. Hawthorne reacted, as he often did to emotionally shattering experiences, by shutting himself up in the study and writing "immensely."[18] Having for some time thought vaguely of yet another collection of tales, he set about adding to his meager stock of new material a story elaborated from an incident in "Endicott and the Red Cross" involving a woman condemned to wear a badge of sin and guilt. The story grew under his hands until (as his new publisher, James T. Fields, was the first to see) it had crowded out the other tales and become a book in itself.

This crowding out proved to be emblematic of a significant turn in Hawthorne's career. The critical and commercial success of *The Scarlet Letter*, the money and the fame that it brought, led him very quickly to the conclusion that he could no longer "afford" to write short stories.[19] Mainly to take advantage of his new found popularity and the aggressiveness of his new publishers, he gathered what uncollected tales remained (including a twenty-year-old story entitled "My Kinsman, Major Molineux") in *The Snow-Image* (1851).

Among the other circumstances that prompted Hawthorne to abandon the short form were the rapidly changing conditions of the publishing world. The period of his activity as a writer of tales and sketches, 1825–50, was also the period in which publishing submitted to the industrial revolution—the period in which the full capacities of machine-press methods of production, of distribution of books by rail, and of systematic advertising were all realized. By the end of this period and no earlier, the modern system of commercial publishing was in place, and the best-seller, in the familiar sense of that term, was born. *The Scarlet Letter* was the first of Hawthorne's books to fall into the hands of competent modern publishers, and if the result fell somewhat short of bestsellerdom, it was gratifying and surprising enough to the author to alter the way he wrote from that point on. Within two years, Harriet Beecher Stowe's *Uncle Tom's Cabin* would show what the new methods could do—would indeed virtually define the best-seller—and would establish the novel as the preeminent economic unit for writers of fiction. It was not Hawthorne alone who was turning away from short stories, nor was his decision an altogether private or personal one.

The same forces that halted Hawthorne's production of short stories—at bottom, the forces of money and prestige—also conspired to throw the preceding quarter-century of his production into a sort of critical eclipse. Apart from *Mosses*, which was belatedly discovered by Melville (at a time when everyone else was talking about *The Scarlet Letter*), Hawthorne's short fiction seemed to elicit less and less attention as it was progressively overshadowed by his romances. The high esteem in which the romances were held did not, by and large, seem to make the tales more interesting, and Hawthorne's reputation—which had practically been founded on *The Scarlet Letter*—became permanently attached, for purposes of general discussion, to what now seemed the work of his maturity: the four major romances.

The tales were of course known, and even occasionally commented upon, by readers of the middle and end of the century, but they seemed somehow screened off from serious critical attention by an aesthetic derived from, or reinforced by, novel reading. A case in point is the prejudice against "allegory," as it was loosely conceived. Poe had the honor of first denouncing its effect on Hawthorne's writings, but by the time Henry James seconded the opinion, it had virtually become a national prejudice. Hawthorne's best efforts, opined Henry Tuckerman in 1870, "are those in which the human predominates. Ingenuity and moral significancy are finely displayed, it is true, in his allegories; but sometimes they are coldly fanciful, and do not win the sympathies as in those instances where the play of the heart relieves the dim workings of the abstract and the supernatural."[20] Melville himself, a lover of the allegories, called attention to Hawthorne's two moods, the light and the dark, and manfully defended the unfashionably dark, naysaying Calvinist temper. But Hawthorne was closer to the public mind when he saw that inveterate element as a fault and tried to work against it, as he did in certain of his most popular sketches and in the equally popular autobiographical prefaces.

In the absence of a strong critical establishment, late-nineteenth-century opinion tended to follow the lead of biographers such as George Parsons Lathrop (Hawthorne's son-in-law) and Henry James (who followed Lathrop) in assigning the tales to a period of virtually pathologic social isolation in Hawthorne's life.[21] James chose to emphasize the cultural rather than the personal or psychological implications of this point in his discussion of the young Hawthorne's provincialism, which James saw as an effect of living in a primitive, culturally unfurnished New England. It was hard to make the same point about the later Hawthorne, who in addition to being an internationally celebrated writer, was the personal friend of an American President (Franklin Pierce) and—yet more decisively in James's view— a European tourist. But it was easy to see the young Hawthorne, the unknown writer, as a romantic solipsist by default, spinning stories, in morbid reclusion, out of a subtle but unstocked intelligence, preferring allegories only because he did not know how the world worked.

The effect of the myth of Hawthorne's brooding isolation on general critical opinion was all but determinative. Typical of the post-Jamesian commentary are the remarks of Henry A. Beers in 1895: "The 'Twice-Told Tales,' " he wrote, "are the work of a recluse, who makes guesses at life from a knowledge of his own heart, acquired by a habit of introspection, but who has had little contact with men. Many of [the tales] were shadowy, and others were morbid and unwholesome."[22] In 1912 William B. Cairns bracketed Hawthorne with Longfellow and Holmes among the "Miscellaneous New England Writers" in his *History of American Literature*. His sparse commentary includes an objection to Hawthorne's penchant for placing his characters "in some peculiar situation with reference to their fellow men, or to moral problems," though he has a good word (following Poe) for the writer's "suggestiveness" and instances the falling of the rose leaves in "The May-Pole of Merry Mount."[23] To Fred Lewis Pattee, the short story in Hawthorne's hands was "pale and unreal . . . , unworldly even to ghostliness, a weird growth of the darkness." Pattee's discussion, written in the early 1920s, is emphatically guided by critical observations contained in eighty-year-old reviews by Poe and Longfellow, and is contextualized by frequent reference both to Hawthorne's "brooding years of solitude" and to the oddity of his family situation, which seems to him "like a fragment from Mrs. Wilkins-Freeman's studies in New England abnormality." The concluding praise for Hawthorne's contribution to the development of the American short story (he credits Hawthorne with legitimizing the genre) seems disproportionate, if not illogically related, to his emphasis on eccentricity.[24]

The standard literary histories were remarkably slow in coming to terms with Hawthorne's short fiction. In 1936 Percy Boynton could be openly abusive, rejecting Hawthorne's "use of history, his resort to fantasy, his weakness for allegory, his unreality, his coldness or lack of passion, his faint yet unspontaneous humor, his rather labored forcing of the pen in the cross-section surveys of human experience that pushes him back on vague generalization, and the resultant thinness of the tales and sketches." The persistent influence of James's devastatingly misapplied critique is evident in Boynton's belief that before 1846 "Hawthorne's work was, of a truth, comparable to the embroidery of the samplers of those days, those pathetic marvels of needlework wrought with who knows what tears and travail by the little girls."[25] Not even F. O. Matthiessen, whose *American Renaissance* (1941) made strong claims for Hawthorne's centrality, was prepared in such a critical climate to do much with the tales: his Hawthorne, and thus the canonical Hawthorne, was by and large the author of the romances written in the 1850s.

The modern recovery of the younger Hawthorne—and therefore of the tales—dates to 1948 and the appearance of Randall Stewart's biography, which met head-on the myth of Hawthorne's morbid solitude and largely dispelled it. This setting straight of the record effectively turned biographical "facts" into literary problems.[26] It also made room for the work of appreciative critics such as Malcolm Cowley, Marius Bewley, and perhaps most influential of all, Q. D. Leavis, whose "Hawthorne as Poet" in 1951 emphatically shifted attention from the artist to the art and inspired an enormously productive reexamination of Hawthorne's work as an artist and historian in the tales.[27] An almost equally influential essay by Donald A. Ringe, "Hawthorne's Psychology of the Head and Heart," gave critics of the fifties a much-needed vocabulary with which to begin discussion of Hawthorne's themes. Working from a popular version of the faculty psychology of the period, Ringe focused renewed attention on Hawthorne's strengths—long recognized in the romances—as a psychologist and moral diagnostician in the tales.[28] In effect, the rehabilitated younger Hawthorne had arisen from the couch and changed places with the analyst. It remained for Frederick Crews in *The Sins of the Fathers: Hawthorne's Psychological Themes* (1966) to develop in Freudian terms the classic acknowledgment by Henry James of Hawthorne's mastery of "the deeper psychology."[29]

The 1950s produced the first book-length critical treatments: Richard Harter Fogle's *Hawthorne's Fiction: The Light and the Dark* (1952; revised in 1964), Hyatt Waggoner's *Hawthorne: A Critical Study* (1955; revised in 1963), and Roy R. Male's *Hawthorne's Tragic Vision* (1957). Each includes an examination of the tales from a New Critical or formalist perspective, and each continues to be of value to the student of Hawthorne, particularly for their attention to ambiguity and irony.[30]

During the sixties, new approaches to Hawthorne's work seemed frequently to center on thematic issues. Among the more notable of these studies, Millicent Bell's *Hawthorne's View of the Artist* (1962) opened a subject—Hawthorne's aesthetic theories—that had received surprisingly little prior treatment.[31] Crews's Freudian study appeared in the context of a general interest in dreams and dream imagery as a key to Hawthorne's aesthetic.[32] Laughter in the tales has been another fruitful theme.[33]

Critics have been concerned as well with gender issues, noticing that while Hawthorne's portrayal of women is often controlled by cultural and archetypal conceptions (the division between "light" and "dark" types, for example), he manages more often and more convincingly than most of his male contemporaries to depict strong female characters. In life his relations with women were strikingly rich and complex—far more so, certainly, than can be indicated here. He had, for example, deep and lasting emotional ties to a family consisting of a passive mother and two lively sisters; he married and idolized a highly intelligent yet also quite passive woman of delicate health; he was familiarly acquainted, on the other hand, with Margaret Fuller and Elizabeth Peabody, perhaps the two most forceful female personalities of the age, to whom he reacted strongly yet ambivalently; and, finally and most notoriously, he came to resent the "damned mob of scribbling women," the writers of the sentimental best-sellers of the 1850s, because he felt that women (and his daughter in particular) ought not to be authors, ought not to be public figures. Gloria C. Erlich traces many of these and other related issues in a well-researched biographical study, *Family Themes and Hawthorne's Fiction: The Tenacious Web* (New Brunswick, N.J.: Rutgers University Press, 1984).[34]

Much of what has been written about Hawthorne as an interpreter of New England history has of course focused on *The Scarlet Letter* and, rather less frequently, on *The House of the Seven Gables.* But critics, keeping pace with the rising academic interest in colonial history, have discovered that the tales constitute an equally rewarding, and certainly a more extensive, exploration of the meaning of America's Puritan past. In the 1930s, at a time when Perry Miller was beginning to rescue the first hundred and fifty years of New England history from the antiquarians, what little interest there was in Hawthorne's Puritan settings revolved around witchcraft.[35] By the time of Miller's death in 1963, however, critics had a much better grasp of the subject and could begin to make sense of Hawthorne's historicity.[36] A number of important essays on Hawthorne and the American Revolution, most of them concerned with "My Kinsman, Major Molineux," appeared at the time of the Bicentennial to remind us that Hawthorne's "sense of the past" was not confined to the seventeenth century.[37]

This kind of investigation of Hawthorne's moral and imaginative uses of history, urged at very the beginning of the Hawthorne revival by Q. D. Leavis, has generally seemed more rewarding and profitable than the ahistorical (or antihistorical) approaches associated with poststructuralism.[38] The vitality of the historicist approach has recently been demonstrated in two especially important treatments: Michael Colacurcio's *Province of Piety: Moral History in Hawthorne's Early Tales* (Cambridge: Harvard University Press, 1985), and Frederick Newberry's *Hawthorne's Divided Loyalties: England and America in His Works* (Rutherford, N.J.: Fairleigh Dickinson University Press, 1987). The former, denying that Puritanism was, for Hawthorne, either an inherited and inevitable collection of self-defining myths or a safe haven from contemporary reality, argues in great detail that it was rather a subject that Hawthorne approached with a good deal of intellectual detachment, very much in the spirit of sane historical inquiry.[39] Newberry's study interprets the historical tales as the record—the tragic record—of the loss of such English cultural values as might have sustained a more humane and artistic tradition in America and might at the same time have saved New England from much violence and bigotry.

It remains only to point out that by far the largest body of commentary on Hawthorne's tales consists of the innumerable essays devoted to individual sketches and short stories. The best guide to this literature, though incomplete and in need of updating, is Lea Bertani Vozar Newman's *A Reader's Guide to the Short Stories of Nathaniel Hawthorne* (Boston: G. K. Hall, 1979), which helpfully surveys the criticism relating to each of the stories separately.[40]

Washington State University   ALBERT J. VON FRANK

Notes

1. Many of the early memoirs by Hawthorne's friends and relatives retain considerable biographical value, particularly Horatio Bridge, *Personal Recollections of Nathaniel Hawthorne* (New York: Harper & Bros., 1893), Rose Hawthorne Lathrop, *Memories of Hawthorne* (Boston: Houghton Mifflin, 1897), Julian Hawthorne, *Nathaniel Hawthorne and His Wife*, 2 vols. (Boston: Houghton Mifflin, 1884), and, by the same author, *Hawthorne and His Circle* (New York: Harper & Bros. 1903). See also Randall Stewart, "Recollections of Hawthorne by His Sister, Elizabeth," *American Literature* 16 (1945): 316–31. Long regarded as the standard life, Randall Stewart, *Nathaniel Hawthorne: A Biography* (New Haven: Yale University Press, 1948) has been superseded by the more extensive treatments of Arlin Turner, *Nathaniel Hawthorne: A Biography* (New York: Oxford University Press, 1980), and James R. Mellow, *Nathaniel Hawthorne in His Times* (Boston: Houghton Mifflin, 1980). Vernon Loggins, *The Hawthornes* (New York: Columbia University Press, 1951) is a history of the family.

2. Austin Warren opened up the question of "Hawthorne's Reading" in the *New England Quarterly* 8 (1935): 480–97; Marion L. Kesselring drew on library charge records in compiling her standard work, *Hawthorne's Reading: 1828–1850* (New York: New York Public Library, 1949).

3. Many of the notes and articles written about individual tales analyze their sources. The pioneering effort among source studies is the still-valuable work of

Elizabeth L. Chandler, *A Study of the Sources of the Tales and Romances Written by Nathaniel Hawthorne Before 1853* (George Banta: Manasha, Wisconsin, 1926). Arlin Turner examined "Hawthorne's Literary Borrowings" in *PMLA* 51 (1936): 543–62 and "Hawthorne's Method of Using His Source Material" in *Studies for W. A. Read* (Baton Rouge: Louisiana State University Press, 1940). The influence of Spenser and Bunyan has attracted considerable attention over the years; see Randall Stewart, "Hawthorne and the *Faerie Queene*," *Philological Quarterly* 12 (1933): 196–206; Herbert A. Leibowitz, "Hawthorne and Spenser: Two Sources," *American Literature* 30 (1959): 459–66; Rod Wilson, "Further Spenserian Parallels in Hawthorne," *Nathaniel Hawthorne Journal* 2 (1972): 195–201; Charles E. Mounts, "Hawthorne's Echoes of Spenser and Milton," *Nathaniel Hawthorne Journal* 3 (1973): 162–71; Jane Chambers, "Two Legends of Temperance: Spenser's and Hawthorne's," *ESQ: A Journal of the American Renaissance* 20 (1974): 275–79; Buford Jones, "Hawthorne and Spenser: From Allusion to Allegory," *Nathaniel Hawthorne Journal* 5 (1975): 71–90; Raymond Himelick, "Hawthorne, Spenser, and Christian Humanism," *ESQ: A Journal of the American Renaissance* 21 (1975): 21–28; James Duban, Hawthorne's Debt to Edmund Spenser and Charles Chauncy in 'The Gentle Boy,' " *Nathaniel Hawthorne Journal* 6 (1976): 189–95; Robert C. Roulston, "Hawthorne's Use of Bunyan's Symbols in 'The Celestial Railroad,' " *Kentucky Philological Association Bulletin* 1 (1975): 17–24; W. Stacy Johnson, "Hawthorne and The Pilgrim's Progress," *Journal of English and Germanic Philology* 50 (1951): 156–66; Robert Stanton, "Hawthorne, Bunyan and the American Romances," *PMLA* 71 (1956): 155–65; and David E. Smith, "Bunyan and Hawthorne," in *John Bunyan in America* (Bloomington: University of Indiana Press, 1966), pp. 45–89. Also useful on this topic is John O. Rees, Jr., "Hawthorne's Concept of Allegory: A Reconsideration," *Philological Quarterly* 54 (1975): 495–510.

Other English influences are glanced at by David Cody, "Invited Guests at Hawthorne's 'Christmas Banquet': Sir Thomas Browne and Jeremy Taylor," *Modern Language Notes* 11 (1980–81): 17–26; Frederick Asals, "Jeremy Taylor and Hawthorne's Early Tales," *American Transcendental Quarterly* 14 (1972): 15–23; B. Bernard Cohen, "*Paradise Lost* and 'Young Goodman Brown,' " *Essex Institute Historical Collections* 94 (1958): 282–96; Sheldon W. Liebman, "Hawthorne's *Comus*: A Miltonic Source for 'The Maypole of Merrymount,' " *Nineteenth-Century Fiction* 27 (1972): 345–51; Robert H. Deming, "The Use of the Past: Herrick and Hawthorne," *Journal of Popular Culture* 2 (1968): 278–91; Alice L. Cooke, "Some Evidence of Hawthorne's Indebtedness to Swift," *University of Texas Studies in English* 18 (1938): 140–62; Frank Davidson, "Hawthorne's Use of Patterns from *The Rambler*," *Modern Language Notes* 63 (1948): 545–58; Marvin Fisher, "The Pattern of Conservatism in Johnson's *Rasselas* and Hawthorne's Tales," *Journal of the History of Ideas* 19 (1958): 173–96; Mark Evan Johnston, "The Recording Narrator: *The Spectator, The Rambler*, and Hawthorne's Shorter Fiction," *Essays in Arts and Sciences* 6 (1977): 20–46; Richard Harter Fogle, "Hawthorne's Sketches and the English Romantics," in *Towards a New American Literary History*, ed. Louis J. Budd et al. (Durham, N.C.: Duke University Press, 1980), 129–39; and Fogle, "Art and Illusion: Coleridgean Assumptions in Hawthorne's Tales and Sketches," in *Ruined Eden of the Present: Hawthorne, Melville, and Poe*, ed. G.R. Thompson and Virgil Lokke (West Lafayette, Ind.: Purdue University Press, 1981), pp. 109–27.

4. See Nelson F. Adkins, "The Early Projected Works of Nathaniel Hawthorne," *Papers of the Bibliographical Society of America* 39 (1945): 119–55, (excerpted below), and Richard P. Adams, "Hawthorne's Provincial Tales," *New England Quarterly* 30 (1957): 39–57. Of the three projected collections, the last, "The Story-Teller," has attracted sustained interest, both because more information is available about it and because it seems to have been, with its elaborate framing device, a more ambitious and artistically significant effort; see Alfred Weber, *Die Entwicklung der Rahmener-*

zählungen Nathaniel Hawthornes: "The Story Teller" und andere frühe Werke (Berlin: Erich Schmidt, 1973).

5. See Seymour L. Gross, "Hawthorne's Income from *The Token*," *Studies in Bibliography* 8 (1956): 236–38, and Wayne Allen Jones, "The Hawthorne-Goodrich Relationship and a New Estimate of Hawthorne's Income from *The Token*," *Nathaniel Hawthorne Journal* 5 (1975): 91–140. Hawthorne's connection with Goodrich also resulted in Hawthorne's editorship of the *American Magazine of Useful and Entertaining Knowledge* in 1836; see Arlin Turner, *Hawthorne as Editor* (Baton Rouge: Louisiana State University, 1941).

6. A number of early reviews may be conveniently consulted in J. Donald Crowley, ed., *Hawthorne: The Critical Heritage* (New York: Barnes & Noble, 1970). The reviews are discussed by Crowley in his introduction and also, more extensively, by Bertha Faust in *Hawthorne's Contemporaneous Reputation* (1939; rpt. New York: Octagon Books, 1968). See also B. Bernard Cohen, ed., *The Recognition of Nathaniel Hawthorne* (Ann Arbor: University of Michigan Press, 1969).

7. See Wayne Allen Jones, "Sometimes Things Just Don't Work Out: Hawthorne's Income from *Twice-told Tales* (1837), and Another 'Good Thing' for Hawthorne," *Nathaniel Hawthorne Journal* 5 (1975): 11–26. The "Historical Commentary" essays by J. Donald Crowley, included in the Tales volumes (9–11) of the *Centenary Edition of the Works of Nathaniel Hawthorne* (Columbus: Ohio State University Press, 1974), are exceptionally full and reliable in giving what information is known about the composition, publication, and reception of the tales. The *Centenary Edition*, edited by Fredson Bowers et al., is standard.

8. *North American Review* 35 (July 1837): 59–73. Jane Tompkins, in *Sensational Designs: The Cultural Work of American Fiction, 1790–1860* (New York: Oxford University Press, 1985), pp. 3–39, sees this review as the beginning of a conspiracy by the male establishment, lasting the better part of a century, to canonize Hawthorne. It is at least true that at a time when women were not permitted the benefits of a college education, Hawthorne's experience at Bowdoin and the relationships he established there were persistently fortunate. But the fact is that Longfellow could and would do little of real value for Hawthorne's standing with the public as a writer; the entrepreneurship of poet-capitalist James T. Fields was far more responsible for permanently fixing Hawthorne's reputation. Richard H. Brodhead's discussion of these matters (*The School of Hawthorne* [New York: Oxford University Press, 1986], esp. ch. 3) is finally more credible than Tompkins's, although neither takes fully into account the different ways in which the tales and the romances have been regarded critically.

9. Poe's review of *Twice-told Tales* (1842) in *Graham's Magazine* 20 (April and May 1842): 254, 298–300, excerpted in this book.

10. "Tale-Writing—Nathaniel Hawthorne," *Godey's Lady's Book* 35 (1847): 252–56, reprinted in this book.

11. The comparison with Tieck had been drawn by several others before Poe, including G. P. R. James and Henry F. Chorley (see Crowley, ed., *Hawthorne: The Critical Heritage*, 95, 101, and 105). The subject of Hawthorne's knowledge of German literature has been examined by several scholars: Alfred H. Marks, "German Romantic Irony in Hawthorne's Tales," *Symposium* 7 (November 1953): 274–305; Percy Matenko, "Tieck, Poe, and Hawthorne," in *Ludwig Tieck and America* (Chapel Hill: University of North Carolina Press, 1954), 71–88; Henry A. Pochmann, *German Culture in America: Philosophical and Literary Influences, 1600–1900* (Madison: University of Wisconsin Press, 1957), 381–88; and Thomas Baginski, "Was Hawthorne a Puritan Tieck? Aspects of Nature Imagery in Hawthorne's Tales and Tieck's Marchen," *Literatur in Wissenschaft und Uterricht* (Kiel, GDR) 18 (1985): 175–91.

12. A number of articles discuss the "Legends" as a unit: Robert H. Fossum,

"Time and the Artist in 'Legends of the Province House,' " *Nineteenth-Century Fiction* 21 (1967): 337–48; Julian Smith, "Hawthorne's Legends of the Province House," *Nineteenth-Century Fiction* 24 (1969): 31–44; Margaret V. Allen, "Imagination and History in Hawthorne's 'Legends of the Province House,' " *American Literature* 43 (1971): 432–37; Jane D. Eberwein, "Temporal Perspective in 'The Legends of the Province House,' " *American Transcendental Quarterly* 14 (1972): 41–45; P. L. Reed, "The Telling Frame of Hawthorne's 'Legends of the Province House,' " *Studies in American Fiction* 4 (1976): 105–11.

13. Quoted in Randall Stewart, *Hawthorne: A Biography* (New Haven: Yale University Press, 1948), 61–62.

14. While it is generally conceded that Hawthorne was not particularly attracted to the transcendental movement (occasionally to the dismay of his more liberal wife), he did himself suggest some affinities in his humorous preface to "Rappaccini's Daughter" (see the Centenary Edition of *Mosses from an Old Manse* [Columbus: Ohio State University Press, 1974], 91–93). The literature bearing on Hawthorne's connection with the movement is surveyed by Joel Myerson in Myerson, ed., *The Transcendentalists: A Review of Research and Criticism* (New York: The Modern Language Association of America, 1984), 328–35. See also Michael Colacurcio, "A Better Mode of Evidence," *Emerson Society Quarterly* 22 (1969): 12–22, and Kermit Vanderbilt, "Hawthorne's Ironic Mode: With Side-Trips into Emerson," *Thalia* 4 (1982): 40–45.

15. Anyone concerned with this period of Hawthorne's career will find a series of essays by John J. McDonald extremely useful: "The Old Manse Period Canon," *Nathaniel Hawthorne Journal* 2 (1972): 13–39; " 'The Old Manse' and Its Mosses: The Inception and Development of *Mosses from an Old Manse*," *Texas Studies in Literature and Language* 16 (1974): 77–108, and "A Guide to Primary Source Materials for the Study of Hawthorne's Old Manse Period," in *Studies in the American Renaissance*, ed. Joel Myerson (Boston: G. K. Hall & Co., 1977), 261–312. See also R. P. Adams, "Hawthorne: The Old Manse Period," *Tulane Studies in English* 8 (1958): 115–51.

16. For discussions of "The Old Manse" essay, see Alfred Weber, "Hawthornes Briefe uber The Old Manse," in *Festschrift fur Walter Hubner*, eds. Dieter Riesner and Helmut Gneuss (Berlin: Schmidt, 1963), 234–38; John C. Willoughby, " 'The Old Manse' Revisited: Some Analogues for Art," *New England Quarterly* 46 (1973): 45–61; Teresa Toulouse, "Spatial Relations in 'The Old Manse,' " *ESQ: A Journal of the American Renaissance* 28 (1982): 154–67; James Walters, " 'The Old Manse': The Pastoral Precinct of Hawthorne's Fiction," *American Transcendental Quarterly* 51 (1983): 195–209, and Frederick Newberry, *Hawthorne's Divided Loyalties: England and America in His Works* (Rutherford, NJ: Fairleigh Dickinson University Press, 1987), ch. 4. Two articles examine the revelations about other Concordians in "The Old Manse" essay, and two relate it to "The Custom House": John S. Martin, "The Other Side of Concord: A Critique of Emerson in Hawthorne's 'The Old Manse,' " *New England Quarterly* 58 (1985): 453–58; G. Thomas Couser, " 'The Old Manse,' *Walden*, and the Hawthorne-Thoreau Relationship," *ESQ: A Journal of the American Renaissance* 21 (1975): 11–20; Roberta F. Weldon, "From 'The Old Manse' to 'The Custom-House': The Growth of the Artist's Mind," *Texas Studies in Language and Literature* 20 (1978): 36–47, and James M. Cox, "The Scarlet Letter: Through the Old Manse and the Custom House," *Virginia Quarterly Review* 51 (1975): 432–47.

17. See Tom Quirk, "Hawthorne's Last Tales and 'The Custom-House,' " *ESQ: A Journal of the American Renaissance* 30 (1984): 220–31.

18. The characterization is Sophia's, from a letter to her mother, quoted in Turner, *Nathaniel Hawthorne: A Biography*, p. 189.

19. Offering his last short story ("Feathertop") to Rufus W. Griswold in 1851, Hawthorne said, "I cannot afford [to sell] it for less than $100, and would not write

another for the same price" (*The Letters, 1843–1853*, ed. Thomas Woodson et al., vol. 16 of *The Centenary Edition of the Works of Nathaniel Hawthorne.* [Columbus: Ohio State University Press, 1985], 518–19).

20. Henry T. Tuckerman, "Nathaniel Hawthorne," *Lippincott's Magazine* 5 (May 1870): 500; reprinted in Crowley, ed., *Hawthorne: The Critical Heritage*, p. 469.

21. George Parsons Lathrop, *A Study of Hawthorne* (Boston: J. R. Osgood, 1876), and Henry James, *Hawthorne* (New York: Macmillan, 1879), excerpted below.

22. *Initial Studies in American Letters* (New York: The Chatauqua Press, 1895), 120.

23. Cairns, *A History of American Literature* (New York: Oxford University Press, 1912), 310–11.

24. Pattee, *The Development of the American Short Story* (New York: Harper & Bros., 1923), 91–114.

25. Boynton, *Literature and American Life* (Boston: Ginn & Co., 1936), 528–29. Appearing very early in the body of Hawthorne commentary is the curious notion that Hawthorne is somehow hermaphroditic. Longfellow alludes to it in his 1837 review of the *Twice-told Tales*, as does Lowell in the *Fable for Critics;* it occurred to many others as well. It was mainly a way of talking about Hawthorne's delicacy of observation and purity of expression, though it was also more complicated than that.

26. See Darrell Abel, "The Theme of Isolation in Hawthorne," *Personalist* 32 (1951): 42–59, 182–90, and D. K. Anderson, "Hawthorne's Crowds," *Nineteenth-Century Fiction* 7 (1952): 39–50.

27. Q. D. Leavis, "Hawthorne as Poet," *Sewanee Review* 59 (1951): 179–205, excerpted in this book.

28. *PMLA* 65 (1950): 366–73; see also Nina Baym, "The Head, the Heart, and the Unpardonable Sin," *New England Quarterly* 40 (1967): 31–47.

29. "The Logic of Compulsion," a particularly brilliant and influential essay on "Roger Malvin's Burial," is excerpted from *The Sins of the Fathers* in this book.

30. See also, among shorter treatments, Robert Allen Durr, "Hawthorne's Ironic Mode," *New England Quarterly* 30 (1957): 486–95.

31. The only notable prior studies of the subject are Roy R. Male, Jr., " 'From the Innermost Germ': The Organic Principle in Hawthorne's Fiction," *Journal of English Literature* 20 (1953): 218–36; Annette K. Baxter, "Independence vs. Isolation: Hawthorne and James on the Problem of the Artist," *Nineteenth-Century Fiction* 10 (1955): 225–31; and Harry Hayden Clark, "Hawthorne's Literary and Aesthetic Doctrines as Embodied in His Tales," *Transactions of the Wisconsin Academy of Sciences, Arts, and Letters* 50 (1961): 251–75. Later discussions include Terence Martin, "The Method of Hawthorne's Tales," in *Hawthorne Centenary Essays*, ed. Harvey Pearce (Columbus: Ohio State University Press, 1964), 7–30; Mary Rohrberger, "Hawthorne's Literary Theory and the Nature of His Short Stories," *Studies in Short Fiction* 3 (1965): 23–30; Rohrberger's *Hawthorne and the Modern Short Story: A Study in Genre* (The Hague: Mouton, 1966); Leo B. Levy, "Hawthorne and the Sublime," *American Literature* 37 (1966): 391–402; R. K. Gupta, "Hawthorne's Treatment of the Artist," *New England Quarterly* 45 (1972): 65–80; Max L. Autrey, "Hawthorne and the Beautiful Impulse," *American Transcendental Quarterly* 14 (1972): 48–54; Harry C. West, "Hawthorne's Magic Circle: The Artist as Magician," *Criticism* 16 (1974): 311–25; Nancy L. Bunge, "Unreliable Artist-Narrators in Hawthorne's Short Stories," *Studies in Short Fiction* 14 (1977): 145–50; Shannon Burns, "Hawthorne's Literary Theory in the Tales," *Nathaniel Hawthorne Journal* 7 (1977): 261–77; Thelma J. Shinn, "A Fearful Power: Hawthorne's Views on Art and the Artist as Expressed in His Sketches and Short Stories," *Nathaniel Hawthorne Journal* 8 (1978): 121–35; and Brian Way, "Art and the Spirit of Anarchy:

A Reading of Hawthorne's Short Stories," *Nathaniel Hawthorne: New Critical Essays* (London: Vision Press, 1982), 11–30.

32. See Ted-Larry Pebworth, " 'The Soul's Instinctive Perception': Dream, Actuality, and Reality in Four Tales from Hawthorne's *Mosses from an Old Manse*," *South Central Bulletin* 23 (1963): 18–23; Joseph C. Pattison, "Point of View in Hawthorne," *PMLA* 82 (1967): 363–69; B. H. Fairchild, "A Technique of Discovery: The Dream Vision in Hawthorne's Fiction," *Essays in Literature* (University of Denver) 1 (1973): 17–28; Jerry A. Herndon, "Hawthorne's Dream Imagery," *American Literature* 46 (1975): 538–45; Nancy Bunge, "Dreams in Hawthorne's Tales," *Nathaniel Hawthorne Journal* 7 (1977): 279–87, and finally and most completely, Rita Gollin, *Nathaniel Hawthorne and the Truth of Dreams* (Baton Rouge: Louisiana State University Press, 1979).

33. Robert Dusenbery, "Hawthorne's Merry Company: The Anatomy of Laughter in the Tales and Short Stories," *PMLA* 82 (1967): 285–88; Mary Allen, "Smiles and Laughter in Hawthorne," *Philological Quarterly* 52 (1973): 119–28, and R. K. Gupta, "Laughter in Hawthorne's Fiction: A Psycho-Literary Approach," *Nathaniel Hawthorne Journal* 8 (1978): 205–17. Closely related are several studies of Hawthorne's sense of humor: William L. Vance, "The Comic Element in Hawthorne's Sketches," *Studies in Romanticism* 3 (1964): 144–60; James G. Janssen, "The 'Dismal Merry-Making' in Hawthorne's Comic Vision," *Studies in American Humor* 1 (1973): 107–17; Samuel I. Bellman, " 'The Joke's on *You!*': Sudden Revelation in Hawthorne," *Nathaniel Hawthorne Journal* 5 (1975): 192–99; and Henning Cohen, "A Comic Mode of the Romantic Imagination," in *Comic Imagination*, ed. Louis Rubin (New York, 1975), 85–99.

34. Among the more recent discussions of these matters, see also Ehrlich, "Deadly Innocence: Hawthorne's Dark Women," *New England Quarterly* 41 (1968): 163–79; Nina Baym, "Hawthorne's Women: The Tyranny of Social Myths," *Centennial Review* 15 (1971): 250–72; Darrell Abel, "Hawthorne and the Strong Division-Lines of Nature," *American Transcendental Quarterly* 14 (1972): 23–31; Allen Flint, "The Saving Grace of Marriage in Hawthorne's Fiction," *ESQ: A Journal of the American Renaissance* 19 (1973): 112–16; Sheldon Leibman, "The Forsaken Maiden in Hawthorne's Stories," *American Transcendental Quarterly* 19 (1973): 13–19; Paul John Eakin, *The New England Girl: Cultural Ideals in Hawthorne, Stowe, Howells and James* (Athens: University of Georgia Press, 1978); Kristin Herzog, "Primitive Strength in Hawthorne's Women," in *Women, Ethnics, and Exotics* (New Brunswick, N.J.: Rutgers University Press, 1984), 3–54; Joyce W. Warren, *The American Narcissus: Individualism and Women in Nineteenth-Century American Fiction* (New Brunswick, N.J.: Rutgers University Press, 1984); and Leland S. Person, Jr., *Aesthetic Headaches: Women and a Masculine Poetics in Poe, Melville, and Hawthorne* (Athens: University of Georgia Press, 1988), Ch. 5. Nina Baym has been the most consistent feminist interpreter of Hawthorne; in addition to the title mentioned above, see her essay "Nathaniel Hawthorne and His Mother: A Biographical Speculation," *American Literature* 54 (1982): 105–15, and *The Shape of Hawthorne's Career* (Ithaca, N.Y.: Cornell University Press, 1976).

35. See, for example, G. Harrison Orians, "New England Witchcraft in Fiction," *American Literature* 2 (1930): 54–71, and Tremaine McDowell, "Nathaniel Hawthorne and the Witches of Colonial Salem," *Notes and Queries* 166 (1934): 152. A somewhat later example is Orians, "Hawthorne and Puritan Punishments," *College English* 13 (1952): 424–32.

36. Robert H. Fossum, "The Shadow of the Past: Hawthorne's Historical Tales," *Claremont Quarterly* 11 (1963): 45–56; Joseph Schwartz, "Three Aspects of Hawthorne's Puritanism," *New England Quarterly* 36 (1963): 192–208; Roy Harvey Pearce, "Romance and the Study of History" in *Hawthorne Centenary Essays*, ed. Pearce (Columbus: Ohio State University Press, 1964); Nelson F. Adkins, "Hawthorne's Democratic New England Puritans," *Emerson Society Quarterly* 44 (1966): 364–67; Johannes

Kjorven, "Hawthorne and the Significance of History," in *America Norvegica: Norwegian Contributions to American Studies* (Philadelphia: University of Pennsylvania Press, 1966), 110–60; Michael Davitt Bell, *Hawthorne and the Historical Romance of New England* (Princeton, N.J.: Princeton University Press, 1971); John E. Becker, *Hawthorne's Historical Allegory* (Port Washington, NY: Kennikat Press, 1971); Priscilla M. Jones, "Hawthorne's Mythic Use of Puritan History," *Cithera* 12 (1972): 59–73, and Paula K. White, "Puritan Theories of History in Hawthorne's Fiction," *Canadian Review of American Studies* 9 (1978): 135–53.

37. See, for example, John P. McWilliams, Jr., " 'Thorough-Going Democrat' and 'Modern Tory': Hawthorne and the Puritan Revolution of 1776," *Studies in Romanticism* 15 (1976): 549–71; Blair Rouse, "Hawthorne and the American Revolution: An Exploration," *Nathaniel Hawthorne Journal* 6 (1976): 17–61; Donald G. Darnell, " 'Visions of Hereditary Rank': The Loyalist in the Fiction of Hawthorne, Cooper, and Frederick," *South Atlantic Bulletin* 42 (1977): 54–45; Peter Shaw, "Hawthorne's Ritual Typology of the American Revolution," *Prospects*, ed. Jack Salzman (New York: Burt Franklin, 1977), 483–98; Celeste Loughman, "Hawthorne's Patriarchs and the American Revolution," *American Transcendental Quarterly* 40 (1978): 335–44, and Michael Kammen, *A Season of Youth: The American Revolution and the Historical Imagination* (New York: Alfred A. Knopf, 1978), ch. 7.

38. It has often been remarked that scholars and critics specializing in early nineteenth-century American literature have been notably resistant to deconstruction and related critical approaches. This has been especially true in Hawthorne scholarship. Among the relatively few critical works informed by such approaches, however, are Kenneth Dauber, *Rediscovering Hawthorne* (Princeton, N.J.: Princeton University Press, 1977) and Edgar Dryden, *Nathaniel Hawthorne: The Poetics of Enchantment* (Ithaca, N.Y.: Cornell University Press, 1977).

39. Colacurcio's book is only the second study wholly devoted to the tales; the first, Neal Frank Doubleday's *Hawthorne's Early Tales, A Critical Study* (Durham, N.C.: Duke University Press, 1972), while much shorter and less speculative, is still useful and informative.

40. For a general overview of writings about Hawthorne, nothing has yet superseded Walter Blair's chapter in *Eight American Authors: A Review of Research and Criticism*, ed. James Woodress (New York: Norton, 1971), 85–128. Work done since 1971 can be traced in the annual volumes of the *Nathaniel Hawthorne Journal* and its successor, the *Hawthorne Society Newsletter*. The Hawthorne chapter in the annual *American Literary Scholarship* evaluates the work it considers but is selective; the listings in the annual *MLA International Bibliography* are generally more complete. Less useful are Buford Jones, *A Checklist of Hawthorne Criticism, 1951–1966* (Hartford: Transcendental Books, 1967), and *Nathaniel Hawthorne: A Reference Bibliography, 1900–1971*, compiled by Beatrice Ricks, Joseph D. Adams, and Jack O. Hazling (Boston: G. K. Hall & Co., 1972). The standard primary bibliography is C. E. Frazer Clark, Jr., *Nathaniel Hawthorne: A Descriptive Bibliography* (Pittsburgh: University of Pittsburgh Press, 1978).

NINETEENTH-CENTURY COMMENT

[Hawthorne's Twice-told Tales]

Henry Wadsworth Longfellow[*]

When a new star rises in the heavens, people gaze after it for a season with the naked eye, and with such telescopes as they may find. In the stream of thought, which flows so peacefully deep and clear, through the pages of this book, we see the bright reflection of a spiritual star, after which men will be fain to gaze "with the naked eye, and with the spy-glasses of criticism." This star is but newly risen; and ere long the observations of numerous star-gazers, perched up on arm-chairs and editors' tables, will inform the world of its magnitude and its place in the heaven of poetry, whether it be in the paw of the Great Bear, or on the forehead of Pegasus, or on the strings of the Lyre, or in the wing of the Eagle. Our own observations are as follows.

To this little work we would say, "Live ever, sweet, sweet book." It comes from the hand of a man of genius. Every thing about it has the freshness of morning and of May. These flowers and green leaves of poetry have not the dust of the highway upon them. They have been gathered fresh from the secret places of a peaceful and gentle heart. There flow deep waters, silent, calm, and cool; and the green trees look into them, and "God's blue heaven." The book, though in prose, is written nevertheless by a poet. He looks upon all things in the spirit of love, and with lively sympathies; for to him external form is but the representation of internal being, all things having a life, an end and aim. The true poet is a friendly man. He takes to his arms even cold and inanimate things, and rejoices in his heart, as did St. Bernard of old, when he kissed his Bride of Snow. To his eye all things are beautiful and holy; all are objects of feeling and of song, from the great hierarchy of the silent, saint-like stars, that rule the night, down to the little flowers which are "stars in the firmament of the earth." . . .

[*] Reprinted from *North American Review* 45 (July 1837): 59–73.

There are some honest people into whose hearts "Nature cannot find the way." They have no imagination by which to invest the ruder forms of earthly things with poetry. . . . But it is one of the high attributes of the poetic mind, to feel a universal sympathy with Nature, both in the material world and in the soul of man. It identifies itself likewise with every object of its sympathy, giving it new sensation and poetic life, whatever that object may be, whether man, bird, beast, flower, or star. As to the pure mind all things are pure, so to the poetic mind all things are poetical. To such souls no age and no country can be utterly dull and prosaic. They make unto themselves their age and country; dwelling in the universal mind of man, and in the universal forms of things. Of such is the author of this book.

There are many who think that the ages of Poetry and Romance are gone by. They look upon the Present as a dull, unrhymed, and prosaic translation of a brilliant and poetic Past. Their dreams are of the days of Eld; of the Dark Ages, of the days of Chivalry, and Bards, and Troubadours and Minnesingers. . . . We also love ancient ballads. Pleasantly to our ears sounds the voice of the people in song, swelling fitfully through the desolate chambers of the past, like the wind of evening among ruins. And yet this voice does not persuade us that the days of balladry were more poetic than our own. The spirit of the past pleads for itself, and the spirit of the present likewise. If poetry be an element of the human mind, and consequently in accordance with nature and truth, it would be strange indeed, if, as the human mind advances, poetry should recede. The truth is, that when we look back upon the Past, we see only its bright and poetic features. All that is dull, prosaic, and common-place is lost in the shadowy distance. . . . We see the tree-tops waving in the wind, and hear the merry birds singing under their green roofs; but we forget that at their roots there are swine feeding upon acorns. With the Present it is not so. We stand too near to see objects in a picturesque light. What to others at a distance is a bright and folded summer cloud, is to us, who are in it, a dismal, drizzling rain. Thus to many this world, all beautiful as it is, seems a poor, working-day world. . . . Thus has it been since the world began. Ours is not the only Present, which has seemed dull, common-place, and prosaic.

The truth is, the heaven of poetry and romance still lies around us and within us. If people would but lay aside their "abominable spectacles," the light of The Great Carbuncle[1] would flash upon their sight with astonishing brightness. So long as truth is stranger than fiction, the elements of poetry and romance will not be wanting in common life. If, invisible ourselves, we could follow a single human being through a single day of its life, and know all its secret thoughts, and hopes, and anxieties, its prayers, and tears, and good resolves, its passionate delights and struggles against temptation,—all that excites, and all that soothes the heart of man,—we should have poetry enough to fill a volume. Nay, set the imagination free, like another Bottle-imp, and bid it lift for you the roofs of the city, street by street, and after a single night's observation you shall sit you down and write poetry and romance for the rest of your life.

We deem these few introductory remarks important to a true understanding of Mr. Hawthorne's character as a writer. It is from this point that he goes forth; and if we would go with him, and look upon life and nature as he does, we also must start from the same spot. In order to judge of the truth and beauty of his sketches, we must at least know the point of view, from which he drew them. Let us now examine the sketches themselves.

The Twice-told Tales are so called, we presume, from having been first published in various annuals and magazines, and now collected together, and told a second time in a volume by themselves. And a very delightful volume do they make; one of those, which excite in you a feeling of personal interest for the author. A calm, thoughtful face seems to be looking at you from every page; with now a pleasant smile, and now a shade of sadness stealing over its features. Sometimes, though not often, it glares wildly at you, with a strange and painful expression. . . .

One of the most prominent characteristics of these tales is, that they are national in their character. The author has wisely chosen his themes among the traditions of New England; the dusty legends of "the good Old Colony times, when we lived under a king." This is the right material for story. It seems as natural to make tales out of old tumble down traditions, as canes and snuff-boxes out of old steeples, or trees planted by great men. The puritanical times begin to look romantic in the distance. . . . Who would not like to have seen the time, when Thomas Taylor was presented to the grand jury "for abusing Captain Raynes, being in authority, by *thee-ing* and *thou-ing* him"; and John Wardell likewise, for denying Cambridge College to be an ordinance of God; and when some were fined for winking at comely damsels in church; and others for being common-sleepers there on the Lord's day? Truly, many quaint and quiet customs, many comic scenes and strange adventures, many wild and wondrous things, fit for humorous tale, and soft, pathetic story, lie all about us here in New England. There is no tradition of the Rhine nor of the Black Forest, which can compare in beauty with that of the Phantom Ship. The Flying Dutchman of the Cape, and the Klabotermann of the Baltic, are nowise superior. The story of Peter Rugg, the man who could not find Boston, is as good as that told by Gervase of Tilbury, of a man who gave himself to the devils by an unfortunate imprecation, and was used by them as a wheelbarrow; and the Great Carbuncle of the White Mountains shines with no less splendor, than that which illuminated the subterranean palace in Rome, as related by William of Malmesbury. Truly, from such a Fortunatus's pocket and wishing-cap, a tale-bearer may furnish forth a sufficiency of "peryllous adventures right espouventables, bryfefly compyled and pyteous for to here."

Another characteristic of this writer is the exceeding beauty of his style. It is as clear as running waters are. Indeed he uses words as mere stepping-stones, upon which, with a free and youthful bound, his spirit crosses and recrosses the bright and rushing stream of thought. Some writers of the present day have introduced a kind of Gothic architecture into their style. All is fantastic, vast, and wondrous in the outward form, and within is mysterious twilight, and the swelling sound of an organ, and a voice chanting hymns in Latin, which need a translation for many of the crowd. To this we do not object. Let the priest chant in what language he will, so long as he understands his own mass-book. But if he wishes the world to listen and be edified, he will do well to choose a language that is generally understood.

And now let us give some specimens of the bright, poetic style we praise so highly. Here is the commencement of a sketch entitled "The Vision of the Fountain." What a soft and musical flow of language! And yet all as simple as a draught of water from the fountain itself. [Quotes the first four paragraphs.]

Here are a few passages from a sketch called "Sunday at Home." [Quotes most of the sketch.]

We are obliged to forego the pleasure of quoting from the Tales. A tale must be given entire, or it is ruined. We wish we had room for "The Great Carbuncle," which is our especial favorite among them all. It is, however, too long for this use. Instead thereof, we will give one of those beautiful sketches, which are interspersed among the stories, like green leaves among flowers. But which shall we give? Shall it be "David Swan"; or "Little Annie's Ramble"; or "The Vision of the Fountain"; or "Fancy's Show-Box"; or "A Rill from the Town Pump"? We decide in favor of the last. [Quotes the entire sketch.]

These extracts are sufficient to show the beautiful and simple style of the book before us, its vein of pleasant philosophy, and the quiet humor, which is to the face of a book what a smile is to the face of man. In speaking in terms of such high praise as we have done, we have given utterance not alone to our own feelings, but we trust to those of all gentle readers of the Twice-told Tales. Like children we say, "Tell us more."

Notes

1. See Mr. Hawthorne's story with this title. If some persons, like the cynic here mentioned, cannot see the gems of poetry which shine before them, because of their

colored spectacles, others resemble the alchymist in the same tale, who "returned to his laboratory with a prodigious fragment of granite which he ground to powder, dissolved in acids, melted in the crucible, and burnt with the blowpipe, and published the result of his experiments in one of the heaviest folios of the day."

[Twice-told Tales]   Elizabeth Palmer Peabody[*]

The Story without an End, of which all true stories are but episodes, is told by Nature herself. She speaks now from the depths of the unmeasured heavens, by stars of light, who sing in a distance that the understanding cannot measure, but which the spirit realises; now from clouds, that, dropping sweetness, or catching light—to soften it to weak eyes—bend with revelations of less general truth over particular regions of earth's surface; and now from the infinitely varied forms, and hues, with which vegetable life has clothed the nakedness of the dark unknown of this rock-ribbed earth, (whose secrets who may tell?) And not only does she speak to the eye and ear, but to the heart of man; for taking human voice and form, she tells of love, and desire, and hate; of grief, and joy, and remorse; and even of human wilfulness and human caprice, when, as sometimes, these break the iron chains of custom, and scatter, with the breath of their mouths, the cobwebs of conventionalism.

Therefore must every true story-teller, like the child of the German tale, go out of his narrow hut into Nature's universal air, and follow whatsoever guides may woo him: her humble-bee, her butterfly, her dragon-fly, each in their turn; lying down in her caverns, and with heart couchant on her verdant breast, ever listening for her mighty voice. If, like one class of modern novelists, he prefers to listen to his own narrow individuality, to generalise his own petty experience, to show us the universe through the smoky panes of a Cockney window, he shall not give us any of that immortal story; its sphere-music will be drowned in that discord. Or if, like another class, he is mainly intent on some theory of political economy—some new experiment in social science—the dogmas of some philosophical or theological sect, he shall not make a work of art—he shall not open or clear up the eye of Reason, but rather thicken that crowd of phenomena that overwhelms it with fatigue. The confessions of egotism, and the demonstrations of modern science, have their place, but not where the true story-teller—who is the ballad-singer of the

[*] Reprinted from New-Yorker 5 (24 March 1838): 1–2. The attribution was made by Arlin Turner in "Elizabeth Peabody Reviews Twice-told Tales," Nathaniel Hawthorne Journal 4 (1974):75–84.

time—has *his*. He sits at the fountain-head of national character, and he must never stoop below the highest aim, but for ever seek the primal secret—for ever strive to speak the word which is answered by nothing less than a creation.

In this country, the state of things is so peculiarly unfavorable to that quiet brooding of the spirit over the dark waters, which must precede the utterance of a word of power;—our young men are so generally forced into the arena of business or politics before they have ever discriminated the spirit that they are, from the formless abyss in which they are, that it argues a genius of a high order to soar over the roaring gulf of transition in which the elements of society are boiling, into the still heaven of beauty. Such genius, however, there is amongst us. The harmonies of Nature, like the musical sounds in the ancient rites of Cybele, so fill the souls of her chosen priests, that they are insensible to all meaner sounds; and one of these true priests is the sweet story-teller, with the flowery name, whose little book of caged melodies we are now to review.

We have heard that the author of these tales has lived the life of a recluse; that the inhabitants of his native town have never been able to catch a glimpse of his person; that he is not seen at any time in the walks of men. And, indeed, his knowledge of the world is evidently not the superficial one acquired by that perpetual presence in good society—so called—which is absence from all that is profound in human feeling and thought; but, on the contrary, it is the wisdom which comes from knowing some few hearts well—from having communed with the earnest spirits of the past, and mainly studied in the light of that Pythian temple "not built with hands—eternal in the spirit," whose initiation is—"know thyself." There is throughout the volume a kindliness and even heartiness of human sympathy—a healthy equilibrium of spirits, and above all, a humor, so exquisitely combined of airy wit and the "sad, sweet music of humanity," that it contradicts the notion of misanthropical or whimsical seclusion. We will venture our reputation for sagacity on the assertion that he is frank and communicative in his character, winning thereby the experience of whatsoever hearts come in his path, to subject it to his Wordsworthian philosophy.

Wordsworthian philosophy we say, and with consideration; not that we would imply that he has taken it from Wordsworth. We mean to speak of the kind of philosophy, which cannot be learnt except in the same school of Nature where Wordsworth studied, and by the same pure light. We mean that he illustrates the principle defended by Wordsworth in his prose writings, as well as manifested by him in his metrical compositions, viz: that the ideal beauty may be seen clearest and felt most profoundly in the common incidents of actual life, if we will but "purge our visual ray with euphrasie and rue."

Mr. Hawthorne seems to have been born to this faith. His stories, generally speaking, have no dramatic pretension. Their single incident is the window through which he looks "into the mind of man— / *His* haunt, and the main region of *his* song."

In none of the little pieces before us has he succeeded more completely in suggesting the most general ideas, than in the "Sunday at Home," the "Sights from a Steeple," and "Little Annie's Ramble." These pieces also exhibit in perfection the objective power of his mind. With what a quiet love and familiar power he paints that sunrise stealing down the steeple opposite his chamber window! We turn to this passage, as we do to a painting upon canvass, for the pleasure it affords to the eye. The motion and sentiment so mingled with the forms and hues do not obscure the clear outlines—the sharp light and shade. What a living as well as tangible being does that meeting-house become, even during its week-day silence! The author does not go to church, he says; but no one would think he stayed at home for a vulgar reason. What worship there is in his stay at home! How livingly he teaches others to go, if they do go! What a hallowed feeling he sheds around the venerable institution of public worship! How gentle and yet effective are the touches by which he rebukes all that is inconsistent with its beautiful ideal! His "Sunday at Home" came from a heart alive through all its depths with a benignant Christian faith. *"Would that the Sabbath came twice as often, for the sake of that sorrowful old soul!"* This is worth a thousand sermons on the duty of going to church. It quickens the reader's love of religion; it shows the adaptation of Christianity to our nature, by adding to the common phenomena of the sacred day the pathos and grace which are to be drawn up from the wells of sympathy, and reproduces the voice that said "the Sabbath is made for man," in its very tones of infinite love, even to our senses. And "Little Annie's Ramble," though still lighter in execution, is no less replete with heart-touching thought. We feel as if to dwell upon it in our prosaic manner would be to do some injury to its airy structure. The more times we have read it, the more fully we have realised the force of its last paragraph:

> Sweet has been the charm of childhood on my spirit throughout my ramble with little Annie! Say not that it has been a waste of precious moments, an idle matter, a babble of childish talk, and a reverie of childish imaginations, about topics unworthy of a grown man's notice. Has it been merely this? Not so—not so. They are not truly wise who would affirm it. As the pure breath of children revives the life of aged men, so is our moral nature revived by their free and simple thoughts, their native feeling, their airy mirth for little cause or none, their grief soon roused and soon allayed. Their influence on us is at least reciprocal with ours on them. When

our infancy is almost forgotten, and our boyhood long departed, though it seems but as yesterday;—when life settles darkly down upon us, and we doubt whether to call ourselves young any more, then it is good to steal away from the society of bearded men, and even of gentle woman, and spend an hour or two with children. After drinking from these fountains of still fresh existence, we shall return into the crowd, as I do now, to struggle onward, and do our part in life, perhaps as fervently as ever, but, for a time, with a kinder and purer heart, and a spirit more lightly wise. All this by thy sweet magic, dear little Annie!

Not so grave is the effect of the "Vision of the Fountain." But who would ask for more than meets the eye and touches the heart in that exquisite little fancy? "Sure, if our eyes were made for seeing, / Then Beauty is its own excuse for being."

But nothing about our author delights us so much as the quietness—the apparent leisure, with which he lingers around the smallest point of fact, and unfolds therefrom a world of thought, just as if nothing else existed in the outward universe but that of which he is speaking. The hurried manner that seems to have become the American habit—the spirit of the steam-engine and railroad, has never entered into him. He seems to believe and act upon what is seldom ever apprehended, that every man's mind is the centre of the whole universe—the *primum mobile*—itself at rest, which wheels all phenomena, in lesser or greater circles, around it. Thus, "David Swan" goes down from his father's house in the New Hampshire hills, to seek his fortune in his uncle's grocery in Boston; and being tired with his walk, lies down by a fountain near the way-side for an hour's repose. Our philosophic, or, more accurately, our poetical story-teller, marks him for his own, and sitting down by his side, notes the several trains of phenomena which pass by and involve the unconscious sleeper; and comparing these with that train in which he is a conscious actor, reads the great lesson of superintending Providence, with the relation thereto of the human foresight. Again, his eye is struck with an odd action related in a newspaper, and his attentive mind is awakened, and may not rest until he has harmonised it with the more generally obeyed laws of human nature. Thus we have "Wakefield," and the terror-striking observation with which it closes: "Amid the seeming confusion of our mysterious world, individuals are so nicely adjusted to a system, and systems to one another, and to a whole, that *by stepping aside for a moment*, a man exposes himself to a fearful risk of losing his place for ever. Like Wakefield, he may become, as it were, the outcast of the universe."

"The Rill from the Town Pump" has been praised so much— not too much, however—that we have hardly anything left to say. It shows that genius may redeem to its original beauty the most hackneyed subject. We have here what would make the best temperance tract; and it is a work of the fine arts too—something we could hardly have believed possible beforehand.

"The Gray Champion," "The Maypole of Merry Mount," and "The Great Carbuncle," from another class of stories, for which it has often been said that this country gives no material. When we first read them, we wanted to say to the author, "This is your work:— with the spirit of the past, chrystallized thus, to gem the hills and plains of your native land; especially let every scene of that great adventure which settled and finally made free our country, become a symbol of the spirit which is too fast fading—the spirit that in Hugh Peters and Sir Henry Vane laid down mortal life, to take up the life which is infinitely communicable of itself." But, on second thought, we feel that we cannot spare him from the higher path, to confine him to this patriotic one; although we would recommend him frequently to walk in it. Why will he not himself give us the philosophical romance of Mt. Wallaston, of which he speaks? We can see but one objection; and that is, that into his little tale of "The Maypole," he has already distilled all the beauty with which he might have garnished the volume. "The Great Carbuncle" combines the wild imagination of Germany, and its allegoric spirit, with the common sense that the English claim as their characteristic; and these diverse elements are harmonized by the reliance on natural sentiment which we love to believe will prove in the end to be the true American character. The story awakens first that feeling and thought which is too fine in its essence for words to describe. A practical philosophy of life, that gives its due place and time to imagination and science, but rests on the heart as a solid foundation, is the light that flashes from the "Great Carbuncle" upon the true soul; which absorbing it, leaves the outward rock only "opaque stone, with particles of mica glittering on its surface."

The momentous questions with which "Fancy's Show Box" commences, and the "sad and awful truths" interwoven with its light frame-work, and the expressed hope with which the author relieves these at the end, where he suggests "that all the dreadful consequences of sin may not be incurred unless the act have set its seal upon the thought," would make the story interesting, even if it were not half so well done. Yet it does not denote a character of genius so high as the others that we have mentioned. It is as much inferior to the "Great Carbuncle" as the faculty of fancy is below the imagination. In quite an opposite vein is Mr. Higginbotham's catastrophe; but the variety of power proves the soundness of the author's mind. Where there is not the sense and power of the ludicrous, we always may fear weakness.

"The Gentle Boy" we have not neglected so long because we

like it least. It is more of a story than any of the rest; and we, perhaps, are the most fond of it, because it was the first of the author's productions we saw. We took it up in the Token, where it was first told, not expecting much, and found ourselves charmed by a spell of power. That sad, sweet, spiritual Ilbrahim, with "eyes melting into the moonlight," seeking a home on the cold tomb of his murdered father, while his deluded mother is wandering over the earth to awaken, with the concentrated force of all human passions that she has baptized into the name of the Holy Ghost, the spiritually dead to spiritual life, is worth a thousand homilies on fanaticism in all its forms, contrasted with the divinity of the natural sentiments, and the institutions growing therefrom. In this angelic child, we see human nature in its perfect holiness, its infinite tenderness, its martyr power, pleading, with all the eloquence of silent suffering, against the time-hallowed sins and ever renewed errors of men. On the judgment seat sits Time; and he shows himself, as usual, a very Pilate, delivering up the innocent victim to the furies of the present. They crucify him, and bury him in its stony bosom. Bury him, did we say? No—we saw his feet "pressing on the soil of Paradise," and again his soothing spirit coming "down from heaven, to teach his parent a true religion."

We have now spoken, as we could, of our chief favorites in this volume. A few more stories are left, which are indeed treated with great skill and power, and with as severe a taste as their subjects admit—especially the "Prophetic Pictures," a masterpiece in its way. As specimens of another vein of the author's art, we would not give them up. But we cannot avoid saying that these subjects are dangerous for his genius. There is a meretricious glare in them, which is but too apt to lead astray. And for him to indulge himself in them, will be likely to lower the sphere of his power. First-rate genius should leave the odd and peculiar, and especially the fantastic and horrible, to the inferior talent which is obliged to make up its own deficiency by the striking nature of the subject matter. Doubtless, we are requiring of genius some self-denial. These very tales are probably the most effective of the volume, at least with readers of Tokens and Magazines. They are the first read and oftenest spoken of, perhaps, by all persons; and yet, we would venture to say, they are the least often recurred to. They never can leave the reader in so high a mood of mind as the "Sunday at Home," or "Little Annie's Ramble." The interest they excite, in comparison with the latter, is somewhat analogous to the difference between the effect of Byron and Wordsworth's poetry.

But it is with diffidence we offer counsel to Mr. Hawthorne. We prefer to express gratitude. Can we do it more strongly, than to say, "We would hear more and more and forever"? Nor do we doubt that we shall hear more. Talent may tire in its toils, for it is ascending a weary hill. But genius wells up at the top of the hill; and in this instance descends in many streams—and the main stream is augmented and widened and deepened at every conflux. As it approaches the dwelling places of men, and spreads out to bear the merchandise of nations on its bosom, may it preserve the sweetness and purity of its fountains, far up in the solitudes of nature! We can wish nothing better for Mr. Hawthorne or for ourselves. He will then take his place amongst his contemporaries, as the greatest artist of his line; for not one of our writers indicates so great a variety of the elements of genius.

And this is a high quarry at which to aim. The greatest artist will be the greatest benefactor of our country. Art is the highest interest of our state, for it is the only principle of conservatism our constitution allows—a beauty which at once delights the eye, touches the heart, and projects the spirit into the world to come, will be something too precious to be weighed against the gains of a breakneck commerce, or the possible advantages held out by empirical politicians. While all the other excitements of the time tend to change and revolution, this will be a centre of unity. Let the poetic storyteller hasten, then, to bind with the zone of Beauty whatever should be permanent amongst us. In order to discharge his high office worthily, he will draw his materials from the wells of nature, and involve the sanctities of religion in all his works. Being, thinking, loving, seeing, uttering himself, without misgiving, without wearisomeness, and, like the spirit which hangs the heavens and clothes the earth with beauty, for ever assiduous; he yet need do nothing with special foresight. We would not yoke Pegasus to the dray-cart of utility; for the track of his footsteps will be hallowed, and every thing become sacred which he has touched.—Then, and not till then, we shall have a country; for then, and not till then, there will be a national character, defending us alike from the revolutionist within, and the invader without our borders.

[Hawthorne's Twice-told Tales, 1842]

Edgar Allan Poe°

We have always regarded the *Tale* (using this word in its popular acceptation) as affording the best prose opportunity for display of the highest talent. It has peculiar advantages which the novel does

° Reprinted from *Graham's Magazine* 20 (April and May 1842): 254, 298–300.

not admit. It is, of course, a far finer field than the essay. It has even points of superiority over the poem. An accident has deprived us, this month, of our customary space for review; and thus nipped in the bud a design long cherished of treating this subject in detail; taking Mr. Hawthorne's volumes as a text. In May we shall endeavor to carry out our intention. At present we are forced to be brief.

With rare exception—in the case of Mr. Irving's "Tales of a Traveller," and a few other works of a like cast—we have had no American tales of high merit. We have had no skilful compositions— nothing which could bear examination as works of art. Of twattle called tale-writing we have had, perhaps, more than enough. We have had a superabundance of the Rosa-Matilda effusions—gilt-edged paper all *couleur de rose:* a full allowance of cut-and-thrust blue-blazing melodramaticisms; a nauseating surfeit of low miniature copying of low life, much in the manner, and with about half the merit, of the Dutch herrings and decayed cheeses of Van Tuyssel—of all this, *eheu jam satis!*

Mr. Hawthorne's volumes appear to us misnamed in two respects. In the first place they should not have been called "Twice-Told Tales"—for this is a title which will not bear *repetition.* If in the first collected edition they were twice-told, of course now they are thrice-told.—May we live to hear them told a hundred times! In the second place, these compositions are by no means *all* "Tales." The most of them are essays properly so called. It would have been wise in their author to have modified his title, so as to have reference to all included. This point could have been easily arranged.

But under whatever titular blunders we receive this book, it is most cordially welcome. We have seen no prose composition by any American which can compare with *some* of these articles in the higher merits, or indeed in the lower; while there is not a single piece which would do dishonor to the best of the British essayists.

"The Rill from the Town Pump" which, through the *ad captandum* nature of its title, has attracted more of public notice than any one other of Mr. Hawthorne's compositions, is perhaps, the *least* meritorious. Among his best, we may briefly mention "The Hollow of the Three Hills;" "The Minister's Black Veil;" "Wakefield;" "Mr. Higginbotham's Catastrophe," "Fancy's Show-Box;" "Dr. Heidegger's Experiment;" "David Swan;" "The Wedding Knell;" and "The White Old Maid." It is remarkable that all these, with one exception, are from the first volume.

The style of Mr. Hawthorne is purity itself. His *tone* is singularly effective—wild, plaintive, thoughtful, and in full accordance with his themes. We have only to object that there is insufficient diversity in these themes themselves, or rather in their character. His *originality* both of incident and of reflection is very remarkable; and this trait alone would ensure him at least *our* warmest regard and commendation. We speak here chiefly of the tales; the essays are not so markedly novel. Upon the whole we look upon him as one of the few men of indisputable genius to whom our country has as yet given birth. As such, it will be our delight to do him honor; and lest, in these undigested and cursory remarks, without proof and without explanation, we should appear to do him *more* honor than is his due, we postpone all further comment until a more favorable opportunity.

o   o   o

We said a few hurried words about Mr. Hawthorne in our last number, with the design of speaking more fully in the present. We are still, however, pressed for room, and must necessarily discuss his volumes more briefly and more at random than their high merits deserve.

The book professes to be a collection of *tales,* yet is, in two respects, misnamed. These pieces are now in their third republication, and, of course, are thrice-told. Moreover, they are by no means *all* tales, either in the ordinary or in the legitimate understanding of the term. Many of them are pure essays; for example, "Sights from a Steeple," "Sunday at Home," "Little Annie's Ramble," "A Rill from the Town-Pump," "The Toll-Gatherer's Day," "The Haunted Mind," "The Sister Years," "Snow-Flakes," "Night Sketches," and "Foot-Prints on the Sea-Shore." We mention these matters chiefly on account of their discrepancy with that marked precision and finish by which the body of the work is distinguished.

Of the Essays just named, we must be content to speak in brief. They are each and all beautiful, without being characterised by the polish and adaptation so visible in the tales proper. A painter would at once note their leading or predominant feature, and style in *repose.* There is no attempt at effect. All is quiet, thoughtful, subdued. Yet this repose may exist simultaneously with high originality of thought; and Mr. Hawthorne has demonstrated the fact. At every turn we meet with novel combinations; yet these combinations never surpass the limits of the quiet. We are soothed as we read; and withal is a calm astonishment, that ideas so apparently obvious have never occurred or been presented to us before. Herein our author differs materially from Lamb or Hunt or Hazlitt—who, with vivid originality of manner and expression, have less of the true novelty of thought than is generally supposed, and whose originality, at best, has an uneasy and meretricious quaintness, replete with startling effects unfounded in nature, and inducing trains of reflection which lead to no satisfactory result. The Essays of Hawthorne have much of the character of Irving, with more of originality, and less of finish; while, compared with the Spectator, they have a vast superiority at all points. The Spectator, Mr. Irving, and Mr. Hawthorne have in common that tranquil and subdued manner which we have chosen to denominate *repose;* but, in the case of the two former, this repose is attained rather by the absence of novel combination, or of originality, than otherwise, and consists chiefly in the calm, quiet, unostentatious expression of commonplace thoughts, in an unambitious unadulterated Saxon. In them, by strong effort, we are made to conceive the absence of all. In the essays before us the absence of effort is too obvious to be mistaken, and a strong under-current of *suggestion* runs continuously beneath the upper stream of the tranquil thesis. In short, these effusions of Mr. Hawthorne are the product of a truly imaginative intellect, restrained, and in some measure repressed, by fastidiousness of taste, by constitutional melancholy and by indolence.

But it is of his tales that we desire principally to speak. The tale proper, in our opinion, affords unquestionably the fairest field for the exercise of the loftiest talent, which can be afforded by the wide domains of mere prose. Were we bidden to say how the highest genius could be most advantageously employed for the best display of its own powers, we should answer, without hesitation—in the composition of a rhymed poem, not to exceed in length what might be perused in an hour. Within this limit alone can the highest order of true poetry exist. We need only here say, upon this topic, that, in almost all classes of composition, the unity of effect or impression is a point of the greatest importance. It is clear, moreover, that this unity cannot be thoroughly preserved in productions whose perusal cannot be completed at one sitting. We may continue the reading of a prose composition, from the very nature of prose itself, much longer than we can persevere, to any good purpose, in the perusal of a poem. This latter, if truly fulfilling the demands of the poetic sentiment, induces an exaltation of the soul which cannot be long sustained. All high excitements are necessarily transient. Thus a long poem is a paradox. And, without unity of impression, the deepest effects cannot be brought about. Epics were the offspring of an imperfect sense of Art, and their reign is no more. A poem *too* brief may produce a vivid, but never an intense or enduring impression. Without a certain continuity of effort—without a certain duration or repetition of purpose—the soul is never deeply moved. There must be the dropping of the water upon the rock. De Béranger has wrought brilliant things—pungent and spirit-stirring—but, like all immassive bodies, they lack *momentum,* and thus fail to satisfy the Poetic Sentiment. They sparkle and excite, but, from want of continuity, fail deeply to impress. Extreme brevity will degenerate into epigrammatism; but the sin of extreme length is even more unpardonable. *In medio tutissimus ibis.*

Were we called upon, however, to designate that class of composition which, next to such a poem as we have suggested, should best fulfil the demands of high genius—should offer it the most advantageous field of exertion—we should unhesitatingly speak of the prose tale, as Mr. Hawthorne has here exemplified it. We allude to the short prose narrative, requiring from a half-hour to one or two hours in its perusal. The ordinary novel is objectionable, from its length, for reasons already stated in substance. As it cannot be read at one sitting, it deprives itself, of course, of the immense force derivable from *totality*. Worldly interests intervening during the pauses of perusal, modify, annul, or counteract, in a greater or less degree, the impressions of the book. But simple cessation in reading would, of itself, be sufficient to destroy the true unity. In the brief tale, however, the author is enabled to carry out the fulness of his intention, be it what it may. During the hour of perusal the soul of the reader is at the writer's control. There are no external or extrinsic influences—resulting from weariness or interruption.

A skilful literary artist has constructed a tale. If wise, he has not fashioned his thoughts to accommodate his incidents; but having conceived, with deliberate care, a certain unique or single *effect* to be wrought out, he then invents such incidents—he then combines such events as may best aid him in establishing this preconceived effect. If his very initial sentence tend not to the outbringing of this effect, then he has failed in his first step. In the whole composition there should be no word written, of which the tendency, direct or indirect, is not to the one pre-established design. And by such means, with such care and skill, a picture is at length painted which leaves in the mind of him who contemplates it with a kindred art, a sense of the fullest satisfaction. The idea of the tale has been presented unblemished, because undisturbed; and this is an end unattainable by the novel. Undue brevity is just as exceptionable here as in the poem; but undue length is yet more to be avoided.

We have said that the tale has a point of superiority even over the poem. In fact, while the *rhythm* of this latter is an essential aid in the development of the poem's highest idea—the idea of the Beautiful—the artificialities of this rhythm are an inseparable bar to the development of all points of thought or expression which have their basis in *Truth*. But Truth is often, and in very great degree, the aim of the tale. Some of the finest tales are tales of ratiocination. Thus the field of this species of composition, if not in so elevated a region on the mountain of Mind, is a table-land of far vaster extent than the domain of the mere poem. Its products are never so rich, but infinitely more numerous, and more appreciable by the mass of mankind. The writer of the prose tale, in short, may bring to his theme a vast variety of modes or inflections of thought and expression—(the ratiocinative, for example, the sarcastic or the humorous) which are not only antagonistical to the nature of the poem, but absolutely forbidden by one of its most peculiar and indispensable adjuncts; we allude of course, to rhythm. It may be added, here, *par parenthese,* that the author who aims at the purely beautiful in a prose tale is laboring at great disadvantage. For Beauty can be better treated in the poem. Not so with terror, or passion, or horror, or a multitude of such other points. And here it will be seen how full of prejudice are the usual animadversions against those *tales of effect* many fine examples of which were found in the earlier numbers of Blackwood. The impressions produced were wrought in a legitimate sphere of action, and constituted a legitimate although sometimes an exaggerated interest. They were relished by every man of genius: although there were found many men of genius who condemned them without just ground. The true critic will but demand that the design intended be accomplished, to the fullest extent, by the means most advantageously applicable.

We have very few American tales of real merit—we may say, indeed, none, with the exception of "The Tales of a Traveller" of Washington Irving, and these "Twice-Told Tales" of Mr. Hawthorne. Some of the pieces of Mr. John Neal abound in vigor and originality; but in general, his compositions of this class are excessively diffuse, extravagant, and indicative of an imperfect sentiment of Art. Articles at random are, now and then, met with in our periodicals which might be advantageously compared with the best effusions of the British Magazines; but, upon the whole, we are far behind our progenitors in this department of literature.

Of Mr. Hawthorne's Tales we would say, emphatically, that they belong to the highest region of Art—an Art subservient to genius of a very lofty order. We had supposed, with good reason for so supposing, that he had been thrust into his present position by one of the impudent *cliques* which beset our literature, and whose pretensions it is our full purpose to expose at the earliest opportunity; but we have been most agreeably mistaken. We know of few compositions which the critic can more honestly commend than these "Twice-Told Tales." As Americans, we feel proud of the book.

Mr. Hawthorne's distinctive trait is invention, creation, imagination, originality—a trait which, in the literature of fiction, is positively worth all the rest. But the nature of originality, so far as regards its manifestation in letters, is but imperfectly understood. The inventive or original mind as frequently displays itself in novelty of *tone* as in novelty of matter. Mr. Hawthorne is original at *all* points.

It would be a matter of some difficulty to designate the best of these tales; we repeat that, without exception, they are beautiful. "Wakefield" is remarkable for the skill with which an old idea—a well-known incident—is worked up or discussed. A man of whims conceives the purpose of quitting his wife and residing *incognito,* for twenty years, in her immediate neighborhood. Something of this kind actually happened in London. The force of Mr. Hawthorne's tale lies in the analysis of the motives which must or might have impelled the husband to such folly, in the first instance, with the possible causes of his perseverance. Upon this thesis a sketch of singular power has been constructed.

"The Wedding Knell" is full of the boldest imagination—an imagination fully controlled by taste. The most captious critic could find no flaw in this production.

"The Minister's Black Veil" is a masterly composition of which the sole defect is that to the rabble its exquisite skill will be *caviare.* The *obvious* meaning of this article will be found to smother its insinuated one. The *moral* put into the mouth of the dying minister will be supposed to convey the *true* import of the narrative; and that a crime of dark dye, (having reference to the "young lady") has been committed, is a point which only minds congenial with that of the author will perceive.

"Mr. Higginbotham's Catastrophe" is vividly original and managed most dexterously.

"Dr. Heidegger's Experiment" is exceedingly well imagined, and executed with surpassing ability. The artist breathes in every line of it.

"The White Old Maid" is objectionable, even more than the "Minister's Black Veil," on the score of its mysticism. Even with the thoughtful and analytic, there will be much trouble in penetrating its entire import.

"The Hollow of the Three Hills" we would quote in full, had we space;—not as evincing higher talent than any of the other pieces, but as affording an excellent example of the author's peculiar ability. The subject is commonplace. A witch subjects the Distant and the Past to the view of a mourner. It has been the fashion to describe, in such cases, a mirror in which the images of the absent appear; or a cloud of smoke is made to arise, and thence the figures are gradually unfolded. Mr. Hawthorne has wonderfully heightened his effect by making the ear, in place of the eye, the medium by which the fantasy is conveyed. The head of the mourner is enveloped in the cloak of the witch, and within its magic folds there arise sounds which have an all-sufficient intelligence. Throughout this article also, the artist is conspicuous—not more in positive than in negative merits. Not only is all done that should be done, but (what perhaps is an end with more difficulty attained) there is nothing done which should not be. Every word *tells,* and there is not a word which does *not* tell. . . .

In the way of objection we have scarcely a word to say of these tales. There is, perhaps, a somewhat too general or prevalent *tone*—

a tone of melancholy and mysticism. The subjects are insufficiently varied. There is not so much of *versatility* evinced as we might well be warranted in expecting from the high powers of Mr. Hawthorne. But beyond these trivial exceptions we have really none to make. The style is purity itself. Force abounds. High imagination gleams from every page. Mr. Hawthorne is a man of the truest genius. We only regret that the limits of our Magazine will not permit us to pay him that full tribute of commendation, which, under other circumstances, we should be so eager to pay.

[Review of *Twice-told Tales*, 1842]

Margaret Fuller°

Ever since the "Gentle Boy" first announced among us the presence of his friend and observer, the author of the "Twice-told Tales" has been growing more and more dear to his readers, who now have the pleasure of seeing all the leaves they had been gathering up here and there collected in these two volumes.

It is not merely the soft grace, the playfulness, and genial human sense for the traits of individual character that have pleased, but the perception of what is rarest in this superficial, bustling community, a great reserve of thought and strength never yet at all brought forward. Landor says, "He is not over-rich in knowledge who cannot afford to let the greater part lie fallow, and to bring forward his produce according to the season and the demand." We can seldom recur to such a passage as this with pleasure, as we turn over the leaves of a new book. But here we may. Like gleams of light on a noble tree which stands untouched and self-sufficing in its fulness of foliage on a distant hill-slope,—like slight ripples wrinkling the smooth surface, but never stirring the quiet depths of a wood-embosomed lake, these tales distantly indicate the bent of the author's mind, and the very frankness with which they impart to us slight outward details and habits shows how little yet is told. He is a favorite writer for children, with whom he feels at home, as true manliness always does; and the "Twice-told Tales" scarce call him out more than the little books for his acquaintance of fairy stature.

In the light of familiar letters, written with ready hand, by a friend, from the inns where he stops, in a journey through the varied world-scenes, the tales are most pleasing; but they seem to promise

° Reprinted from *Dial* 3 (July 1842):130–31.

more, should their author ever hear a voice that truly calls upon his solitude to ope his study door.

In his second volume, "The Village Uncle," "Lily's Quest," "Chippings with a Chisel," were new to us, and pleasing for the same reasons as former favorites from the same hand. We again admired the sweet grace of the little piece, "Footprints on the Seashore."

"Chippings with a Chisel," from its mild, common-sense philosophy, and genial love of the familiar plays of life, would have waked a brotherly smile on the lips of the friend of Dr. Dry-as-dust.

It is in the studies of familiar life that there is most success. In the mere imaginative pieces, the invention is not clearly woven, far from being all compact, and seems a phantom or shadow, rather than a real growth. The men and women, too, flicker large and unsubstantial, like "shadows from the evening firelight," seen "upon the parlor wall." But this would be otherwise, probably, were the genius fully roused to its work, and initiated into its own life, so as to paint with blood-warm colors. This frigidity and thinness of design usually bespeaks a want of the deeper experiences, for which no talent at observation, no sympathies, however ready and delicate, can compensate. We wait new missives from the same hand.

[Review of *Mosses from an Old Manse*]

Margaret Fuller°

We have been seated here the last ten minutes, pen in hand, thinking what we can possibly say about this book that will not be either superfluous or impertinent.

Superfluous, because the attractions of Hawthorne's writings cannot fail of one and the same effect on all persons who possess the common sympathies of men. To all who are still happy in some groundwork of unperverted Nature, the delicate, simple, human tenderness, unsought, unbought and therefore precious morality, the tranquil elegance and playfulness, the humor which never breaks the impression of sweetness and dignity, do an inevitable message which requires no comment of the critic to make its meaning clear. Impertinent, because the influence of this mind, like that of some loveliest aspects of Nature, is to induce silence from a feeling of repose. We do not think of any thing particularly worth saying about this that has been so fitly and pleasantly said.

° Reprinted from *New-York Daily Tribune*, 22 June 1846, 1.

Yet it seems *un*fit that we, in our office of chronicler of intellectual advents and apparitions, should omit to render open and audible honor to one whom we have long delighted to honor. It may be, too, that this slight notice of ours may awaken the attention of those distant or busy who might not otherwise search for the volume, which comes betimes in the leafy month of June.

So we will give a slight account of it, even if we cannot say much of value. Though Hawthorne has now a standard reputation, both for the qualities we have mentioned and the beauty of the style in which they are embodied, yet we believe he has not been very widely read. This is only because his works have not been published in the way to insure extensive circulation in this new, hurrying world of ours. The immense extent of country over which the reading (still very small in proportion to the mere working) community is scattered, the rushing and pushing of our life at this electrical stage of development, leave no work a chance to be speedily and largely known that is not trumpeted and placarded. And, odious as are the features of a forced and artificial circulation, it must be considered that it does no harm in the end. Bad books will not be read if they are bought instead of good, while the good have no abiding life in the log-cabin settlements and Red River steamboat landings, to which they would in no other way penetrate. Under the auspices of Wiley and Putnam, Hawthorne will have a chance to collect all his own public about him, and that be felt as a presence which before was only a rumor.

The volume before us shares the charms of Hawthorne's earlier tales; the only difference being that his range of subjects is a little wider. There is the same gentle and sincere companionship with Nature, the same delicate but fearless scrutiny of the secrets of the heart, the same serene independence of petty and artificial restrictions, whether on opinions or conduct, the same familiar, yet pensive sense of the spiritual or demoniacal influences that haunt the palpable life and common walks of men, not by many apprehended except in results. We have here to regret that Hawthorne, at this stage of his mind's life, lay no more decisive hand upon the apparition—brings it no nearer than in former days.—We had hoped that we should see, no more as in a glass darkly, but face to face. Still, still brood over his page the genius of revery and the nonchalance of Nature, rather than the ardent earnestness of the human soul which feels itself born not only to see and disclose, but to understand and interpret such things. Hawthorne intimates and suggests, but he does not lay bare the mysteries of our being.

The introduction to the "Mosses," in which the old Manse, its inhabitants and visitants are portrayed, is written with even more than his usual charm of placid grace and many strokes of his admirable good sense. Those who are not, like ourselves, familiar with the scene and its denizens, will still perceive how true that picture must be; those of us who are thus familiar will best know how to prize the record of objects and influences unique in our country and time.

"The Birth Mark" and "Rappaccini's Daughter" embody truths of profound importance in shapes of aerial elegance. In these, as here and there in all these pieces, shines the loveliest ideal of love and the beauty of feminine purity, (by which we mean no mere acts or abstinences, but perfect single truth felt and done in gentleness) which is its root.

"The Celestial Railroad," for its wit, wisdom, and the graceful adroitness with which the natural and material objects are interwoven with the allegories, has already won its meed of admiration.—"Fireworship" is a most charming essay for its domestic sweetness and thoughtful life. "Goodman Brown" is one of those disclosures we have spoken of, of the secrets of the breast. Who has not known such a trial that is capable indeed of sincere aspiration toward that only good, that infinite essence, which men call God. Who has not known the hour when even that best-beloved image cherished as the one precious symbol left, in the range of human nature, believed to be still pure gold when all the rest have turned to clay, shows, in severe ordeal, the symptoms of alloy. Oh hour of anguish, when the old familiar faces grow dark and dim in the lurid light—when the gods of the hearth, honored in childhood, adored in youth, crumble, and nothing, nothing is left which the daily earthly feelings can embrace—can cherish with unbroken Faith! Yet some survive that trial more happily than young Goodman Brown. They are those who have not sought it—have never of their own accord walked forth with the Tempter into the dim shades of Doubt. Mrs. Bull-Frog is an excellent humorous picture of what is called to be "content at last with substantial realities"!! The "Artist of the Beautiful" presents in a form that is, indeed, beautiful, the opposite view as to what *are* the substantial realities of life. Let each man choose between them according to his kind: Had Hawthorne written "Roger Malvin's Burial" alone, we should be pervaded with the sense of the poetry and religion of his soul.

As a critic, the style of Hawthorne, faithful to his mind, shows repose, a great reserve of strength, a slow secure movement. Though a very refined, he is also a very clear writer, showing, as we said before, a placid grace, and an indolent command of language.

And now, beside the full, calm yet romantic stream of his mind, we will rest. It has refreshment for the weary, islets of fascination no less than dark recesses and shadows for the imaginative, pure reflections for the pure of heart and eye, and, like the Concord he so well describes, many exquisite lilies for him who knows how to get at them.

Tale-Writing— Nathaniel Hawthorne

Edgar A. Poe°

In the preface to my sketches of New York Literati, while speaking of the broad distinction between the seeming public and real private opinion respecting our authors, I thus alluded to Nathaniel Hawthorne:—

> For example, Mr. Hawthorne, the author of "Twice-told Tales," is scarcely recognized by the press or by the public, and when noticed at all, is noticed merely to be damned by faint praise. Now, my own opinion of him is, that although his walk is limited and he is fairly to be charged with mannerism, treating all subjects in a similar tone of dreamy *innuendo*, yet in this walk he evinces extraordinary genius, having no rival either in America or elsewhere; and this opinion I have never heard gainsaid by any one literary person in the country. That this opinion, however, is a spoken and not a written one, is referable to the facts, first, that Mr. Hawthorne *is* a poor man, and secondly, that he *is not* an ubiquitous quack.

The reputation of the author of "Twice-told Tales" has been confined, indeed, until very lately, to literary society; and I have not been wrong, perhaps, in citing him as *the* example, *par excellence*, in this country, of the privately-admired and publicly-unappreciated man of genius. Within the last year or two, it is true, an occasional critic has been urged, by honest indignation, into very warm approval. Mr. Webber, for instance, (than whom no one has a keener relish for that kind of writing which Mr. Hawthorne has best illustrated,) gave us, in a late number of "The American Review," a cordial and certainly a full tribute to his talents; and since the issue of the "Mosses from an Old Manse," criticisms of similar tone have been by no means infrequent in our more authoritative journals. I can call to mind few reviews of Hawthorne published *before* the "Mosses." One I remember in "Arcturus" (edited by Matthews and Duyckinck) for May, 1841; another in the "American Monthly" (edited by Hoffman and Herbert) for March, 1838; a third in the ninety-sixth number of the "North American Review." These criticisms, however, seemed to have little effect on the popular taste—at least, if we are to form any idea of the popular taste by reference to its expression in the newspapers, or by the sale of the author's book. It was never the fashion (until lately) to speak of him in any summary of our best authors. The daily critics would say, on such occasions, "Is there not Irving and Cooper, and Bryant and Paulding, and—Smith?" or, "Have we not Halleck and Dana, and Longfellow and—Thompson?" or,

° Reprinted from *Godey's Lady's Book* 35 (November 1847): 252–56.

"Can we not point triumphantly to our own Sprague, Willis, Channing, Bancroft, Prescott and—Jenkins?" but these unanswerable queries were never wound up by the name of Hawthorne.

Beyond doubt, this inappreciation of him on the part of the public arose chiefly from the two causes to which I have referred—from the facts that he is neither a man of wealth nor a quack—but these are insufficient to account for the whole effect. No small portion of it is attributable to the very marked idiosyncrasy of Mr. Hawthorne himself. In one sense, and in great measure, to be peculiar is to be original, and than the true originality there is no higher literary virtue. This true or commendable originality, however, implies not the uniform, but the continuous peculiarity—a peculiarity springing from ever-active vigor of fancy—better still if from ever-present force of imagination, giving its own hue, its own character to everything it touches, and, especially, *self impelled to touch everything.*

It is often said, inconsiderately, that very original writers always fail in popularity—that such and such persons are too original to be comprehended by the mass. "Too peculiar," should be the phrase, "too idiosyncratic." It is, in fact, the excitable, undisciplined and child-like popular mind which most keenly feels the original. The criticism of the conservatives, of the hackneys, of the cultivated old clergymen of the "North American Review," is precisely the criticism which condemns and alone condemns it. "It becometh not a divine," said Lord Coke, "to be of a fiery and salamandrine spirit." Their conscience allowing them to move nothing themselves, these dignitaries have a holy horror of being moved. "Give us *quietude,*" they say. Opening their mouths with proper caution, they sigh forth the word *"Repose."* And this is, indeed, the one thing they should be permitted to enjoy, if only upon the Christian principle of give and take.

The fact is, that if Mr. Hawthorne were really original, he could not fail of making himself felt by the public. But the fact is, he is *not* original in any sense. Those who speak of him as original, mean nothing more than that he differs in his manner or tone, and in his choice of subjects, from any author of their acquaintance—their acquaintance not extending to the German Tieck, whose manner, in *some* of his works, is absolutely identical with that *habitual* to Hawthorne. But it is clear that the element of the literary originality is novelty. The element of its appreciation by the reader is the reader's sense of the new. Whatever gives him a new and insomuch a pleasurable emotion, he considers original, and whoever frequently gives him such emotion, he considers an original writer. In a word, it is by the sum total of these emotions that he decides upon the writer's claim to originality. I may observe here, however, that there is clearly a point at which even novelty itself would cease to produce the legitimate originality, if we judge this originality, as we should, by the effect designed: this point is that at which *novelty becomes nothing novel;* and here the artist, *to preserve his originality,* will subside into the common-place. No one, I think, has noticed that, merely through inattention to this matter, Moore has comparatively failed in his "Lalla Rookh." Few readers, and indeed few critics, have commended this poem for originality—and, in fact, the effect, originality, is not produced by it—yet no work of equal size so abounds in the happiest originalities, individually considered. They are so excessive as, in the end, to deaden in the reader all capacity for their appreciation.

These points properly understood, it will be seen that the critic (unacquainted with Tieck) who reads a single tale or essay by Hawthorne, may be justified in thinking him original; but the tone, or manner, or choice of subject, which induces in this critic the sense of the new, will—if not in a second tale, at least in a third and all subsequent ones—not only fail of inducing it, but bring about an exactly antagonistic impression. In concluding a volume, and more especially in concluding all the volumes of the author, the critic will abandon his first design of calling him "original," and content himself with styling him "peculiar."

With the vague opinion that to be original is to be unpopular, I could, indeed, agree, were I to adopt an understanding of originality which, to my surprise, I have known adopted by many who have a right to be called critical. They have limited, in a love for mere words, the literary to the metaphysical originality. They regard as original in letters, only such combinations of thought, of incident, and so forth, as are, in fact, absolutely novel. It is clear, however, not only that it is the novelty of *effect* alone which is worth consideration, but that this effect is *best* wrought, for the end of all fictitious composition, pleasure, by shunning rather than by seeking the absolute novelty of combination. Originality, thus understood, tasks and startles the intellect, and so brings into undue action the faculties to which, in the lighter literature, we least appeal. And thus understood, it cannot fail to prove unpopular with the masses, who, seeking in this literature amusement, are positively offended by instruction. But the true originality—true in respect of its purposes—is that which, in bringing out the half-formed, the reluctant, or the unexpressed fancies of mankind, or in exciting the more delicate pulses of the heart's passion, or in giving birth to some universal sentiment or instinct in embryo, thus combines with the pleasurable effect of *apparent* novelty, a real egoistic delight. The reader, in the case first supposed, (that of the absolute novelty,) is excited, but embarrassed, disturbed, in some degree even pained at his own want of perception, at his own folly in not having himself hit upon the idea. In the second case, his pleasure is doubled. He is filled with an intrinsic and extrinsic delight.

He feels and intensely enjoys the seeming novelty of the thought, enjoys it as really novel, as absolutely original with the writer—*and* himself. They two, he fancies, have, alone of all men, thought thus. They two have, together, created this thing. Henceforward there is a bond of sympathy between them, a sympathy which irradiates every subsequent page of the book.

There is a species of writing which, with some difficulty, may be admitted as a lower degree of what I have called the true original. In its perusal, we say to ourselves, not "how original this is!" nor "here is an idea which I and the author have alone entertained," but "here is a charmingly obvious fancy," or sometimes even, "here is a thought which I am not sure has ever occurred to myself, but which, of course, has occurred to all the rest of the world." This kind of composition (which still appertains to a high order) is usually designated as "the natural." It has little external resemblance, but strong internal affinity to the true original, if, indeed, as I have suggested, it is not of this latter an inferior degree. It is best exemplified, among English writers, in Addison, Irving and *Hawthorne.* The "ease" which is so often spoken of as its distinguishing feature, it has been the fashion to regard as ease in appearance alone, as a point of really difficult attainment. This idea, however, must be received with some reservation. The natural style is difficult only to those who should never intermeddle with it—to the unnatural. It is but the result of writing with the understanding, or with the instinct, that the *tone,* in composition, should be that which, at any given point or upon any given topic, would be the tone of the great mass of humanity. The author who, after the manner of the North Americans, is merely at *all* times *quiet,* is, of course, upon *most* occasions, merely silly or stupid, and has no more right to be thought "easy" or "natural" than has a cockney exquisite or the sleeping beauty in the wax-works.

The "peculiarity" or sameness, or monotone of Hawthorne, would, in its mere character of "peculiarity," and without reference to what *is* the peculiarity, suffice to deprive him of all chance of popular appreciation. But at his failure to be appreciated, we can, *of course,* no longer wonder, when we find him monotonous at decidedly the worst of all possible points—at that point which, having the least concern with Nature, is the farthest removed from the popular intellect, from the popular sentiment and from the popular taste. I allude to the strain of allegory which completely overwhelms the greater number of his subjects, and which in some measure interferes with the direct conduct of absolutely all.

In defence of allegory, (however, or for whatever object, employed,) there is scarcely one respectable word to be said. Its best appeals are made to the fancy—that is to say, to our sense of adaptation, not of matters proper, but of matters improper for the purpose, of the real with the unreal; having never more of intelligible connection than has something with nothing, never half so much of effective affinity as has the substance for the shadow. The deepest emotion aroused within us by the happiest allegory, *as* allegory, is a very, very imperfectly satisfied sense of the writer's ingenuity in overcoming a difficulty we should have preferred his not having attempted to overcome. The fallacy of the idea that allegory, in any of its moods, can be made to enforce a truth—that metaphor, for example, may illustrate as well as embellish an argument—could be promptly demonstrated: the converse of the supposed fact might be shown, indeed, with very little trouble—but these are topics foreign to my present purpose. One thing is clear, that if allegory ever establishes a fact, it is by dint of overturning a fiction. Where the suggested meaning runs through the obvious one in a *very* profound under-current, so as never to interfere with the upper one without our own volition, so as never to show itself unless *called* to the surface, there only, for the proper uses of fictitious narrative, is it available at all. Under the best circumstances, it must always interfere with that unity of effect which, to the artist, is worth all the allegory in the world. Its vital injury, however, is rendered to the most vitally important point in fiction—that of earnestness or verisimilitude. That "The Pilgrim's Progress" is a ludicrously over-rated book, owing its seeming popularity to one or two of those accidents in critical literature which by the critical are sufficiently well understood, is a matter upon which no two thinking people disagree; but the pleasure derivable from it, in any sense, will be found in the direct ratio of the reader's capacity to smother its true purpose, in the direct ratio of his ability to keep the allegory out of sight, or of his inability to comprehend it. Of allegory properly handled, judiciously subdued, seen only as a shadow or by suggestive glimpses, and making its nearest approach to truth in a not obtrusive and therefore not unpleasant *appositeness*, the "Undine" of De La Motte Fouqué is the best, and undoubtedly a very remarkable specimen.

The obvious causes, however, which have prevented Mr. Hawthorne's *popularity*, do not suffice to condemn him in the eyes of the few who belong properly to books, and to whom books, perhaps, do not quite so properly belong. These few estimate an author, not as do the public, altogether by what he does, but in great measure—indeed, even in the greatest measure—by what he evinces a capability of doing. In this view, Hawthorne stands among literary people in America much in the same light as did Coleridge in England. The few, also, through a certain warping of the taste, which long pondering upon books as books merely never fails to induce, are not in condition to view the errors of a scholar as errors altogether. At any time these gentlemen are prone to think the public not right rather than an educated author wrong. But the simple truth is, that the writer who aims at impressing the people, is *always* wrong when he fails in forcing that people to receive the impression. How far Mr. Hawthorne has addressed the people at all, is, of course, not a question for me to decide. His books afford strong internal evidence of having been written to himself and his particular friends alone.

There has long existed in literature a fatal and unfounded prejudice, which it will be the office of this age to overthrow—the idea that the mere bulk of a work must enter largely into our estimate of its merit. I do not suppose even the weakest of the Quarterly reviewers weak enough to maintain that in a book's size or mass, abstractly considered, there is anything which especially calls for our admiration. A mountain, simply through the sensation of physical magnitude which it conveys, does, indeed, affect us with a sense of the sublime, but we cannot admit any such influence in the contemplation even of "The Columbiad." The Quarterlies themselves will not admit it. And yet, what else are we to understand by their continual prating about "sustained effort?" Granted that this sustained effort has accomplished an epic—let us then admire the effort, (if this be a thing admirable,) but certainly not the epic on the effort's account. Common sense, in the time to come, may possibly insist upon measuring a work of art rather by the object it fulfils, by the impression it makes, than by the time it took to fulfil the object, or by the extent of "sustained effort" which became necessary to produce the impression. The fact is, that perseverance is one thing and genius quite another; nor can all the transcendentalists in Heathendom confound them.

Full of its bulky ideas, the last number of the "North American Review," in what it imagines a criticism on Simms, "honestly avows that it has little opinion of the mere tale;" and the honesty of the avowal is in no slight degree guarantied by the fact that this Review has never yet been known to put forth an opinion which was *not* a very little one indeed.

The tale proper affords the fairest field which can be afforded by the wide domains of mere prose, for the exercise of the highest genius. Were I bidden to say how this genius could be most advantageously employed for the best display of its powers, I should answer, without hesitation, "in the composition of a rhymed poem not to exceed in length what might be persued in an hour." Within this limit alone can the noblest order of poetry exist. I have discussed this topic elsewhere, and need here repeat only that the phrase "a long poem" embodies a paradox. A poem must intensely excite. Excitement is its province, its essentiality. Its value is in the ratio of its (elevating) excitement. But all excitement is, from a psychal necessity, transient. It cannot be sustained through a poem of great length. In the course of an hour's reading, at most, it flags, fails; and then the poem is, in effect, no longer such. Men admire, but are wearied with the "Paradise Lost;" for platitude follows platitude, *inevitably*, at regular interspaces, (the depressions between the waves of excitement,) until the poem, (which, properly considered, is but a succession of brief poems,) having been brought to an end, we discover that the sums of our pleasure and of displeasure have been very nearly equal. The absolute, ultimate or aggregate effect of any epic under the sun is, for these reasons, a nullity. "The Iliad," in its form of epic, has but an imaginary existence; granting it real, however, I can only say of it that it is based on a primitive sense of Art. Of the modern epic nothing can be so well said as that it is a blindfold imitation of a "come-by-chance." By and by these propositions will be understood as self-evident, and in the meantime will not be essentially damaged as truths by being generally condemned as falsities.

A poem *too* brief, on the other hand, may produce a sharp or vivid, but never a profound or enduring impression. Without a certain continuity, without a certain duration or repetition of the cause, the soul is seldom moved to the effect. There must be the dropping of the water on the rock. There must be the pressing steadily down of the stamp upon the wax. De Béranger has wrought brilliant things, pungent and spirit-stirring, but most of them are too immassive to have *momentum*, and, as so many feathers of fancy, have been blown aloft only to be whistled down the wind. Brevity, indeed, may degenerate into epigrammatism, but this danger does not prevent extreme length from being the one unpardonable sin.

Were I called upon, however, to designate that class of composition which, next to such a poem as I have suggested, should best fulfil the demands and serve the purposes of ambitious genius, should offer it the most advantageous field of exertion, and afford it the fairest opportunity of display, I should speak at once of the brief prose tale. History, philosophy, and other matters of that kind, we leave out of the question, of course. *Of course*, I say, and in spite of the graybeards. These graver topics, to the end of time, will be best illustrated by what a discriminating world, turning up its nose at the drab pamphlets, has agreed to understand as *talent.* The ordinary novel is objectionable, from its length, for reasons analogous to those which render length objectionable in the poem. As the novel cannot be read at one sitting, it cannot avail itself of the immense benefit of *totality.* Worldly interests, intervening during the pauses of perusal, modify, counteract and annul the impressions intended. But simple cessation in reading would, of itself, be sufficient to destroy the true unity. In the brief tale, however, the author is enabled to carry out his full design without interruption. During the hour of perusal, the soul of the reader is at the writer's control.

A skillful artist has constructed a tale. He has not fashioned his thoughts to accommodate his incidents, but having deliberately conceived a certain *single effect* to be wrought, he then invents such incidents, he then combines such events, and discusses them in such tone as may best serve him in establishing this preconceived effect. If his very first sentence tend not to the outbringing of this effect, then in his very first step has he committed a blunder. In the whole composition there should be no word written of which the tendency, direct or indirect, is not to the one pre-established design. And by such means, with such care and skill, a picture is at length painted which leaves in the mind of him who contemplates it with a kindred art, a sense of the fullest satisfaction. The idea of the tale, its thesis, has been presented unblemished, because undisturbed—an end absolutely demanded, yet, in the novel, altogether unattainable.

Of skillfully-constructed tales—I speak now without reference to other points, some of them more important than construction—there are very few American specimens. I am acquainted with no better one, upon the whole, than the "Murder Will Out" of Mr. Simms, and this has some glaring defects. The "Tales of a Traveler," by Irving, are graceful and impressive narratives—"The Young Italian" is especially good—but there is not one of the series which can be commended as a whole. In many of them the interest is subdivided and frittered away, and their conclusions are insufficiently *climactic.* In the higher requisites of composition, John Neal's magazine stories excel—I mean in vigor of thought, picturesque combination of incident, and so forth—but they ramble too much, and invariably break down just before coming to an end, as if the writer had received a sudden and irresistible summons to dinner, and thought it incumbent upon him to make a finish of his story before going. One of the happiest and best-sustained tales I have seen, is "Jack Long; or, The Shot in the Eye," by Charles W. Webber, the assistant editor of Mr. Colton's "American Review." But in general skill of construction, the tales of Willis, I think, surpass those of any American writer—with the exception of Mr. Hawthorne.

I must defer to the better opportunity of a volume now in hand, a full discussion of his individual pieces, and hasten to conclude this paper with a summary of his merits and demerits.

He is peculiar and *not* original—unless in those detailed fancies and detached thoughts which his want of general originality will deprive of the appreciation due to them, in preventing them forever reaching the *public* eye. He is infinitely too fond of allegory, and can never hope for popularity so long as he persists in it. This he will not do, for allegory is at war with the whole tone of his nature, which disports itself never so well as when escaping from the mysticism of his Goodman Browns and White Old Maids into the hearty, genial, but still Indian-summer sunshine of his Wakefields and Little Annie's Rambles. Indeed, *his* spirit of "metaphor run-mad" is clearly imbibed from the phalanx and phalanstery atmosphere in which he has been so long struggling for breath. He has not half the material for the exclusiveness of authorship that he possesses for its universality. He has the purest style, the finest taste, the most available scholarship, the most delicate humor, the most touching pathos, the most radiant imagination, the most consummate ingenuity; and with these varied good qualities he has done *well* as a mystic. But is there any one of these qualities which should prevent his doing doubly as well in a career of honest, upright, sensible, prehensible and comprehensible things? Let him mend his pen, get a bottle of visible ink, come out from the Old Manse, cut Mr. Alcott, hang (if possible) the editor of "The Dial," and throw out of the window to the pigs all his odd numbers of "The North American Review."

Hawthorne and His Mosses: By a Virginian Spending July in Vermont
Herman Melville°

A papered chamber in a fine old farm-house, a mile from any other dwelling, and dipped to the eaves in foliage—surrounded by mountains, old woods, and Indian ponds—this, surely, is the place to write of Hawthorne. Some charm is in this northern air, for love and duty seem both impelling to the task. A man of a deep and noble nature has seized me in this seclusion. His wild, witch-voice rings through me; or, in softer cadences, I seem to hear it in the songs of the hillside birds that sing in the larch trees at my window.

Would that all excellent books were foundlings, without father or mother, that so it might be we could glorify them, without including their ostensible authors! Nor would any true man take exception to this; least of all, he who writes, "When the Artist rises high enough to achieve the Beautiful, the symbol by which he makes it perceptible to mortal senses becomes of little value in his eyes, while his spirit possesses itself in the enjoyment of the reality."

But more than this. I know not what would be the right name to put on the title-page of an excellent book; but this I feel, that the names of all fine authors are fictitious ones, far more so than that of

° Reprinted from *Literary World*, 17 and 24 August 1850, 125–27 and 145–47.

Junius; simply standing, as they do, for the mystical, ever-eluding spirit of all beauty, which ubiquitously possesses men of genius. Purely imaginative as this fancy may appear, it nevertheless seems to receive some warranty from the fact, that on a personal interview no great author has ever come up to the idea of his reader. But that dust of which our bodies are composed, how can it fully express the nobler intelligences among us? With reverence be it spoken, that not even in the case of one deemed more than man, not even in our Saviour, did his visible frame betoken anything of the augustness of the nature within. Else, how could those Jewish eyewitnesses fail to see heaven in his glance!

It is curious how a man may travel along a country road, and yet miss the grandest or sweetest of prospects by reason of an intervening hedge, so like all other hedges, as in no way to hint of the wide landscape beyond. So has it been with me concerning the enchanting landscape in the soul of this Hawthorne, this most excellent Man of Mosses. His "Old Manse" has been written now four years, but I never read it till a day or two since. I had seen it in the book-stores—heard of it often—even had it recommended to me by a tasteful friend, as a rare, quiet book, perhaps too deserving of popularity to be popular. But there are so many books called "excellent," and so much unpopular merit, that amid the thick air of other things, the hint of my tasteful friend was disregarded; and for four years the Mosses on the Old Manse never refreshed me with their perennial green. It may be, however, that all this while the book, likewise,[1] was only improving in flavor and body. At any rate, it so chanced that this long procrastination eventuated in a happy result. At breakfast the other day, a mountain girl, a cousin of mine, who for the last two weeks has every morning helped me to strawberries and raspberries, which, like the roses and pearls in the fairy tale, seemed to fall into the saucer from those strawberry-beds, her cheeks—this delightful creature, this charming Cherry says to me—"I see you spend your mornings in the haymow; and yesterday I found there 'Dwight's Travels in New England.' Now I have something far better than that, something more congenial to our summer on these hills. Take these raspberries, and then I will give you some moss." "Moss!" said I. "Yes, and you must take it to the barn with you, and good-by to 'Dwight.'"

With that she left me, and soon returned with a volume, verdantly bound, and garnished with a curious frontispiece in green; nothing less than a fragment of real moss, cunningly pressed to a fly-leaf. "Why, this," said I, spilling my raspberries, "this is the 'Mosses from an Old Manse.'" "Yes," said cousin Cherry, "yes, it is that flowery Hawthorne." "Hawthorne and Mosses," said I, "no more: it is morning: it is July in the country: and I am off for the barn."

Stretched on that new mown clover, the hill-side breeze blowing over me through the wide barn-door, and soothed by the hum of the bees in the meadows around, how magically stole over me this Mossy Man! and how amply, how bountifully, did he redeem that delicious promise to his guests in the Old Manse, of whom it is written—"Others could give them pleasure, or amusement, or instruction—these could be picked up anywhere—but it was for me to give them rest. Rest, in a life of trouble! What better could be done for weary and world-worn spirits? What better could be done for anybody, who came within our magic circle, than to throw the spell of a magic spirit over him!" So all that day, half-buried in the new clover, I watched this Hawthorne's "Assyrian dawn, and Paphian sunset and moonrise, from the summit of our Eastern Hill."

The soft ravishments of the man spun me round about in a web of dreams, and when the book was closed, when the spell was over, this wizard "dismissed me with but misty reminiscences, as if I had been dreaming of him."

What a wild moonlight of contemplative humor bathes that Old Manse!—the rich and rare distillment of a spicy and slowly-oozing heart. No rollicking rudeness, no gross fun fed on fat dinners, and bred in the lees of wine,—but a humor so spiritually gentle, so high, so deep, and yet so richly relishable, that it were hardly inappropriate in an angel. It is the very religion of mirth; for nothing so human but it may be advanced to that. The orchard of the Old Manse seems the visible type of the fine mind that has described it—those twisted and contorted old trees "that stretch out their crooked branches, and take such hold of the imagination, that we remember them as humorists and odd-fellows." And then, as surrounded by these grotesque forms, and hushed in the noon-day repose of this Hawthorne's spell, how aptly might the still fall of his ruddy thoughts into your soul be symbolized by "the thump of a great apple, in the stillest afternoon, falling without a breath of wind, from the mere necessity of perfect ripeness!" For no less ripe than ruddy are the apples of the thoughts and fancies in this sweet Man of Mosses—"Buds and Bird-voices"— What a delicious thing is that! "Will the world ever be so decayed, that Spring may not renew its greenness?" And the "Fire-Worship." Was ever the hearth so glorified into an altar before? The mere title of that piece is better than any common work in fifty folio volumes. How exquisite is this:—"Nor did it lessen the charm of his soft, familiar courtesy and helpfulness, that the mighty spirit, were opportunity offered him, would run riot through the peaceful house, wrap its inmates in his terrible embrace, and leave nothing of them save their whitened bones. This possibility of mad destruction only made his domestic kindness the more beautiful and touching. It was so sweet of him, being endowed with such power, to dwell, day after day, and one long, lonesome night after another, on the dusky hearth, only now and then betraying his wild nature, by thrusting his red tongue out of the chimney-top! True, he had done much mischief in the world, and was pretty certain to do more, but his warm heart atoned for all; He was kindly to the race of man."

But he has still other apples, not quite so ruddy, though full as ripe;—apples, that have been left to wither on the tree, after the pleasant autumn gathering is past. The sketch of "The Old Apple-Dealer" is conceived in the subtlest spirit of sadness; he whose "subdued and nerveless boyhood prefigured his abortive prime, which, likewise, contained within itself the prophecy and image of his lean and torpid age." Such touches as are in this piece cannot proceed from any common heart. They argue such a depth of tenderness, such a boundless sympathy with all forms of being, such an omnipresent love, that we must needs say that this Hawthorne is here almost alone in his generation,—at least, in the artistic manifestation of these things. Still more. Such touches as these,—and many, very many similar ones, all through his chapters—furnish clues whereby we enter a little way into the intricate, profound heart where they originated. And we see that suffering, some time or other and in some shape or other,—this only can enable any man to depict it in others. All over him, Hawthorne's melancholy rests like an Indian-summer, which, though bathing a whole country in one softness, still reveals the distinctive hue of every towering hill and each far-winding vale.

But it is the least part of genius that attracts admiration. Where Hawthorne is known, he seems to be deemed a pleasant writer, with a pleasant style,—a sequestered, harmless man, from whom any deep and weighty thing would hardly be anticipated—a man who means no meanings. But there is no man, in whom humor and love, like mountain peaks, soar to such a rapt height as to receive the irradiations of the upper skies;—there is no man in whom humor and love are developed in that high form called genius; no such man can exist without also possessing, as the indispensible complement of these, a great, deep intellect, which drops down into the universe like a plummet. Or, love and humor are only the eyes through which such an intellect views this world. The great beauty in such a mind is but the product of its strength. What, to all readers, can be more charming than the piece entitled "Monsieur du Miroir;" and to a reader at all capable of fully fathoming it, what, at the same time, can possess more mystical depth of meaning?—yes, there he sits and looks at me,—this "shape of mystery," this "identical Monsieur du Miroir." "Methinks I should tremble now, were his wizard power of gliding through all impediments in search of me, to place him suddenly before my eyes."

How profound, nay appalling, is the moral evolved by the Earth's Holocaust; where—beginning with the hollow follies and affectations of the world,—all vanities and empty theories and forms are, one after another, and by an admirably graduated, growing comprehensiveness, thrown into the allegorical fire, till, at length, nothing is left but the all-engendering heart of man; which remaining still unconsumed, the great conflagration is naught.

Of a piece with this, is the "Intelligence Office," a wondrous symbolizing of the secret workings in men's souls. There are other sketches still more charged with ponderous import.

"The Christmas Banquet," and "The Bosom Serpent," would be fine subjects for a curious and elaborate analysis, touching the conjectural parts of the mind that produced them. For spite of all the Indian-summer sunlight on the hither side of Hawthorne's soul, the other side—like the dark half of the physical sphere—is shrouded in a blackness, ten times black. But this darkness but gives more effect to the ever-moving dawn, that for ever advances through it, and circumnavigates his world. Whether Hawthorne has simply availed himself of this mystical blackness as a means to the wondrous effects he makes it to produce in his lights and shades; or whether there really lurks in him, perhaps unknown to himself, a touch of Puritanic gloom,—this, I cannot altogether tell. Certain it is, however, that this great power of blackness in him derives its force from its appeals to that Calvinistic sense of Innate Depravity and Original Sin, from whose visitations, in some shape or other, no deeply thinking mind is always and wholly free. For, in certain moods, no man can weigh this world without throwing in something, somehow like Original Sin, to strike the uneven balance. At all events, perhaps no writer has ever wielded this terrific thought with greater terror than this same harmless Hawthorne. Still more: this black conceit pervades him through and through. You may be witched by his sunlight,—transported by the bright gildings in the skies he builds over you; but there is the blackness of darkness beyond; and even his bright gildings but fringe and play upon the edges of thunder-clouds. In one word, the world is mistaken in this Nathaniel Hawthorne. He himself must often have smiled at its absurd misconception of him. He is immeasurably deeper than the plummet of the mere critic. For it is not the brain that can test such a man; it is only the heart. You cannot come to know greatness by inspecting it; there is no glimpse to be caught of it, except by intuition; you need not ring it, you but touch it; and you find it is gold.

Now, it is that blackness in Hawthorne, of which I have spoken, that so fixes and fascinates me. It may be, nevertheless, that it is too largely developed in him. Perhaps he does not give us a ray of his light for every shade of his dark. But however this may be, this blackness it is that furnishes the infinite obscure of his back-ground,—that back-ground, against which Shakspeare plays his grandest conceits, the things that have made for Shakspeare his loftiest but most circumscribed renown, as the profoundest of thinkers. For by philosophers Shakspeare is not adored as the great man of tragedy and comedy.—"Off with his head; so much for Buckingham!" This sort of rant, interlined by another hand, brings down the house,—those mistaken souls, who dream of Shakspeare as a mere man of Richard-the-Third humps and Macbeth daggers. But it is those deep far-away things in him; those occasional flashings-forth of the intuitive Truth in him; those short, quick probings at the very axis of reality;—these are the things that make Shakspeare, Shakspeare. Through the mouths of the dark characters of Hamlet, Timon, Lear, and Iago, he craftily says, or sometimes insinuates the things which we feel to be so terrifically true, that it were all but madness for any good man, in his own proper character, to utter, or even hint of them. Tormented into desperation, Lear, the frantic king, tears off the mask, and speaks the same madness of vital truth. But, as I before said, it is the least part of genius that attracts admiration. And so, much of the blind, unbridled admiration that has been heaped upon Shakspeare, has been lavished upon the least part of him. And few of his endless commentators and critics seem to have remembered, or even perceived, that the immediate products of a great mind are not so great as that undeveloped and sometimes undevelopable yet dimly-discernible greatness, to which those immediate products are but the infallible indices. In Shakspeare's tomb lies infinitely more than Shakspeare ever wrote. And if I magnify Shakspeare, it is not so much for what he did do as for what he did not do, or refrained from doing. For in this world of lies, Truth is forced to fly like a scared white doe in the woodlands; and only by cunning glimpses will she reveal herself, as in Shakspeare and other masters of the great Art of Telling the Truth,—even though it be covertly and by snatches.

But if this view of the all-popular Shakspeare be seldom taken by his readers, and if very few who extol him have ever read him deeply, or perhaps, only have seen him on the tricky stage (which alone made, and is still making him his mere mob renown)—if few men have time, or patience, or palate, for the spiritual truth as it is in that great genius;—it is then no matter of surprise, that in a contemporaneous age, Nathaniel Hawthorne is a man as yet almost utterly mistaken among men. Here and there, in some quiet armchair in the noisy town, or some deep nook among the noiseless mountains, he may be appreciated for something of what he is. But unlike Shakspeare, who was forced to the contrary course by circumstances, Hawthorne (either from simple disinclination, or else from inaptitude) refrains from all the popularizing noise and show of broad farce and blood-besmeared tragedy; content with the still, rich utterance of a great intellect in repose, and which sends a few thoughts into circulation, except they be arterialized at his large warm lungs, and expanded in his honest heart.

Nor need you fix upon that blackness in him, if it suit you not. Nor, indeed, will all readers discern it; for it is, mostly, insinuated to those who may best understand it, and account for it; it is not obtruded upon every one alike.

Some may start to read of Shakspeare and Hawthorne on the same page. They may say, that if an illustration were needed, a lesser light might have sufficed to elucidate this Hawthorne, this small man of yesterday. But I am not willingly one of those who, as touching Shakspeare at least, exemplify the maxim of Rochefoucault, that "we exalt the reputation of some, in order to depress that of others;"— who, to teach all noble-souled aspirants that there is no hope for them, pronounce Shakspeare absolutely unapproachable. But Shakspeare has been approached. There are minds that have gone as far as Shakspeare into the universe. And hardly a mortal man, who, at some time or other, has not felt as great thoughts in him as any you will find in Hamlet. We must not inferentially malign mankind for the sake of any one man, whoever he may be. This is too cheap a purchase of contentment for conscious mediocrity to make. Besides, this absolute and unconditional adoration of Shakspeare has grown to be a part of our Anglo-Saxon superstitions. The Thirty-Nine articles are now Forty. Intolerance has come to exist in this matter. You must believe in Shakspeare's unapproachability, or quit the country. But what sort of a belief is this for an American, a man who is bound to carry republican progressiveness into Literature as well as into Life? Believe me, my friends, that men, not very much inferior to Shakspeare, are this day being born on the banks of the Ohio. And the day will come when you shall say, Who reads a book by an Englishman that is a modern? The great mistake seems to be, that even with those Americans who look forward to the coming of a great literary genius among us, they somehow fancy he will come in the costume of Queen Elizabeth's day; be a writer of dramas founded upon old English history or the tales of Boccaccio. Whereas, great geniuses are parts of the times, they themselves are the times, and possess a correspondent coloring. It is of a piece with the Jews, who, while their Shiloh was meekly walking in their streets, were still praying for his magnificent coming; looking for him in a chariot, who was already among them on an ass. Nor must we forget that, in his own lifetime, Shakspeare was not Shakspeare, but only Master William Shakspeare of the shrewd, thriving, business firm of Condell, Shakspeare & Co., proprietors of the Globe Theatre in London; and by a courtly author, of the name of Chettle, was looked at[2] as an "upstart crow," beautified "with other birds' feathers." For, mark it well, imitation is often the first charge brought against real originality. Why this is so, there is not space to set forth here. You must have plenty of sea-room to tell the Truth in; especially when it seems to have an aspect of newness, as America did in 1492, though it was then just as old, and perhaps older than Asia, only those sagacious philosophers, the common sailors, had never seen it before, swearing it was all water and moonshine there.

◦　◦　◦

Now I do not say that Nathaniel of Salem is a greater than William of Avon, or as great. But the difference between the two men is by no means immeasurable. Not a very great deal more, and Nathaniel were verily William.

This, too, I mean, that if Shakspeare has not been equalled, give the world time, and he is sure to be surpassed, in one hemisphere or the other. Nor will it at all do to say, that the world is getting grey and grizzled now, and has lost that fresh charm which she wore of old, and by virtue of which the great poets of past times made themselves what we esteem them to be. Not so. The world is as young to-day as when it was created; and this Vermont morning dew is as wet to my feet, as Eden's dew to Adam's. Nor has nature been all over ransacked by our progenitors, so that no new charms and mysteries remain for this latter generation to find. Far from it. The trillionth part has not yet been said; and all that has been said, but multiplies the avenues to what remains to be said. It is not so much paucity as superabundance of material that seems to incapacitate modern authors.

Let America, then, prize and cherish her writers; yea, let her glorify them. They are not so many in number as to exhaust her good-will. And while she has good kith and kin of her own, to take to her bosom, let her not lavish her embraces upon the household of an alien. For believe it or not, England, after all, is in many things an alien to us. China has more bonds[3] of real love for us than she. But even were there no strong literary individualities among us, as there are some dozens[4] at least, nevertheless, let America first praise mediocrity even, in her own children, before she praises (for every-where, merit demands acknowledgement from every one) the best excellence in the children of any other land. Let her own authors, I say, have the priority of appreciation. I was much pleased with a hot-headed Carolina cousin of mine, who once said,—"If there were no other American to stand by, in literature, why, then, I would stand by Pop Emmons and his 'Fredoniad,' and till a better epic came along, swear it was not very far behind the Iliad." Take away the words, and in spirit he was sound.

Not that American genius needs patronage in order to expand. For that explosive sort of stuff will expand though screwed up in a vice, and burst it, thought it were triple steel. It is for the nation's sake, and not for her authors' sake, that I would have America be heedful of the increasing greatness among her writers. For how great the shame, if other nations should be before her, in crowning her heroes of the pen! But this is almost the case now. American authors have received more just and discriminating praise (however loftly and ridiculously given, in certain cases) even from some Englishmen, than from their own countrymen. There are hardly five critics in America; and several of them are asleep. As for patronage, it is the American author who now patronizes his country, and not his country him. And if at times some among them appeal to the people for more recognition, it is not always with selfish motives, but patriotic ones.

It is true, that but few of them as yet have evinced that decided originality which merits great praise. But that graceful writer, who perhaps of all Americans has received the most plaudits from his own country for his productions,—that very popular and amiable writer, however good and self-reliant in many things, perhaps owes his chief reputation to the self-acknowledged imitation of a foreign model, and to the studied avoidance of all topics but smooth ones. But it is better to fail in originality, than to succeed in imitation. He who has never failed somewhere, that man cannot be great. Failure is the true test of greatness. And if it be said, that continual success is a proof that a man wisely knows his powers,—it is only to be added that, in that case, he knows them to be small. Let us believe it, then, once for all, that there is no hope for us in these smooth, pleasing writers that know their powers. Without malice, but to speak the plain fact, they but furnish an appendix to Goldsmith, and other English authors. And we want no American Goldsmiths; nay, we want no American Miltons. It were the vilest thing you could say of a true American author, that he were an American Tompkins. Call him an American and have done, for you cannot say a nobler thing of him. But it is not meant that all American writers should studiously cleave to nationality in their writings; only this, no American writer should write like an Englishman or a Frenchman; let him write like a man, for then he will be sure to write like an American. Let us away with this leaven of literary flunkeyism towards England. If either must play the flunkey in this thing, let England do it, not us. While we are rapidly preparing for that political supremacy among the nations which prophetically awaits us at the close of the present century, in a literary point of view, we are deplorably unprepared for it; and we seem studious to remain so. Hitherto, reasons might have existed why this should be; but no good reason exists now. And all that is requisite to amendment in this matter, is simply this: that while fully[5] acknowledging all excellence everywhere, we should refrain from unduly lauding foreign writers, and, at the same time, duly recognize the meritorious writers that are our own;—those writers who breathe that unshackled, democratic spirit of Christianity in all things, which now takes the practical lead in this world, though at the same time led by ourselves—us Americans. Let us boldly contemn all imitation, though it comes to us graceful and fragrant as the morning; and foster all originality, though at first it be crabbed and ugly as our own pine knots. And if any of our authors fail, or seem to fail, then, in the words of my Carolina cousin, let us clap him on the shoulder, and back him against all Europe for his second round. The truth is, that in one point of view, this matter of a national literature has come to such a pass with us, that in some sense we must turn bullies, else the day is lost, or superiority so far beyond us, that we can hardly say it will ever be ours.

And now, my countrymen, as an excellent author of your own flesh and blood,—an unimitating, and perhaps, in his way, an inimitable man—whom better can I commend to you, in the first place, than Nathaniel Hawthorne. He is one of the new, and far better generation of your writers. The smell of your beeches and hemlocks is upon him; your own broad prairies are in his soul; and if you travel away inland into his deep and noble nature, you will hear the far roar of his Niagara. Give not over to future generations the glad duty of acknowledging him for what he is. Take that joy to yourself, in your own generation; and so shall he feel those grateful impulses on him,[6] that may possibly prompt him to the full flower of some still greater achievement in your eyes. And by confessing him you thereby confess others; you brace the whole brotherhood. For genius, all over the world, stands hand in hand, and one shock of recognition runs the whole circle round.

In treating of Hawthorne, or rather of Hawthorne in his writings (for I never saw the man; and in the chances of a quiet plantation life, remote from his haunts, perhaps never shall); in treating of his works, I say, I have thus far omitted all mention of his "Twice-told Tales," and "Scarlet Letter." Both are excellent, but full of such manifold, strange, and diffusive beauties, that time would all but fail me to point the half of them out. But there are things to those two books, which, had they been written in England a century ago, Nathaniel Hawthorne had utterly displaced many of the bright names we now revere on authority. But I am content to leave Hawthorne to himself, and to the infallible finding of posterity; and however great may be the praise I have bestowed upon him, I feel that in so doing I have more served and honored myself, than him. For, at bottom, great excellence is praise enough to itself; but the feeling of a sincere and appreciative love and admiration towards it, this is relieved by utterance; and warm, honest praise, ever leaves a pleasant flavor in the mouth; and it is an honorable thing to confess to what is honorable in others.

But I cannot leave my subject yet. No man can read a fine author, and relish him to his very bones while he reads, without subsequently fancying to himself some ideal image of the man and his mind. And if you rightly look for it, you will almost always find that the author himself has somewhere furnished you with his own picture. For poets (whether in prose or verse), being painters of nature, are like their bethren of the pencil, the true portrait-painters, who, in the multitude of likenesses to be sketched, do not invariably omit their own; and in all high instances, they paint them without any vanity, though at times with a lurking something that would take several pages to properly define.

I submit it, then, to those best acquainted with the man personally, whether the following is not Nathaniel Hawthorne;—and to himself, whether something involved in it does not express the temper of his mind,—that lasting temper of all true, candid men—a seeker, not a finder yet:—"A man now entered, in neglected attire, with the aspect of a thinker, but somewhat too rough-hewn and brawny for a scholar. His face was full of sturdy vigor, with some finer and keener attribute beneath; though harsh at first, it was tempered with the glow of a large, warm heart, which had force enough to heat his powerful intellect through and through. He advanced to the Intelligencer, and looked at him with a glance of such stern sincerity, that perhaps few secrets were beyond its scope. 'I seek for Truth,' said he."

Twenty-four hours have elapsed since writing the foregoing. I have just returned from the hay-mow, charged more and more with love and admiration of Hawthorne. For I have just been gleaning through the Mosses, picking up many things here and there that had previously escaped me. And I found that but to glean after this man, is better than to be in at the harvest of others. To be frank (though, perhaps, rather foolish) notwithstanding what I wrote yesterday of these Mosses, I had not then culled them all, but had, nevertheless, been sufficiently sensible of the subtle essence in them, as to write as I did. To what infinite height of loving wonder and admiration I may yet be borne, when by repeatedly banqueting on these Mosses I shall have thoroughly incorporated their whole stuff into my being,— that, I cannot tell. But already I feel that this Hawthorne has dropped germinous seeds into my soul. He expands and deepens down, the more I contemplate him; and further and further, shoots his strong New England roots into the hot soil in my Southern soul.

By careful reference to the "Table of Contents," I now find that I have gone through all the sketches; but that when I yesterday wrote, I had not at all read two particular pieces, to which I now desire to call special attention,—"A Select Party," and "Young Goodman Brown." Here, be it said, to all those whom this poor fugitive scrawl of mine may tempt to the perusal of the "Mosses," that they must on no account suffer themselves to be trifled with, disappointed, or deceived by the triviality of many of the titles to these sketches. For in more than one instance, the title utterly belies the piece. It is as if rustic demijohns containing the very best and costliest of Falernian and Tokay, were labelled "Cider," "Perry," and "Elderberry wine." The truth seems to be, that like many other geniuses, this Man of Mosses takes great delight in hoodwinking the world,— at least, with respect to himself. Personally, I doubt not that he rather prefers to be generally esteemed but a so-so sort of author; being willing to reserve the thorough and acute appreciation of what he is, to that party most qualified to judge—that is, to himself. Besides, at the bottom of their natures, men like Hawthorne, in many things, deem the plaudits of the public such strong presumptive evidence of mediocrity in the object of them, that it would in some degree render them doubtful of their own powers, did they hear much and vociferous braying concerning them in the public pastures. True, I have been braying myself (if you please to be witty enough to have it so), but then I claim to be the first that has so brayed in this particular matter; and therefore, while pleading guilty to the charge, still claim all the merit due to originality.

But with whatever motive, playful or profound, Nathaniel Hawthorne has chosen to entitle his pieces in the manner he has, it is certain that some of them are directly calculated to deceive—egregiously deceive, the superficial skimmer of pages. To be downright and candid once more, let me cheerfully say, that two of these titles did dolefully dupe no less an eager-eyed[7] reader than myself; and that, too, after I had been impressed with a sense of the great depth and breadth of this American man. "Who in the name of thunder" (as the country-people say in this neighborhood), "who in the name of thunder, would anticipate any marvel in a piece entitled 'Young Goodman Brown?' " You would of course suppose that it was a simple little tale, intended as a supplement to "Goody Two Shoes." Whereas, it is deep as Dante; nor can you finish it, without addressing the author in his own words—"It is yours to penetrate, in every bosom, the deep mystery of sin." And with Young Goodman, too, in allegorical pursuit of his Puritan wife, you cry out in your anguish: " 'Faith!' shouted Goodman Brown, in a voice of agony and desperation; and the echoes of the forest mocked him, crying—'Faith! Faith!' as if bewildered wretches were seeking her all through the wilderness."

Now this same piece, entitled "Young Goodman Brown," is one of the two that I had not all read yesterday; and I allude to it now, because it is, in itself, such a strong positive illustration of that blackness in Hawthorne, which I had assumed from the mere occasional shadows of it, as revealed in several of the other sketches. But had I previously perused "Young Goodman Brown," I should have been at no pains to draw the conclusion, which I came to at a time when I was ignorant that the book contained one such direct and unqualified manifestation of it.

The other piece of the two referred to, is entitled "A Select Party," which, in my first simplicity upon originally taking hold of the book, I fancied must treat of some pumpkin-pie party in old Salem, or some chowder-party on Cape Cod. Whereas, by all the gods of Peedee, it is the sweetest and sublimest thing that has been written since Spenser wrote. Nay, there is nothing in Spenser that surpasses it, perhaps nothing that equals it. And the test is this: read any canto in "The Faery Queen," and then read "A Select Party," and decide which pleases you most,—that is, if you are qualified to judge. Do not be frightened at this; for when Spenser was alive, he was thought of very much as Hawthorne is now,—was generally accounted just such a "gentle" harmless man. It may be, that to common eyes, the sublimity of Hawthorne seems lost in his sweetness,—as perhaps in that same "Select Party" of his; for whom he has builded so august a dome of sunset clouds, and served them on richer plate than Belshazzar when he banqueted his lords in Babylon.

But my chief business now, is to point out a particular page in this piece, having reference to an honored guest, who under the name of "The Master Genius," but in the guise "of a young man of poor attire, with no insignia of rank or acknowledged eminence," is introduced to the man of Fancy, who is the giver of the feast. Now, the page having reference to this "Master Genius," so happily expresses much of what I yesterday wrote, touching the coming of the literary Shiloh of America, that I cannot but be charmed by the coincidence; especially, when it shows such a parity of ideas, at least in this one point, between a man like Hawthorne and a man like me.

And here, let me throw out another conceit of mine touching this American Shiloh, or "Master Genius," as Hawthorne calls him. May it not be, that this commanding mind has not been, is not, and never will be, individually developed in any one man? And would it, indeed, appear so unreasonable to suppose, that this great fulness and overflowing may be, or may be destined to be, shared by a plurality of men of genius? Surely, to take the very greatest example on record, Shakspeare cannot be regarded as in himself the concretion of all the genius of his time; nor as so immeasurably beyond Marlow, Webster, Ford, Beaumont, Jonson, that these great men can be said to share none of his power? For one, I conceive that there were dramatists in Elizabeth's day, between whom and Shakspeare the distance was by no means great. Let any one, hitherto little acquainted with those neglected old authors, for the first time read them thoroughly, or even read Charles Lamb's Specimens of them, and he will be amazed at the wondrous ability of those Anaks of men, and shocked at this renewed example of the fact, that Fortune has more to do with fame than merit,—though, without merit, lasting fame there can be none.

Nevertheless, it would argue too ill of my country were this maxim to hold good concerning Nathaniel Hawthorne, a man, who already, in some few minds, has shed "such a light, as never illuminates the earth save when a great heart burns as the household fire of a grand intellect."

The words are his,—"in the Select Party," and they are a magnificent setting to a coincident sentiment of my own, but ramblingly expressed yesterday, in reference to himself. Gainsay it who will, as I now write, I am Posterity speaking by proxy—and after times will make it more than good, when I declare, that the American, who up to the present day has evinced, in literature, the largest brain with the largest heart, that man is Nathaniel Hawthorne. Moreover, that whatever Nathaniel Hawthorne may hereafter write, "The Mosses from an Old Manse" will be ultimately accounted his master-piece. For there is a sure, though a secret sign in some works which proves the culmination of the powers (only the developable ones, however) that produced them. But I am by no means desirous of the glory of a prophet. I pray Heaven that Hawthorne may *yet* prove me an impostor in this prediction. Especially, as I somehow cling to the strange fancy, that, in all men, hiddenly reside certain wondrous, occult properties—as in some plants and minerals—which by some happy but very rare accident (as bronze was discovered by the melting of the iron and brass at the burning of Corinth) may chance to be called forth here on earth; not entirely waiting for their better discovery in the more congenial, blessed atmosphere of heaven.

Once more—for it is hard to be finite upon an infinite subject, and all subjects are infinite. By some people this entire scrawl of mine may be esteemed altogether unnecessary, inasmuch "as years ago" (they may say) "we found out the rich and rare stuff in this Hawthorne, whom you now parade forth, as if only *yourself* were the discoverer of his Portuguese diamond in our literature." But even granting all this—and adding to it, the assumption that the books of Hawthorne have sold by the five thousand,—what does that signify? They should be sold by the hundred thousand; and read by the million; and admired by every one who is capable of admiration.

Notes

1. [Ed. note: Printer's error for "like wine."]
2. [Ed. note: Printer's error for "hooted at."]

3. [Ed. note: Printer's error for "bowels."]
4. [Ed. note: Printer's error for "dozen."]
5. [Ed. note: Printer's error for "freely."]
6. [Ed. note: Printer's error for "in him."]
7. [Ed. note: Printer's error for "eagle-eyed."]

[From *Hawthorne:* The Tales]   Henry James°

. . . When I think of it, I almost envy Hawthorne's earliest readers; the sensation of opening upon *The Great Carbuncle, The Seven Vagabonds* or *The Threefold Destiny* in an American annual of forty years ago, must have been highly agreeable.

Among these shorter things (it is better to speak of the whole collection, including the *Snow Image* and the *Mosses from an Old Manse,* at once) there are three sorts of tales, each one of which has an original stamp. There are, to begin with, the stories of fantasy and allegory—those among which the three I have just mentioned would be numbered, and which, on the whole, are the most original. This is the group to which such little masterpieces as *Malvin's Burial, Rappacini's Daughter,* and *Young Goodman Brown* also belong—these two last perhaps representing the highest point that Hawthorne reached in this direction. Then there are the little tales of New England history, which are scarcely less admirable, and of which *The Grey Champion, The Maypole of Merry Mount,* and the four beautiful *Legends of the Province House,* as they are called, are the most successful specimens. Lastly come the slender sketches of actual scenes and of the objects and manners about him, by means of which, more particularly, he endeavoured "to open an intercourse with the world," and which, in spite of their slenderness, have an infinite grace and charm. Among these things *A Rill from the Town Pump, The Village Uncle, The Toll-Gatherer's Day,* the *Chippings with a Chisel,* may most naturally be mentioned. As we turn over these volumes we feel that the pieces that spring most directly from his fancy constitute, as I have said (putting his four novels aside), his most substantial claim to our attention. It would be a mistake to insist too much upon them; Hawthorne was himself the first to recognise that. "These fitful sketches," he says in the preface to the *Mosses from an Old Manse,* "with so little of external life about them, yet claiming no profundity of purpose—so reserved even while they sometimes seem so frank—often but half in earnest, and never, even when most so, expressing satisfactorily the thoughts which they profess to image—such trifles,

° Reprinted from *Hawthorne* (New York: Harper & Brothers, 1880), 55–66.

I truly feel, afford no solid basis for a literary reputation." This is very becomingly uttered; but it may be said, partly in answer to it, and partly in confirmation, that the valuable element in these things was not what Hawthorne put into them consciously, but what passed into them without his being able to measure it—the element of simple genius, the quality of imagination. This is the real charm of Hawthorne's writing—this purity and spontaneity and naturalness of fancy. For the rest, it is interesting to see how it borrowed a particular colour from the other faculties that lay near it—how the imagination, in this capital son of the old Puritans, reflected the hue of the more purely moral part, of the dusky, overshadowed conscience. The conscience, by no fault of its own, in every genuine offshoot of that sombre lineage, lay under the shadow of the sense of *sin*. This darkening cloud was no essential part of the nature of the individual; it stood fixed in the general moral heaven under which he grew up and looked at life. It projected from above, from outside, a black patch over his spirit, and it was for him to do what he could with the black patch. There were all sorts of possible ways of dealing with it; they depended upon the personal temperament. Some natures would let it lie as it fell, and contrive to be tolerably comfortable beneath it. Others would groan and sweat and suffer; but the dusky blight would remain, and their lives would be lives of misery. Here and there an individual, irritated beyond endurance, would throw it off in anger, plunging probably into what would be deemed deeper abysses of depravity. Hawthorne's way was the best; for he contrived, by an exquisite process, best known to himself, to transmute this heavy moral burden into the very substance of the imagination, to make it evaporate in the light and charming fumes of artistic production. But Hawthorne, of course, was exceptionally fortunate; he had his genius to help him. Nothing is more curious and interesting than this almost exclusively *imported* character of the sense of sin in Hawthorne's mind; it seems to exist there merely for an artistic or literary purpose. He had ample cognizance of the Puritan conscience; it was his natural heritage; it was reproduced in him; looking into his soul, he found it there. But his relation to it was only, as one may say, intellectual; it was not moral and theological. He played with it, and used it as a pigment; he treated it, as the metaphysicians say, objectively. He was not discomposed, disturbed, haunted by it, in the manner of its usual and regular victims, who had not the little postern door of fancy to slip through, to the other side of the wall. It was, indeed, to his imaginative vision, the great fact of man's nature; the light element that had been mingled with his own composition always clung to this rugged prominence of moral responsibility, like the mist that hovers about the mountain. It was a necessary condition for a man of Hawthorne's stock that if his imagination should take license to amuse itself, it should at least select this grim precinct of the Puritan morality for its play-ground. He speaks of the dark disapproval with which his old ancestors, in the case of their coming to life, would see him trifling himself away as a story-teller. But how far more darkly would they have frowned could they have understood that he had converted the very principle of their own being into one of his toys!

It will be seen that I am far from being struck with the justice of that view of the author of the *Twice-told Tales*, which is so happily expressed by the French critic to whom I alluded at an earlier stage of this essay. To speak of Hawthorne, as M. Emile Montégut does, as a *romancier pessimiste*, seems to me very much beside the mark. He is no more a pessimist than an optimist, though he is certainly not much of either. He does not pretend to conclude, or to have a philosophy of human nature; indeed, I should even say that at bottom he does not take human nature as hard as he may seem to do. "His bitterness," says M. Montégut, "is without abatement, and his bad opinion of man is without compensation. . . . His little tales have the air of confessions which the soul makes to itself; they are so many little slaps which the author applies to our face." This, it seems to me, is to exaggerate almost immeasurably the reach of Hawthorne's relish of gloomy subjects. What pleased him in such subjects was their picturesqueness, their rich duskiness of colour, their chiaroscuro; but they were not the expression of a hopeless, or even of a predominantly melancholy, feeling about the human soul. Such at least is my own impression. He is to a considerable degree ironical—this is part of his charm—part even, one may say, of his brightness; but he is neither bitter nor cynical—he is rarely even what I should call tragical. There have certainly been story-tellers of a gayer and lighter spirit; there have been observers more humorous, more hilarious— though on the whole Hawthorne's observation has a smile in it oftener than may at first appear; but there has rarely been an observer more serene, less agitated by what he sees and less disposed to call things deeply into question. As I have already intimated, his Note-Books are full of this simple and almost childlike serenity. That dusky preoccupation with the misery of human life and the wickedness of the human heart which such a critic as M. Emile Montégut talks about, is totally absent from them; and if we may suppose a person to have read these Diaries before looking into the tales, we may be sure that such a reader would be greatly surprised to hear the author described as a disappointed, disdainful genius. "This marked love of cases of conscience," says M. Montégut; "this taciturn, scornful cast of mind; this habit of seeing sin everywhere, and hell always gaping open; this dusky gaze bent always upon a damned world, and a nature draped in mourning; these lonely conversations of the imagination with the conscience; this pitiless analysis resulting from a perpetual examination of one's self, and from the tortures of a heart closed before men and open to God—all these elements of the Puritan character have passed into Mr. Hawthorne, or, to speak more justly, have *filtered* into him, through a long succession of generations." This is a very pretty and very vivid account of Hawthorne, superficially considered; and it is just such a view of the case as would commend itself most easily and most naturally to a hasty critic. It is all true indeed, with a difference; Hawthorne was all that M. Montégut says, *minus* the conviction. The old Puritan moral sense, the consciousness of sin and hell, of the fearful nature of our responsibilities and the savage character of our Taskmaster—these things had been lodged in the mind of a man of Fancy, whose fancy had straightway begun to take liberties and play tricks with them—to judge them (Heaven forgive him!) from the poetic and aesthetic point of view, the point of view of entertainment and irony. This absence of conviction makes the difference; but the difference is great.

Hawthorne was a man of fancy, and I suppose that, in speaking of him, it is inevitable that we should feel ourselves confronted with the familiar problem of the difference between the fancy and the imagination. Of the larger and more potent faculty he certainly possessed a liberal share; no one can read *The House of the Seven Gables* without feeling it to be a deeply imaginative work. But I am often struck, especially in the shorter tales, of which I am now chiefly speaking, with a kind of small ingenuity, a taste for conceits and analogies, which bears more particularly what is called the fanciful stamp. The finer of the shorter tales are redolent of a rich imagination.

> Had Goodman Brown fallen asleep in the forest and only dreamed a wild dream of witch-meeting? Be it so, if you will; but, alas, it was a dream of evil omen for young Goodman Brown! a stern, a sad, a darkly meditative, a distrustful, if not a desperate, man, did he become from the night of that fearful dream. On the Sabbath-day, when the congregation were singing a holy psalm, he could not listen, because an anthem of sin rushed loudly upon his ear and drowned all the blessed strain. When the minister spoke from the pulpit, with power and fervid eloquence, and with his hand on the open Bible of the sacred truth of our religion, and of saint-like lives and triumphant deaths, and of future bliss or misery unutterable, then did Goodman Brown grow pale, dreading lest the roof should thunder down upon the gray blasphemer and his hearers. Often, awaking suddenly at midnight, he shrank from the bosom of Faith; and at morning or eventide, when the family knelt down at prayer, he scowled and muttered to himself, and gazed sternly at his wife, and turned away. And when he had lived long, and was borne to his grave a hoary corpse, followed by Faith, an aged woman, and children, and grandchildren, a goodly procession, be-

sides neighbours not a few, they carved no hopeful verse upon his tombstone, for his dying hour was gloom.

There is imagination in that, and in many another passage that I might quote; but as a general thing I should characterise the more metaphysical of our author's short stories as graceful and felicitous conceits. They seem to me to be qualified in this manner by the very fact that they belong to the province of allegory. Hawthorne, in his metaphysical moods, is nothing if not allegorical, and allegory, to my sense, is quite one of the lighter exercises of the imagination. Many excellent judges, I know, have a great stomach for it; they delight in symbols and correspondences, in seeing a story told as if it were another and a very different story. I frankly confess that I have, as a general thing, but little enjoyment of it, and that it has never seemed to me to be, as it were, a first-rate literary form. It has produced assuredly some first-rate works; and Hawthorne in his younger years had been a great reader and devotee of Bunyan and Spenser, the great masters of allegory. But it is apt to spoil two good things—a story and a moral, a meaning and a form; and the taste for it is responsible for a large part of the forcible-feeble writing that has been inflicted upon the world. The only cases in which it is endurable is when it is extremely spontaneous, when the analogy presents itself with eager promptitude. When it shows signs of having been groped and fumbled for, the needful illusion is of course absent, and the failure complete. Then the machinery alone is visible, and the end to which it operates becomes a matter of indifference. There was but little literary criticism in the United States at the time Hawthorne's earlier works were published; but among the reviewers Edgar Poe perhaps held the scales the highest. He, at any rate, rattled them loudest, and pretended, more than any one else, to conduct the weighing-process on scientific principles. Very remarkable was this process of Edgar Poe's, and very extraordinary were his principles; but he had the advantage of being a man of genius, and his intelligence was frequently great. His collection of critical sketches of the American writers flourishing in what M. Taine would call his *milieu* and *moment*, is very curious and interesting reading, and it has one quality which ought to keep it from ever being completely forgotten. It is probably the most complete and exquisite specimen of *provincialism* ever prepared for the edification of men. Poe's judgments are pretentious, spiteful, vulgar; but they contain a great deal of sense and discrimination as well, and here and there, sometimes at frequent intervals, we find a phrase of happy insight imbedded in a patch of the most fatuous pedantry. He wrote a chapter upon Hawthorne, and spoke of him, on the whole, very kindly; and his estimate is of sufficient value to make it noticeable that he should express lively disapproval of the large part allotted to allegory in his tales—in defence of which, he says, "however, or for whatever object employed, there is scarcely one respectable word to be said. . . . The deepest emotion," he goes on, "aroused within us by the happiest allegory *as* allegory, is a very, *very* imperfectly satisfied sense of the writer's ingenuity in overcoming a difficulty we should have preferred his not having attempted to overcome. . . . One thing is clear, that if allegory ever establishes a fact, it is by dint of overturning a fiction;" and Poe has furthermore the courage to remark that the *Pilgrim's Progress* is a "ludicrously overrated book." Certainly, as a general thing, we are struck with the ingenuity and felicity of Hawthorne's analogies and correspondences; the idea appears to have made itself at home in them easily. Nothing could be better in this respect than *The Snow Image* (a little masterpiece), or *The Great Carbuncle, or Doctor Heidegger's Experiment, or Rappacini's Daughter*. But in such things as *The Birth-Mark* and *The Bosom-Serpent* we are struck with something stiff and mechanical, slightly incongruous, as if the kernel had not assimilated its envelope. But these are matters of light impression, and there would be a want of tact in pretending to discriminate too closely among things which all, in one way or another, have a charm. The charm—the great charm—is that they are glimpses of a great field, of the whole deep mystery of man's soul and conscience. They are moral, and their interest is moral; they deal with something more than the mere accidents and conventionalities, the surface occurrences of life. The fine thing in Hawthorne is that he cared for the deeper psychology, and that, in his way, he tried to become familiar with it. This natural, yet fanciful, familiarity with it; this air, on the author's part, of being a confirmed *habitué* of a region of mysteries and subtleties, constitutes the originality of his tales. And then they have the further merit of seeming, for what they are, to spring up so freely and lightly. The author has all the ease, indeed, of a regular dweller in the moral, psychological realm; he goes to and fro in it, as a man who knows his way. His tread is a light and modest one, but he keeps the key in his pocket.

His little historical stories all seem to me admirable; they are so good that you may re-read them many times. They are not numerous, and they are very short; but they are full of a vivid and delightful sense of the New England past; they have, moreover, the distinction, little tales of a dozen and fifteen pages as they are, of being the only successful attempts at historical fiction that have been made in the United States. Hawthorne was at home in the early New England history; he had thumbed its records and he had breathed its air, in whatever odd receptacles this somewhat pungent compound still lurked. He was fond of it, and he was proud of it, as any New Englander must be, measuring the part of that handful of half-starved fanatics who formed his earliest precursors, in laying the foundations of a mighty empire. Hungry for the picturesque as he always was, and not finding any very copious provision of it around him, he turned back into the two preceding centuries, with the earnest determination that the primitive annals of Massachusetts should at least *appear* picturesque. His fancy, which was always alive, played a little with the somewhat meagre and angular facts of the colonial period, and forthwith converted a great many of them into impressive legends and pictures. There is a little infusion of colour, a little vagueness about certain details, but it is very gracefully and discreetly done, and realities are kept in view sufficiently to make us feel that if we are reading romance, it is romance that rather supplements than contradicts history. The early annals of New England were not fertile in legend, but Hawthorne laid his hands upon everything that would serve his purpose, and in two or three cases his version of the story has a great deal of beauty. *The Grey Champion* is a sketch of less than eight pages, but the little figures stand up in the tale as stoutly, at the least, as if they were propped up on half-a-dozen chapters by a dryer annalist; and the whole thing has the merit of those cabinet pictures in which the artist has been able to make his persons look the size of life. Hawthorne, to say it again, was not in the least a realist—he was not to my mind enough of one; but there is no genuine lover of the good city of Boston but will feel grateful to him for his courage in attempting to recount the "traditions" of Washington Street, the main thoroughfare of the Puritan capital. The four *Legends of the Province House* are certain shadowy stories which he professes to have gathered in an ancient tavern lurking behind the modern shop fronts of this part of the city. The Province House disappeared some years ago, but while it stood it was pointed to as the residence of the Royal Governors of Massachusetts before the Revolution. I have no recollection of it; but it cannot have been, even from Hawthorne's account of it—which is as pictorial as he ventures to make it—a very imposing piece of antiquity. The writer's charming touch, however, throws a rich brown tone over its rather shallow venerableness; and we are beguiled into believing, for instance, at the close of *Howe's Masquerade* (a story of a strange occurrence at an entertainment given by Sir William Howe, the last of the Royal Governors, during the siege of Boston by Washington), that "superstition, among other legends of this mansion, repeats the wondrous tale that on the anniversary night of Britain's discomfiture the ghosts of the ancient governors of Massachusetts still glide through the Province House. And last of all comes a figure shrouded in a military cloak, tossing his clenched hands into the air, and stamping his iron-shod boots upon the freestone steps with a semblance of feverish despair, but without the sound of a foot-tramp." Hawthorne had, as regards the two earlier centuries of New England life, that faculty which is called now-a-days the historic consciousness. He never sought to exhibit it on a large scale; he exhibited it, indeed, on a scale so minute that we must not linger too much upon it. His vision of the past was filled with definite images—images none the less definite that they were concerned with events as shadowy as this dramatic passing away of the last of King George's representatives in his long loyal but finally alienated colony.

MODERN COMMENTARY

The Early Projected Works of
Nathaniel Hawthorne

Early in January of 1839, Nathaniel Hawthorne had decided to accept the humble position of measurer in the Boston Custom House. The work, he was told, would not be arduous; perhaps he might hope, he wrote to Longfellow, to employ at least part of his leisure time "in sketches of my new experiences, under some such titles as follow: 'Passages in the Life of a Custom-house Officer,' 'Scenes in Dock,' 'Nibblings of a Wharf-Rat,' 'Trials of a Tide-waiter,' 'Romance of the Revenue Service;' together with an ethical work, in two volumes, on the subject of Duties, ..."[1] These are but a few of the books which resided on "a certain ideal shelf," to which Hawthorne once referred toward the close of his life. Here, he said, "are reposited many . . . shadowy volumes of mine, more in number, and very much superior in quality, to those which I have succeeded in rendering actual."[2] . . .

1

Hawthorne's first fully planned literary project involving the publication of a number of stories was called *Seven Tales of My Native Land*. . . .

There is some uncertainty when the project was conceived and the tales were written. Three biographers state that the stories were composed after he had graduated from college in 1825.[3] Elizabeth Hawthorne, however, in a statement quoted by Julian Hawthorne, asserts that her brother showed her in "the summer of 1825" the tales making up the volume.[4] If this date be correct, the stories must have been virtually completed before he left college, but Miss Hawthorne's recollection of the date on this occasion may well have been incorrect.[5] In any case, this group of tales, which had as their motto the title of Wordsworth's poem *We Are Seven*, dealt with witchcraft and the sea,[6] natural subjects for Hawthorne to turn to in view of

[*] Reprinted by permission from the *Papers of the Bibliographical Society of America* 39 (1945): 119–55.

his ancestry. Elizabeth Hawthorne mentions by name one tale of witchcraft, *Alice Doane*.[7] The stories of the sea were "of pirates and privateers." One tale contained some verses, only one line of which has been preserved: "The pirates of the sea, they were a fearful race."[8] Elizabeth Hawthorne also notes a second title, *Susan Grey*,[9] but whether the story concerned witchcraft or the sea we cannot be certain.

Lathrop gives a circumstantial account of the ultimate disposal of the tales:

> He indeed had the most discouraging sort of search for a publisher; but at last a young printer of Salem promised to undertake the work. His name was Ferdinand Andrews,[10] and he was at one time half-owner with Caleb Cushing of an establishment from which they issued "The Salem Gazette," in 1822, the same journal in which Hawthorne published various papers at a later date, when Mr. Caleb Foote was its editor. Andrews was ambitious, and evidently appreciative of his young townsman's genius; but he delayed issuing the "Seven Tales" so long that the author, exasperated, recalled the manuscript. Andrews, waiting only for better business prospects, was loath to let them go; but Hawthorne insisted, and at last the publisher sent word, "Mr. Hawthorne's manuscript awaits his orders." The writer received it and burned it, to the chagrin of Andrews, who had hoped to bring out many works by the same hand.[11]

Horatio Bridge, Hawthorne's college friend, also alludes to the author's fit of temper which led to the destruction of the tales. When Hawthorne demanded back his manuscript, says Bridge, "The publisher, aroused to a sense of his duty and ashamed of his broken promises, apologized and offered to proceed with the work at once; but Hawthorne was inexorable; and though, as he wrote me at the time, he was conscious of having been too harsh in his censures, he would not recede, and he burned the manuscript, in a mood half savage, half despairing."[12]

It seems right to assume, as Lathrop and others have done, that Hawthorne's tale *The Devil in Manuscript* is a fictional version of the young author's failure to find a publisher for his *Seven Tales*, but the sketch reflects as well Hawthorne's later humiliating experiences of a similar kind. This tale was published in the *New England Magazine* for November, 1835, under the pseudonym of "Ashley A. Royce," and it was not acknowledged until 1852, when it was collected in *The Snow Image and Other Twice-told Tales*. In this partly humorous, partly hysterical story, a young writer, named Oberon,[13] tells of his attempt "to embody the character of a fiend, as represented in our traditions and the written records of witchcraft."[14] Seventeen publishers had rejected these stories of witchcraft, and the poor author at last found himself in a mood of utter despondency and desperation. One publisher to whom Oberon submitted the tales told him frankly that "no American publisher will meddle with an American work,— seldom if by a known writer, and never if by a new one,—unless at the writer's risk."[15] Gradually preparing himself for the act by frequent draughts of champagne, Oberon finally consigned the stories to the flames. But he failed to reckon with the fiend which he had called forth in his tales. Giving the author one glaring look, the devil bolted up the chimney, and in a few moments had wrapped the whole town in flames. Oberon's despair suddenly turned to wild exultation: " 'My tales!' cried Oberon. 'The chimney! The roof! The Fiend has gone forth by night, and startled thousands in fear and wonder from their beds! Here I stand—a triumphant author! Huzza! Huzza! My brain has set the town on fire! . . .' "[16]

The Americanism of Hawthorne's approach to fiction is apparent from the first. Yet in this approach, we must remember, Hawthorne was but following a literary trend already well marked in the 1830's. . . . *Alice Doane's Appeal*, the only extant story we may be quite certain belonged to the *Seven Tales*, uses the matter of New England witchcraft. American authors, by the mid-twenties, had already started to experiment with the fictional possibilities of this subject, and in the course of the next twenty years, it became a theme of considerable popularity.[17]

The story of Alice Doane was one of Hawthorne's earliest excursions into this field he later found so fascinating.[18] But *Alice Doane's Appeal*, which appeared in *The Token* for 1835, could not have been, in form, the same story that had been part of the *Seven Tales*. In *Alice Doane's Appeal*, Hawthorne tells of having once conducted two young ladies to the top of Gallows Hill; and while on this historic spot, he reads to them a story of witchcraft which he had written some years before. In mentioning the many tales of which he had been the author, he remarks, "One great heap had met a brighter destiny; they had fed the flames; . . . The story now to be introduced, and another, chanced to be in kinder custody at the time, and thus, by no conspicuous merits of their own, escaped destruction."[19] Whether we are to take literally what Hawthorne here states, it would be impossible to say. In any case, only fragments of the tale of Alice Doane, with running comment, are presented, as if Hawthorne might have been retelling the story from memory. A number of critics[20] have believed that the other tale which, as Hawthorne avers, "chanced to be in kinder custody," was *The Hollow of the Three Hills*. This was one of his first published stories,[21] again involving witchcraft. *An Old Woman's Tale*,[22] another early story concerned with the supernatural, has also been thought to belong to this group.[23]

The stories which Lathrop asserts concerned the sea are virtually beyond conjecture. It is curious, however, that *The Mermaid*,[24] which was collected in *Twice-told Tales* (1842) as *The Village Uncle*, has for its setting a fishing town not far from Nahant. The story contains some vivid descriptive touches of life by the sea, and introduces a girl named Susan, once a frank and mirthful child of nature, but now grown old. Could this have been the *Susan Grey* mentioned by Elizabeth Hawthorne? Lathrop asserts that the Susan of *The Mermaid* "is said to have had a prototype in the daughter of a Salem fisherman."[25] In any case, although one would be likely to call *Alice Doane's Appeal* and the other supernatural stories which we have associated with the *Seven Tales* essentially gothic, the Wordsworthian portrait of *The Mermaid* seems to suggest that other influence implied in the motto, "We Are Seven." . . .

2

If Hawthorne ultimately abandoned the *Seven Tales of My Native Land* as a literary unit, he quickly entered upon other plans for a collection of his short stories along lines not essentially different from those of the earlier group. "He now gathered from his materials," writes Woodberry, "a new series which he knew as 'Provincial Tales,' in which it remains doubtful how much of the old survived, for the burnt manuscripts of youth have something of the phoenix in their ashes."[26]

Early in December, 1829, Hawthorne disclosed his new literary plans to Samuel Goodrich, the Boston editor and publisher, who had just started his long career. Now Goodrich expressed a willingness to examine Hawthorne's manuscripts, and to aid the young author in whatever way he could, but Goodrich gave him little encouragement regarding publication. Still hoping, however, that Goodrich might find the tales worthy of a publisher, Hawthorne addressed him in this letter:

> Salem, Dec. 20th, 1829
>
> Dear Sir,
>
> I am obliged to you for your willingness to aid me in my affairs, though I perceive that you do not anticipate much success. Very probably you may be in the right, but I have nevertheless concluded to trouble you with some of the tales. These which I send have been completed (except prefixing the titles) a considerable time. There are two or three others, not at present in a condition to be sent. If I ever finish them, I suppose they will be about on a par with the rest.
>
> You will see that one of the stories is founded upon the Superstitions of this part of the country. I do not know that such an attempt has hitherto been made, but, as I have thrown away much

time in listening to such traditions, I could not help trying to put them into some shape. The tale is certainly rather wild and grotesque, but the outlines of many not less so might be picked up hereabouts.

Before returning the tales (for such, I suppose, is the most probable result) will you have the goodness to write to me, and await my answer? I have some idea that I shall be out of town, and it would be inconvenient to have them arrive during my absence. I am &c.

Nath. Hawthorne.

P.S. None of the pieces are shorter than the one first sent you. If I write any of the length you mention, I will send them to you; but I think I shall close my literary labours with what I have already begun.

Mr. Samuel G. Goodrich
Boston
Mass.[27]

On examining Hawthorne's tales, Goodrich experienced far more pleasure than he had anticipated. "I brought the MSS, which you sent me to this place, where I am spending a few weeks," wrote Goodrich from Hartford on January 19, 1830. "I have read them with great interest. 'The Gentle Boy' and 'My Uncle Molineaux' [sic] I liked particularly; about 'Alice Doane' I should be more doubtful as to the public approbation. On my return to Boston in April, I will use my influence to induce a publisher to take hold of the work, who will give it a fair share of success. . . . As a practical evidence of my opinion of the uncommon merit of these tales, I offer you $35 for the privilege of inserting 'The Gentle Boy' in the 'Token,' and you shall be at liberty to publish it with your collection provided it does not appear before the publication of the 'Token.' "[28] Hawthorne, however, did not accept immediately Goodrich's offer, probably because he hoped, before the close of the year, to find a publisher for his collection. In this hope he was disappointed, and the following year he yielded to Goodrich's entreaties. "I have made liberal use of the privilege you gave me as to the insertion of your pieces in the 'Token'," Goodrich wrote to Hawthorne on May 31, 1831. "I have already inserted four of them; namely 'The Wives of the Dead,' 'Roger Malvin's Burial,' 'Major Molineaux' [sic], and 'The Gentle Boy.' "[29] These four tales were published in *The Token* for 1832. Meanwhile, with thoughts of publishing the *Provincial Tales* still fresh in his mind, Hawthorne, apparently at Goodrich's request, had sent the editor two stories, *Sights from a Steeple* and presumedly *The Haunted Quack*.[30] Both appeared in *The Token* for 1831. This move was wholly in accord with Hawthorne's plans for the publication of a larger work, since neither tale sent to Goodrich concerned itself with Colonial history. Hawthorne's letter to Goodrich, which contains the only direct reference we have to *Provincial Tales*, is here presented:

Salem, May 6th, 1830

Dear Sir:—

I send you the two pieces for the token [*sic*]. They were ready some days ago, but I kept them in expectation of hearing from you. I have complied with your wishes in regard to brevity. You can insert them (if you think them worthy a place in your publication) as by the author of 'Provincial Tales'—such being the title I propose to give my volume. I can conceive no objection to your designating them in this manner, even if my tales should not be published as soon as the Token, or, indeed, if they never see the light at all. An unpublished book is not more obscure than many that creep into the world, and your readers will suppose that the 'Provincial Tales' are among the latter.

I am, etc.,

Nath. Hawthorne

S. G. Goodrich, Esq.[31]

In abandoning his plans for the publication of *Provincial Tales*, Hawthorne allowed Goodrich to publish at least some of the individual stories in *The Token*. Those tales printed in the issue for 1832 belonged, we may reasonably assume, to the original collection. *The Gentle Boy* concerned the Puritan persecution of the Quakers in the seventeenth century. *My Kinsman, Major Molineux* concluded with the tarring and feathering of a proud old Tory. *Roger Malvin's Burial* told a tale of the French and Indian War. And *The Wives of the Dead* related a domestic incident occurring, as Hawthorne says, "in a principal seaport town of the Bay Province." *Alice Doane's Appeal*, which had been part of the *Seven Tales*, and of which in 1830 Goodrich had not approved, was not published in *The Token* until 1835.[32] This story, it seems likely, was the one which, in writing to Goodrich in 1829, Hawthorne had referred to as "founded upon the Superstitions of this part of the country." As for the rest of the tales forming the collection, we have little to help us in establishing their identity. Although essentially biographical, *Sir William Pepperell*, contributed to *The Token* for 1833, may have belonged to this series, but *The Canterbury Pilgrims* and *The Seven Vagabonds*, in the same issue of *The Token*, are plainly related to a third project—*The Story Teller*, most of the material of which appeared in the *New England Magazine*. It is not improbable that *The Gray Champion* and *Young Goodman Brown*, included in this new project, were originally items in *Provincial Tales*. *The May-Pole of Merrymount* and *The Minister's Black Veil*, printed in *The Token* for 1836, may possibly have been part of the group, but the four *Tales of the Province House*[33] seem to have been written at too late a date ever to have had a place in *Provincial Tales.*

3

By 1832 Hawthorne had laid new literary plans. Although he did not wholly abandon the historical vein, he now sought, more realistically, to build a volume of tales around excursions he had made and was to make through New England, New York State, and, as he hoped, Canada. "Once a year, or thereabouts," wrote Hawthorne many years later, "I used to make an excursion of a few weeks, in which I enjoyed as much of life as other people do in the whole year's round."[34] But of his earliest journeys, just after he left college, we know little. In fact, Woodberry has remarked, "There is the same dubiousness about these journeys, his earliest ventures in the world, as about his first attempts in the field of authorship."[35] In a letter written early in the 1830's, Hawthorne describes a trip that he took with his uncle, Samuel Manning, through Connecticut, meeting, as he says, "with many marvellous adventures."[36] Other early letters describe trips to a Quaker settlement in New Hampshire,[37] and to the White Mountains.[38] Still another letter, dated June 28, 1832, and addressed to his college friend, Franklin Pierce, reveals more fully the relationship of these travels to his new literary scheme:

> I was making preparations for a Northern tour when this accursed cholera broke out in Canada. It was my intention to go by way of New York and Albany to Niagara; from thence to Montreal and Quebec, and home through Vermont and New Hampshire. I am very desirous of making this journey on account of a book by which I intend to acquire an (undoubtedly) immense literary reputation, but which I cannot commence writing till I have visited Canada. I still hope that the pestilence will disappear, so that it may be safe to go in a month or two.[39]

The special importance Hawthorne here attaches to a trip to Canada has unhappily been lost, but there seems little doubt that he is here alluding to the volume to which he ultimately gave the title of *The Story Teller.* This new group of tales was to derive its unity from "a travelling story-teller, whose shiftings of fortune were to form the interludes and links between the separate stories."[40]

Early in 1834, it would seem, Hawthorne submitted again to Goodrich his new collection of stories. It was a somewhat bulky manuscript, consisting, according to Elizabeth Peabody, of "two volumes."[41] Although Goodrich himself declined to undertake its publication,[42] he displayed sufficient interest in the work to offer the manuscript, or to advise Hawthorne to offer it, to Joseph T. Buckingham. Now Buckingham, who was then the editor of the *New England Magazine*, seems to have agreed to publish the collection serially in that periodical. In the issues of the *New England Magazine* for November and December, 1834, appeared two installments called *The Story Teller*. But unfortunately for Hawthorne, Buckingham, at the close of the year, withdrew as editor, and Dr. Samuel G. Howe and John O. Sargent took over the editorial duties.[43] Then in March of 1835 Park Benjamin became the sole editor and proprietor of the magazine.[44] This shake-up in the editorial staff had a significant effect on the publication of Hawthorne's book. The new editors, and especially Park Benjamin, declined to print any more of the work as a literary unit, with the result that the frame-work of the book was virtually abandoned, and the collection was broken down into such parts as could be printed in the magazine either as stories or essays. Hawthorne especially blamed Park Benjamin for what took place. In writing years later to Elizabeth Peabody, Hawthorne remarked, ". . . it was Park Benjamin, not Goodrich, who cut up the 'Story-teller.' "[45] With the exception of September and October, each 1835 issue of the periodical carried at least one fragment of *The Story Teller*, three numbers publishing two selections, and one number three. At the end of the year, however, the *New England Magazine* was absorbed in the *American Monthly Magazine* of New York. Park Benjamin now shared with Charles Fenno Hoffman the editorship of the paper, and three (possibly four) more parts of Hawthorne's work were published in this periodical in 1836, 1837, and 1838. Hawthorne's reactions to the way in which Benjamin carried to New York the remainder of the manuscripts, some of which appear to have been unpaid for, was decidedly unfavorable, although the exact nature of the affair is not clear.[46] In any case, the book was broken up; and, again according to his sister-in-law, Elizabeth Peabody, Hawthorne "said he cared little for the stories afterwards, which had in their original place in *The Story Teller* a great degree of significance; and he got little or nothing as pay. Then, as nobody reviews stories in magazines, it did not serve the purpose of introducing him into the world of letters."[47]

In a moment, we must examine the fragments of *The Story Teller* as they appeared in the *New England Magazine* and in the *American Monthly Magazine*, in an effort to reconstruct, if possible, something of Hawthorne's original design. This design is partially set forth in the first two installments of the work as published entire by Mr. Buckingham. It is my belief, however, that Hawthorne in *The Seven Vagabonds*, which was contributed to *The Token* for 1833, had made an earlier attempt to write an introduction to his proposed volume. In this delightful sketch, seven people, to escape a summer shower, meet by chance in the wagon of an itinerant showman. All, we learn, are on their way to the camp-meeting in Stamford, Connecticut; and they now agree to travel together, each in his own way contributing to the happiness of what spectators they may chance to find. For they are resolved to take the world as it goes, embracing "the free mind, that preferred its own folly to another's wisdom; the open spirit, that found companions everywhere; above all, the restless impulse"[48] that would not be stilled. The narrator finds his own place in this happy group to be that of the story teller. "My design, in short," he explains, "was to imitate the story-tellers of whom Oriental travellers have told us, and become an itinerant novelist, reciting my own extemporaneous fictions to such audiences as I could collect."[49] Thus Hawthorne seems at first to have launched his story teller on his travels, with this merry company of vagabonds. But later, I feel reasonably confident, he abandoned this plan for another, terminating abruptly a situation which he had so delightfully built up. As the company are about to proceed on their way to Stamford, a Methodist preacher rides up from that direction, and hastily announces that "the camp-meeting is broke up." Whereupon the vagabonds separate, going their several ways.[50] Although rejecting the sketch as an introduction to the work he was to write, Hawthorne doubtless wished to preserve its substance as a tale, and so brought the sketch artificially to a close. In any case, this essentially abortive story reveals the plan for the new collection taking shape in his mind, for he has already begun to associate his travels with the impulse of the *raconteur*. We have noted the letter, written in the early 1830's, in which he relates some of his experiences in Connecticut; and a significant passage in *The Vagabonds*, put into the mouth of the conjurer, suggests again Hawthorne's desire (whether it ever became a reality we may doubt) of including Canada among his travels: "I am taking a trip northward, this warm weather," replied the conjurer, "across the Connecticut first, and then up through Vermont, and may be into Canada before the fall. . . ."[51]

But Hawthorne finally presented his story teller in quite a different way. The first two installments of the work, which appeared unaltered in the *New England Magazine*, not only introduce the narrator, but reveal that Hawthorne intended a dramatic relationship between the framework and the stories making up the collection. These two installments were finally collected as *Passages From a Relinquished Work* in the second edition of *Mosses From an Old Manse* (1854). Here the story teller, similar in character to the young man of *The Seven Vagabonds*, describes himself as "a youth of gay and happy temperament, with an incorrigible levity of spirit, of no vicious propensities, sensible enough, but wayward and fanciful."[52] Indeed, alluding to the earlier sketch, he remarks, "The idea of becoming a wandering story teller had been suggested, a year or two before, by an encounter with several merry vagabonds in a showman's wagon, where they and I had sheltered ourselves during a summer shower."[53] Finding his life in a country village intolerable under the guardianship of Parson Thumpcushion, the young man, one fine June morning, goes forth into the world. Along the way, he meets Eliakim Abbott, a shy young minister of the gospel, who is determined to address all "sinners on the welfare of their immortal souls."[54] Together, this odd pair go from village to village, each eager to fulfill the demands of his calling. After some humiliating failures, they finally enter a town where Eliakim manages to gather in the village schoolhouse "about fifteen hearers, mostly females."[55] While the young preacher struggles in vain to hold the attention of his small group ("at the conclusion of the prayer several of the little audience went out"), the story teller in the village theatre recites with great applause the tale of *Mr. Higginbotham's Catastrophe.*

In this prefatory matter which I have here sought to outline, Hawthorne also sets forth in part the nature of his proposed work. Having expressed his determination to leave his native place, the story teller remarks: "The following pages will contain a picture of my vagrant life, intermixed with specimens, generally brief and slight, of that great mass of fiction to which I gave existence, and which has vanished like cloud shapes."[56]

Experience in his art taught him, as time went on, the range of feeling and power which must be his if he were to be a successful *raconteur:* "No talent or attainment could come amiss; everything, indeed, was requisite—wide observation, varied knowledge, deep thoughts, and sparkling ones; pathos and levity, and a mixture of both, like sunshine in a raindrop; lofty imagination, veiling itself in the garb of common life; and the practised art which alone could render these gifts, and more than these, available."[57]

In the exercise of his art, much was to be left to mother wit— much to sheer inspiration: "I manufactured a great variety of plots and skeletons of tales, and kept them ready for use, leaving the filling up to the inspiration of the moment; though I cannot remember ever to have told a tale which did not vary considerably from my preconceived idea, and acquire a novelty of aspect as often as I repeated it."[58]

And finally the collection as a whole was to have a moral: "But I write the book for the sake of its moral, which many a dreaming youth may profit by, though it is the experience of a wandering story teller."[59]

The second installment of *The Story Teller,* as published in the *New England Magazine,* was broken, at the proper dramatic moment, by the insertion of *Mr. Higginbotham's Catastrophe.* After the recital of the tale, the narrator describes his success. "I never knew the 'magic of a name' till I used that of Mr. Higginbotham. Often as I repeated it, there were louder bursts of merriment than those which responded to what, in my opinion, were more legitimate strokes of humor."[60] When Hawthorne came to publish his *Twice-told Tales* in 1837, *Mr. Higginbotham's Catastrophe* was lifted from its context and included in that volume.

The rest of *The Story Teller*, reduced by the magazine editors to individual tales and sketches, offers a baffling and, I fear, insoluble problem to one who would rebuild Hawthorne's project as a dramatic unit. . . .

The Gray Champion,[61] possibly carried over from *Provincial Tales*, was the first installment to appear after the abandonment of the original plan; and seven more compositions which may be classified strictly as tales were published at intervals: *Young Goodman Brown*,[62] *Wakefield*,[63] *The Ambitious Guest*,[64] *The Old Maid in the Winding Sheet*,[65] *The Vision of the Fountain*,[66] *The Devil in Manuscript*,[67] *A Visit to the Clerk of the Weather*,[68] and possibly *The Three-fold Destiny*.[69] Then occasionally the editors inserted essays, such as *Old News*[70] (three installments), *A Rill from the Town Pump*,[71] and *Graves and Goblins*.[72]

A third group of pieces consisted of travel sketches, which, in Hawthorne's original plan, must have been links and interludes between the stories. Owing to the fragmentary manner in which these sketches were presented, it is now virtually impossible to trace the itinerary of the story teller. When Hawthorne wrote in 1832 regarding his contemplated trip, he expressed the intention of going "by the way of New York and Albany to Niagara; from thence to Montreal and Quebec, and home through Vermont and New Hampshire." But although, as we shall see, he probably made an excursion by boat on Lake Ontario, there is no evidence that he ever crossed the border into Canada. In general, however, the story teller may have followed the route suggested in this letter. If we assume that the narrator had somehow made his way to the State of New York, we now find him on the Grand Canal "about thirty miles below Utica."[73] In the fragment called *The Canal Boat*[74] he describes minutely a number of his fellow passengers, and mentions "traversing the 'long level,' a dead flat between Utica and Syracuse. . . ."[75] This sketch is twice broken by asterisks; and we may reasonably suppose that at these points the story teller held forth for the benefit of those aboard the canal boat, but with what stories he regaled them we cannot say. Just before the boat reached Syracuse, it was found necessary to make a brief stop. The narrator left the boat for a little walk. While he was amusing himself on shore, the boat started on its way again; and he was now stranded "on the 'long level,' at midnight, with the comfortable prospect of a walk to Syracuse, . . ."[76] His next major stop may have been Rochester, for in a sketch of that title,[77] he describes the city, as well as the falls of the Genesee. Here again, we find gaps indicated by asterisks. Then in *My Visit to Niagara*[78] he gives fully his impression of the great falls; and in *A Night Scene*[79] a Lake Erie steamboat is carrying him to Detroit. Finally, his tour of Western New York probably included a trip to the St. Lawrence. In the sketch *An Ontario Steam-Boat*[80] he remarks: ". . . I had embarked at Ogdensburgh, and was voyaging westward, to the other extremity of Lake Ontario . . ."

On his way back, in this hypothetical record of his travels, the story teller stopped at Burlington and Ticonderoga. "It was a bright forenoon," he states in *The Inland Port*,[81] "When I set foot on the beach at Burlington, and took leave of the two boatmen in whose little skiff I had voyaged since daylight from Peru. Not that we had come that morning from South America, but only from the New York shore of Lake Champlain."[82] A brief description of Burlington then follows. In *Old Ticonderoga. A Picture of the Past*,[83] Hawthorne describes the old fort, and ruminates on the historical events with which it had once been connected. This sketch originally had two opening paragraphs, which were deleted when the item was collected. The first is significant: "In returning once to New England, from a visit to Niagara, I found myself, one summer's day, before noon, at Orwell, about forty miles from the southern extremity of Lake Champlain, which has here the aspect of a river or a creek. We were on the Vermont shore, with a ferry, of less than a mile wide, between us and the town of Ti, in New-York."[84]

Assuming that the story teller visited New England as he was returning home, we have next to pause over his visit to the White Mountains. *The Notch* and *Our Evening Party Among the Mountains*[85] are closely related sketches in which he describes the Notch and his stay at Ethan Crawford's inn. *The Ambitious Guest* may have been intended for narration at this juncture in the adventures of the story teller. References in the tale clearly link it to the descriptive matter we have already mentioned. The young man in the story speaks of Burlington, the Notch, and Ethan Crawford's tavern. I am also of the opinion that *The Great Carbuncle*, published in *The Token* for 1837, may have fitted into the frame-work of the project, to be recited at Crawford's inn. Not only does the story teller relate briefly in *Our Evening Party* the legend of the Carbuncle, but he remarks, "On this theme methinks I could frame a tale with a deep moral."[86]

And now for the story teller's return, which is fully described in the second section of *Fragments From the Journal of a Solitary Man*.[87] The youth approaches and enters the village which, some years before, he had left to become a teller of tales. In returning, he makes no allusion to Parson Thumpcushion (possibly the old gentleman had died in his absence), but he does note once more the business establishments of Dominicus Pike and Mr. Nightingale, which he had particularly mentioned as he left his native town. But alas for our hero; he returns a sadder and a wiser man. We are led to believe that he has burned his candle at both ends, and has come home to die. The youth who had left the village with so light a heart, now looks upon himself as an example to some other young man who might follow in his footsteps: " 'He shall be taught,' said I 'by my life, and by my death, that the world is a sad one for him who shrinks from its sober duties. My experience shall warn him to adopt some great and serious aim, such as manhood will cling to, that he may not feel himself, too late, a cumberer of this overladen earth, but a man among men.' "[88] Such was to have been the moral of Hawthorne's book!

Any attempt, it will be seen, to reconstruct accurately the original plan of Hawthorne's project is futile. We cannot be certain that the itinerary of the story teller was ever so clearly defined as we have sought to make it. Even the New England village from which the young man sets forth and to which he finally returns is never localized; and Hawthorne may not have intended the man's travels to form an exact geographical pattern.[89] . . .

4

We need not dwell on the outcome of Hawthorne's successive failures to bring out a collection of his tales. Through the kindly offices of Horatio Bridge, the *Twice-told Tales* appeared in 1837; and in 1842, a second series was published. Hawthorne then went with his wife to live in the Old Manse, and *Mosses From an Old Manse,* brought out in 1846, was the literary fruit of these four years. But during his residence in Concord, Hawthorne seems to have planned another volume of stories, over which we may briefly pause. *Egotism; or the Bosom Serpent*[90] and *The Christmas Banquet*[91] are designated in their titles as coming *From the Unpublished "Allegories of the Heart."* Nowhere else does Hawthorne mention by name *The Allegories of the Heart;* and it is the belief of Miss Elizabeth Chandler that Hawthorne never "projected a separate collection under this title, but merely wished to group the two together. . . ."[92] But of this we cannot be sure. "The human Heart," he suggests in his journal in 1842, might "be allegorized as a cavern."[93] Always fascinated by speculative psychology, Hawthorne, by the early forties, had come to explore with a curious penetration "the gloomy mysteries of the human heart"[94]—a strange and sinister study, since in that gloom there lies estrangement from one's fellows. These gloomy mysteries affecting so profoundly the social life of man were the theme not only of *Egotism* and *The Christmas Banquet,* but also of *The Birth-*

mark,[95] *Rappaccini's Daughter*,[96] and *Earth's Holocaust*[97]—all written
and published during his stay in the Old Manse. Hawthorne could
have drawn numerous other stories into his project, for the ramifications of his theme were many. In this collection, for example, he
might have included *The Antique Ring*, contributed to *Sargent's New
Monthly Magazine*,[98] but never collected by the author. Through one
of his characters the symbolism of this tale is finally revealed: ". . .
we may suppose the Gem to be the human heart, and the Evil Spirit
to be Falsehood, which, in one guise or another, is the fiend that
causes all the sorrow and trouble in the world."[99] Although certainly
written at a somewhat later period, and never associated directly with
the group, *Ethan Brand* was also conceived during these years in
Concord.[100] But Hawthorne had doubtless come to realize the monotony inherent in any collection of stories which derives its unity
from a single theme. Some years later, when Rufus Griswold asked
him to write for the *International Magazine* a series of twelve short
tales, possessing an underlying theme, Hawthorne gave expression to
the opinion to which he had finally come after twenty years of
authorship: "The reader would inevitably be tired to death of the
one prominent idea, if presented to him under different aspects for
a twelve-month together."[101]

5

By 1846 Hawthorne had returned with his family to Salem, and was
working in the Custom House. He now had less time to devote to
writing; in fact, he seems to have grown weary of composing tales
that yielded him so little money. And where, too, was the literary
reputation for which he longed? So far as I can discover, he produced
but three stories at this period: *Main Street*,[102] *The Great Stone Face*,[103]
and *Ethan Brand*.[104] Then early in June of 1849 came the news of
his dismissal from the Custom House. Now deprived of his livelihood,
he once more returned seriously to authorship, and during the following months was wholly absorbed in writing *The Scarlet Letter*. It
was probably toward the close of 1849 that Hawthorne handed to
James T. Fields the first draft of the famous romance. Fields relates
that Hawthorne had originally intended the story to "occupy about
two hundred pages" in a volume "of several short stories." The book
was to be called: "Old-Time Legends: Together with Sketches, Experimental and Ideal."[105] When Fields, however, finally persuaded
Hawthorne to enlarge *The Scarlet Letter*, and publish it as a single
volume, *Old-Time Legends* was abandoned as a project. Hawthorne
and Fields probably came to this decision early in January, 1850.

Whether Hawthorne had entirely made up his mind about the
contents of his new book when he turned over to Fields *The Scarlet*

Letter, it would be hard to say. But we may be reasonably sure that the three tales written during his Custom House years were to be part of the collection. Julian Hawthorne avers that *The Snow Image* was also a product of these years in Salem.[106] If so, it seems very odd that Hawthorne should have allowed so good a tale to remain unpublished as late as August, 1850, when it was transmitted to Griswold for publication in *The Memorial*.[107] I believe it likely that *The Snow Image* was composed in 1850, and hence could not have had a place in *Old-Time Legends*. The descriptive phrases employed in the title of Hawthorne's proposed collection are so vague and colorless as to offer only the most general clues for determining the classification of his material. It seems clear, however, that in using the word *Experimental* he must have referred to *Ethan Brand*. . . .

We have sought to examine and reconstruct, so far as possible, the more important literary plans which Hawthorne failed to bring to completion. Of these, the most ambitious were laid before he had reached middle-age. Naturally, his failure to realize these early ambitions sprang in part from the sensitiveness and immaturity of the young man. Something of the intellectual atmosphere surrounding the earlier projects Hawthorne himself vividly recalled in 1840 in a letter to Sophia, now familiar to every student of the author. He had just returned to the "old accustomed chamber" in his Salem home— to the room where, as he says, "I used to sit in the days gone by. . . . Here I have written many tales,—many that have been burned to ashes, many that doubtless deserved the same fate. This claims to be a haunted chamber, for thousands upon thousands of visions have appeared to me in it, and some few of them have become visible to the world. If ever I should have a biographer, he ought to make great mention of this chamber in my memoirs, because so much of my lonely youth was wasted here, and here my mind and character were formed; and here I have been glad and hopeful, and here I have been despondent."[108] Yet sensitive though he was, quite as much of his failure was due to the fear and procrastination of the publishers who had the handling of his manuscripts. During the 1830's and 1840's, there was but one author in America comparable to Hawthorne in the field of the short story, and that was Edgar Allan Poe. He, too, suffered the same difficulties and disappointments in attempting to bring out his first collection—*Tales of the Folio Club*. That good literature in America had so small an audience, that the economic status of the writer was painfully low and inadequate, were conditions which, of course, in large measure explain the unhappy situation. Yet Hawthorne and Poe but experienced the same weary waiting, the same hopes deferred, that have been the lot of the young artist in every generation. The pursuit of beauty doubtless has its own rewards, but in that pursuit lurk bitterness and despair.

Notes

1. Samuel Longfellow, *Life of Henry Wadsworth Longfellow* (Boston, 1891), I:323.

2. *To a Friend* in *Our Old Home* (1863); see *Our Old Home and English Notebooks*, I:16. The pagination for all references to Hawthorne's writings in this paper, except where otherwise noted, is that of *The Complete Works of Nathaniel Hawthorne*, Riverside Edition, Boston, 1883.

3. Fields, *Yesterdays with Authors* (New York, 1871), p. 65; Lathrop, *A Study of Hawthorne* (Boston, 1876), p. 134; Horatio Bridge, *Personal Recollections of Nathaniel Hawthorne* (New York, 1893), p. 67. See also Lathrop in his *Introductory Note* to *Twice-told Tales* (Riverside Edition), p. 7.

4. Julian Hawthorne, *Nathaniel Hawthorne and His Wife* (Boston, 1885), I:123–124. See also George Woodberry, *Nathaniel Hawthorne* (Boston, 1902), pp. 30–31.

5. Cf. Randall Stewart, *American Literature*, XVI:323, where Elizabeth distinctly says that they were composed soon after he left college.

6. Lathrop, *A Study of Hawthorne*, p. 134. See also Randall Stewart, *American Literature*, XVI:323.

7. J. Hawthorne, *op. cit.*, p. 124.

8. Lathrop *op. cit.*, p. 134.

9. J. Hawthorne, *op. cit.*, p.. 124.

10. For references to Andrews as a Salem publisher and printer, as well as for the titles of some of his early imprints, see Harriet S. Tapley, *Salem Imprints, 1768–1825* (Salem, 1927), *passim.*

11. Lathrop, *op. cit.*, p. 135. Other biographers have related the episode somewhat differently. See Fields, *op. cit.*, p. 65; J. Hawthorne, *op. cit.*, I:124; Moncure Conway, *Life of Nathaniel Hawthorne* (London, 1890), p. 42.

12. Bridge, *op. cit.*, p. 68.

13. "Oberon" was a signature once used by Hawthorne in corresponding with Horatio Bridge. See Bridge, *op. cit.*, p. 49.

14. *The House of the Seven Gables and The Snow Image and Other Twice-told Tales*, p. 575.

15. *Ibid.*, p. 577.

16. *Ibid.*, p. 580.

17. See G. Harrison Orians, *New England Witchcraft in Fiction* in: *American Literature*, II:54–71 (March, 1930).

18. Evert A. Duyckinck once proposed to Hawthorne that he write a history of witchcraft. See a letter of Duyckinck, dated October 2, 1845, in Bridge, *op. cit.*, p. 106. For Hawthorne's rejection of this proposal, dated October 10, see Randall Stewart, *Two Uncollected Reviews* in: *New England Quarterly*, IX:504–505 (September, 1936).

19. *Tales, Sketches, and Other Papers*, p. 282.

20. See Elizabeth Chandler, *A Study of the Sources of the Tales and Romances Written by Nathaniel Hawthorne Before 1853* (Northhampton, 1926), p. 8; Julian Hawthorne, *Hawthorne Reading* (Cleveland, 1902), p. 103; and G. H. Orians, *American Literature*, II:65.

21. *Salem Gazette*, November 12, 1830. Collected in *Twice-told Tales* (1837).

22. Appeared in the *Salem Gazette* for December 21, 1830, and was collected posthumously in *The Dolliver Romance and Other Pieces* (1876).

23. Chandler, *op. cit.*, p. 8.

24. First published in *The Token* for 1835.

25. Lathrop, *op. cit.*, p. 142. Elizabeth Hawthorne, however, identifies the mermaid "Susan" with a girl Hawthorne met on a trip to Swampscott "about the year 1833" (J. Hawthorne, *op. cit.* I:127–128.) See also Randall Stewart, *American Literature*, XVI:326. If the date 1833 be correct, the Susan of the story could not possibly have been the "Susan Grey" of the *Seven Tales* since the project had long been abandoned by that date.

26. Woodberry, *op. cit.*, p. 33.

27. Here published for the first time through the courtesy of Mr. Carroll A. Wilson, owner of the manuscript; and through the kindness of Professors Stanley T. Williams and Randall Stewart, who have in preparation a complete edition of Hawthorne's letters. Professor William Charvat first called my attention to this letter.

28. J. Hawthorne, *op. cit.*, I:131–132.

29. *Ibid.*, I:132.

30. This tale was signed "Joseph Nicholson." Although never acknowledged by Hawthorne, this story, it seems to me, bears unmistakable internal evidence of his authorship. This evidence was first presented by Frank Sanborn in an article entitled *A New "Twice-told Tale" by Nathaniel Hawthorne* in the *New England Magazine*, (n.s.) XVIII:688–696 (August 1898). This tale was included in the Old Manse Edition of Hawthorne's works published in 1904.

31. J. C. Derby, *Fifty Years Among Authors, Books, and Publishers* (New York, 1884), pp. 112–113.

32. *Alice Doane's Appeal* had a strange bibliographical fate. Apparently Hawthorne himself, as well as Goodrich, came to feel that the tale was not an artistic success. This is suggested not only by its delayed publication in *The Token*, but also by the fact that Hawthorne failed to acknowledge the story in later life. It was first reprinted from *The Token* in the posthumous collection, edited by Lathrop in 1883, and entitled *Tales, Sketches, and Other Papers*.

33. *United States Magazine and Democratic Review*, May, July, December, 1838, January, 1839.

34. J. Hawthorne, *op. cit.*, I:97.

35. Woodberry, *op. cit.*, p. 40.

36. Lathrop, *op. cit.*, pp. 143–144.

37. *Ibid.*, pp. 144–145. Lathrop dates the letter 1831.

38. *The American Notebooks by Nathaniel Hawthorne*, edited by Randall Stewart (New Haven, 1932), p. 283. The letter, addressed to his mother, is dated September 16, 1832.

39. James T. Fields, *Underbrush* (Boston, 1877), p. 35.

40. Lathrop, *op. cit.*, pp. 173–174.

41. Conway, *op. cit.*, p. 32.

42. *Ibid.*, p. 32.

43. For Buckingham's editorial valedictory, see the *New England Magazine*, VII:515 (December, 1834).

44. Frank L. Mott, *A History of American Magazines, 1741–1850* (New York, 1930), p. 601.

45. Woodberry, *op. cit.*, p. 70.

46. See Bridge, *op. cit.*, 69; and Mott, *op. cit.*, pp. 602–603.

47. Conway, *op. cit.*, p. 32.

48. *Twice-told Tales*, p. 409.

49. *Ibid.*, p. 409.

50. *Ibid.*, p. 413.

51. *Ibid.*, p. 404.

52. *Mosses From an Old Manse*, p. 459.

53. *Ibid.*, p. 459–460.

54. *Ibid.*, p. 471.

55. *Ibid.*, p. 471.

56. *Ibid.*, p. 460.

57. *Ibid.*, p. 469.

58. *Ibid.*, p. 470.

59. *Ibid.*, p. 461.

60. *Ibid.*, p. 473.

61. *New England Magazine*, January, 1835. Collected in *Twice-told Tales* (1837).

62. *New England Magazine*, April, 1835. Collected in *Mosses From an Old Manse* (1846).

63. *New England Magazine*, May, 1835. Collected in *Twice-told Tales* (1837).

64. *New England Magazine*, June, 1835. Collected in *Twice-told Tales* (1842).

65. *New England Magazine*, July, 1835. Collected in *Twice-told Tales* (1842).

66. *New England Magazine*, August, 1835. Collected in *Twice-told Tales* (1837).

67. *New England Magazine*, November, 1835. Collected in *The Snow Image and Other Twice-told Tales* (1852).

68. *American Monthly Magazine*, May, 1836. Hawthorne's authorship of this tale has been disputed. Although the evidence is not conclusive, the fact that the Clerk of the Weather as a supernatural character appears again in *A Select Party* (*Mosses From an Old Manse*, 1846) would seem to point to Hawthorne's authorship.

69. *American Monthly Magazine*, March, 1838. Collected in *Twice-told Tales* (1842). This tale was published somewhat too late to have belonged originally to *The Story Teller*. Still, it is difficult to understand why it should have been printed at all in this periodical if it had not been part of the project.

70. *New England Magazine*, February, 1835; March, 1835; May, 1835. Collected in *The Snow Image and Other Twice-told Tales* (1852).

71. *New England Magazine*, June, 1835. Collected in *Twice-told Tales* (1937).

72. *New England Magazine*, June, 1835. Collected in *The Dolliver Romance and Other Pieces* (1876).

73. *Mosses From an Old Manse*, p. 485.

74. Part of *Sketches From Memory By A Pedestrian, No. II* in: *New England Magazine*, December, 1835. Collected in *Mosses From an Old Manse* (1854).

75. *Mosses From an Old Manse*, p. 492.

76. *Ibid.*, p. 494.

77. Part of *Sketches From Memory . . . No. II.* Collected in *The Dolliver Romance and Other Pieces* (1876).

78. *New England Magazine*, February, 1835. Collected in *The Dolliver Romance and Other Pieces* (1876). Two brief descriptive pieces also relating to Niagara are to be found in Hawthorne's "Fragments From the Journal of a Solitary Man."

79. Part of *Sketches From Memory . . . No. II.* Collected in *The Dolliver Romance and Other Pieces* (1876).

80. I feel reasonably certain that this sketch belonged originally to *The Story Teller*. It was first published in the *American Magazine of Useful and Entertaining Knowledge* (March, 1836) of which Hawthorne was for a time the editor. During the brief period of his editorship, he often found it difficult to prepare sufficient copy for the printer, and this short descriptive piece, which for some reason he may have had by him, he turned to good use. In this sketch, besides describing some of his fellow passengers, as in *The Canal Boat*, he indulges in contemptuous remarks at the expense of the Irish, as in the *The Inland Port*. For Hawthorne's editorship of the *American Magazine* and for selections from his contributions to the periodical, see *Hawthorne as Editor*, edited by Arlin Turner, University, Louisiana, 1941.

81. Part of *Sketches From Memory* . . . No. II. Collected in *The Dolliver Romance and Other Pieces* (1876).

82. *Tales, Sketches, and Other Papers*, p. 13. Hawthorne himself stopped at Burlington as he returned from the White Mountains in September, 1832. See the letter addressed to his mother in *The American Notebooks* (edited by Randall Stewart), p. 283.

83. *American Monthly Magazine*, February, 1836. Collected in *The Snow Image and Other Twice-told Tales* (1852).

84. *American Monthly Magazine*, (n.s.) I:138 (February, 1836).

85. *Sketches From Memory* . . . No. I in: *New England Magazine*, November, 1835. Collected in *Mosses From an Old Manse* (1854).

86. *Mosses From an Old Manse*, p. 483.

87. *Fragments From the Journal of a Solitary Man* first appeared in the *American Monthly Magazine*, July, 1837; and was collected in *The Dolliver Romance and Other Pieces*. This group of sketches begins with a description of a "sensitive recluse" named "Oberon," with supposed extracts from his journal. The first of these extracts is a morbid piece of self-analysis, evidently written by Hawthorne in a depressed mood. It is difficult to see what place this sketch could possibly have had in *The Story Teller*. Yet, at the close of this selection, Hawthorne, by means of a clumsy interlude has attempted to identify the morbid "Oberon" with what is apparently the story teller. Then follow two descriptive fragments dealing with Niagara, supposedly from the pen of "Oberon," but plainly parts of *The Story Teller*. Finally, in a second section entitled *My Home Return* we have what is, without doubt, the conclusion of *The Story Teller*. This, too, is represented as written by "Oberon." Thus apparently, through the fiction of "Oberon," Hawthorne tried to tie together a number of miscellaneous fragments from his own pen, but it is virtually impossible to reconcile the character of "Oberon" with that of the story teller.

88. *Tales, Sketches, and Other Papers*, p. 40.

89. Such a conclusion, for example, is suggested by the casual opening of *Old Ticonderoga*, already quoted.

90. *United States Magazine and Democratic Review*, March, 1843. Collected in *Mosses From an Old Manse* (1846).

91. *United States Magazine and Democratic Review*, January, 1844. Collected in *Mosses From an Old Manse* (1846).

92. Chandler, *op. cit.*, p. 33.

93. *The American Notebooks* (Edited by Randall Stewart), p. 98.

94. *Mosses From an Old Manse*, p. 322.

95. *Pioneer*, March, 1843. Collected in *Mosses From an Old Manse* (1846).

96. *United States Magazine and Democratic Review*, December, 1844. Collected in *Mosses From an Old Manse* (1846).

97. *Graham's Lady's and Gentleman's Magazine*, May, 1844. Collected in *Mosses From an Old Manse* (1846).

98. February, 1843. Collected in *The Dolliver Romance and Other Pieces.*

99. *Tales, Sketches, and Other Papers*, p. 67.

100. In 1844 Hawthorne made in his journal two entries on which the theme of *Ethan Brand* was later based. See *The American Notebooks* (Edited by Randall Stewart), p. 106.

101. *Passages From the Correspondence and Other Papers of Rufus W. Griswold* (Cambridge, Massachusetts, 1898), p. 280.

102. *Aesthetic Papers, edited by Elizabeth P. Peabody* (Boston, 1849), pp. 145–174.

103. *National Era*, January 24, 1850.

104. *Boston Museum*, January 5, 1850.

105. Fields, *op. cit.*, p. 51.

106. J. Hawthorne, *op. cit.*, I:312, 330.

107. Ralph Thompson, *American Literary Annuals and Gift Books*, p. 140.

108. *Passages From the American Notebooks*, pp. 222–223.

Hawthorne as Poet   Q. D. Leavis°

. . . The essential Hawthorne—and he seems to me a great genius, the creator of a literary tradition as well as a wonderfully original and accomplished artist—is the author of *Young Goodman Brown, The Maypole of Merry Mount, My Kinsman Major Molineux, The Snow-Image, The Blithedale Romance, The Scarlet Letter,* and of a number of sketches and less pregnant stories associated with these works such as *The Gray Champion, Main Street, Old News, Endicott of the Red Cross, The Artist of the Beautiful.* This work is not comparable with the productions of the eighteenth-century "allegorical" essayists nor is it in the manner of Spenser, Milton, or Bunyan—whom of course it can be seen he has not merely studied but assimilated. The first batch of works I specified is essentially dramatic, its use of language is poetic, and it is symbolic, and richly so, as is the dramatic poet's. In fact I should suggest that Hawthorne can have gone to school with no one but Shakespeare for his inspiration and model. Mr. Wilson Knight's approach to Shakespeare's tragedies—each play an expanded metaphor—is a cue for the method of rightly apprehending these works of Hawthorne's, where the "symbol" is the thing itself, with no separable paraphrasable meaning as in an allegory: the language is directly evocative. Rereading this work, one is certainly not conscious of a limited and devitalized talent employing a simple-minded pedestrian technique; one is constantly struck by fresh subtleties of

° Reprinted by permission from *Sewanee Review* 59 (1951): 179–205.

organization, of intention, expression and feeling, of original psychological insight and a new minting of terms to convey it, as well as of a predominantly dramatic construction. Yet of the above-mentioned works, apart from *The Scarlet Letter* which has had a good deal of inadequate attention, I can't find any serious *literary* criticism, even in *The American Renaissance* where Hawthorne is evidently intended in some way to be a focus and key-figure. . . .

The aspect of Hawthorne that I want to stress as the important one, decisive for American literature, and to be found most convincingly in the works I specified, is this: that he was the critic and interpreter of American cultural history and thereby the finder and creator of a literary tradition from which sprang Henry James on the one hand and Melville on the other. I find it impossible to follow Mr. Parkes's argument that "what is lacking in [Hawthorne's] framework of experience is any sense of society as a kind of organic whole to which the individual belongs and in which he has his appointed place. And lacking the notion of social continuity and tradition, [he] lacks also the corresponding metaphysical conception of the natural universe as an ordered unity which harmonizes with human ideals."[1] It is precisely those problems, the relation of the individual to society, the way in which a distinctively American society developed and how it came to have a tradition of its own, the relation of the creative writer to the earlier nineteenth-century American community, and his function and how he could contrive to exercise it—the exploration of these questions and the communication in literary art of his findings—that are his claim to importance. It is true that he is most successful in treating pre-Revolutionary America, but that, after all, is, as he saw it, the decisive period, and *The Blithedale Romance* is the finest test of his dictum in *Old News* that "All philosophy that would abstract mankind from the present is no more than words." As I see it, Hawthorne's sense of being part of the contemporary America could be expressed only in concern for its evolution—he needed to see how it had come about, and by discovering what America had, culturally speaking, started from and with, to find what choices had faced his countrymen and what they had had to sacrifice in order to create that distinctive "organic whole." He was very conscious of the nature of his work; he asserted that to be the function of every great writer, as when in *The Old Manse* he wrote: "A work of genius is but the newspaper of a century, or perchance of a hundred centuries." [Indeed, in some sketches, such as *Old News*, we can see the half-way stage between the newspapers and the work of genius; these sketches have a function like that of the *Letters* of Jane Austen in the evolution of her novels.] And he prepared himself for the task by study, though Providence had furnished him with an eminently usable private Past, in the history of his own family, which epitomized the earlier phases of New England history; this vividly stylized the social history of Colonial America, provided him with a personal mythology, and gave him an emotional stake in the past, a private key to tradition. We know that his first pieces which he later burnt in despair of getting published were called *Seven Tales of My Native Land.* Though he was the very opposite of a Dreiser (whom Mr. Parkes backs in contrast) yet I should choose to describe Hawthorne as a sociological novelist in effect, employing a poetic technique which communicates instead of stating his findings. . . .

The Maypole of Merry Mount is an early work bearing obvious signs of immaturity but it also shows great originality, and it is a root work, proving that Hawthorne had laid the foundations of much later successes, notably *The Scarlet Letter* and *The Blithedale Romance,* in his beginnings almost. It proves also that he decided in his youth on his characteristic technique. We notice that it is essentially a poetic technique: the opening is almost too deliberately poetic in rhythm and word-order. But once the convention has been established in the first two paragraphs, he relaxes and proceeds less artificially. We are, or should be, struck in this early piece by the mastery Hawthorne achieves in a new form of prose art, by the skill with which he manages to convey ironic inflexions and to control transitions from one layer of meaning to another, and by which he turns, as it was to become his great distinction to do, history into myth and anecdote into parable. The essential if not the greatest Hawthorne had so soon found himself.

The tale originally had a sub-title: "A Parable," and in a few prefatory sentences Hawthorne wrote that "the curious history of the early settlement of Mount Wollaston, or Merry Mount" furnishes "an admirable foundation for a philosophic romance"—we see his decision to take for his own from the start the associations of "romance" and not of "novel" or some such term suggesting a disingenuous connection between fiction and daily life. He continued: "In the slight sketch here attempted the facts, recorded on the grave pages of our New England annalists, have wrought themselves, almost spontaneously, into a sort of allegory." If an allegory (unfortunate word), it is a "sort" that no experience of *The Faerie Queen* and *The Pilgrim's Progress* can prepare us for. Its distinctive quality is its use of symbols to convey meaning, and a boldness of imagination and stylization which while drawing on life does not hesitate to rearrange facts and even violate history in that interest. The outline of the historically insignificant Merry Mount affair, whether as recorded by the Puritan historian Governor Bradford or so very differently by the protagonist Thomas Morton in his entertaining *New England Canaan,* was a godsend to Hawthorne, who saw in it a means of precipitating his own reactions to his forefathers' choice. While Hawthorne's imagination was historical in a large sense, he was never an imaginative recreator of the romantic past, a historical novelist: he had always from the first very clearly in view the *criticism* of the past. The past was his peculiar concern since it was the source of his present. . . .

Perhaps the American Puritans, who must if so have had none of the humane qualities of Bunyan and his class that make *Pilgrim's Progress* so pleasing—perhaps those who emigrated were more intensively intolerant than those who remained at home, or perhaps the persecuting aspect of their way of life was peculiarly present to Hawthorne because of the witch-hanging judge and the Quaker-whipping Major among his ancestors. But the essential truth Hawthorne rightly seized on, that the decisive minority set themselves in absolute hostility to the immemorial culture of the English folk with its Catholic and ultimately pagan roots, preserved in song and dance, festivals and superstitions, and especially the rites and dramatic practices of which the May-Day ceremonies were the key. Morton did rear a Maypole at Merry Mount and the fanatic Governor Endicott did indeed (but only after Morton had been seized and shipped home) visit the settlement and have the abominable tree cut down. Moreover the early theologians and historians had dramatized in their writings the elements of the scene in scriptural and theological terms. But this theological myth Hawthorne adapted to convey subtle and often ironic meanings, just as he freely adapts the historical facts. Morton was actually as well as ideally a High Churchman of good birth, a Royalist and deliberately anti-Puritan, but the object of his settlement was profitable trading with the Indians. Having none of the Puritans' conviction of the damned state of the savages, he made friends with them. Thus Hawthorne could make these settlers embody the old way of living as opposed to the new. He starts with the Maypole as the symbol of the pagan religion for "what chiefly characterized the colonists of Merry Mount was their veneration for the Maypole. It has made their true history a poet's tale." A living tree, "venerated" for it is the center of life and changes with the seasons, it is now on the festival of Midsummer's Eve hung with roses, "some that had been gathered in the sunniest spots of the forest and others, of still richer blush, which the colonists had reared from English seed." Here we have the earliest use of one of Hawthorne's chief symbols, the rose, and we notice that the native wild rose and the cultivated rose carried as seed from England (with generations of grafting and cultivation behind it) are in process of being mingled at Merry Mount. Round the tree the worshippers of the natural religion are figured with extraordinary vitality of imagination: "Gothic monsters, though perhaps of Grecian ancestry," the animal-masked figures of mythology and primitive art (man as wolf, bear, stag and he-goat); "And, almost as wondrous, stood a real bear of the dark forest, lending each of his fore-paws to the grasp of a human hand, and as ready for the dance as any in that circle. His inferior nature rose half-way to meet his companions as they stooped"; "the Salvage Man, well known in heraldry, hairy as a baboon and girdled with green leaves"; Indians real and counterfeit. The harmony between man and beast and nature that was once recognized by a religious ritual could hardly be more poetically conjured up. Then the youth and maiden who represent the May Lord and Lady are shown; they are about to be permanently as well as ritually married, by an English priest who wears also "a chaplet of the native vine-leaves." Later on he is named by Endicott as "Blackstone," though Hawthorne protects himself against the fact that the historic Blaxton had nothing to do with Merry Mount by an equivocal footnote: Blackstone here represents a poetic license which Hawthorne is perfectly justified in taking. Blackstone, who is similarly imported into *The Scarlet Letter* in a key passage, was actually not a High Churchman nor "a clerk of Oxford" as he declares in *The Maypole*, but like most New England divines a Cambridge man and anti-Episcopalian. But he must be of Oxford because Hawthorne needs him to represent Catholicism and Royalism, to complete the culture-complex of Merry Mount, which has been shown in every other respect to be ancient, harmonious and traditional, a chain of life from the dim past, from the tree and animal upwards, all tolerated and respected as part of the natural and right order. The reader is expected to take the reference to the historical Blaxton, who like Endicott and Ann Hutchinson, among others, become in Hawthorne's art cultural heroes. How eminently adapted for Hawthorne's purpose he was is seen in this account by the historian of *The Colonial Period of American History:* "The Rev. William Blaxton, M.A. Emmanuel College, Cambridge, removed to the western slope of Shawmut peninsula [Beacon Hill] where, near an excellent spring, he built a house, planted an orchard, raised apples, and cultivated a vegetable garden. Leaving Boston in 1635, disillusioned because of the intolerance of the Puritan magistrates, he went southward saying as he departed, 'I came from England because I did not like the Lord Bishops, but I cannot join with you because I would not be under the Lord Brethren.' He too wanted to worship God in his own way." He represents, among other things, the crowning, the unPuritan virtue of tolerance, one of Hawthorne's main positives. Without what he stands for the dance and drama round the Maypole and the whole pagan year-cycle of "hereditary pastimes" would be negligible in comparison with the Christian culture even of the Puritans.

Meanwhile a band of Puritans in hiding are watching the scene. To them the masquers and their comrades are like "those devils and ruined souls with whom their superstitions peopled the black wilderness." For "Unfortunately there were men in the new world, of a sterner faith than these Maypole worshippers. Not far from Merry Mount was a settlement of Puritans, most dismal wretches, who said their prayers before daylight, and then wrought in the forest or the cornfield, till evening made it prayer time again." This, to judge by the "most dismal wretches," is to be discounted by the reader as probably the prejudiced view of the Maypole worshippers, just as to the Puritans the others appear to be "the crew of Comus." But if so persuaded, we are brought up short by a characteristic taut statement about the Puritans, shocking both in its literal and allegorical implications, that immediately follows: "Their weapons were always at hand to shoot down the straggling savage." At Merry Mount we have seen a life where the "savage," without and within the human breast, is accepted as part of life. Hawthorne continues in the same tone: "When they met in conclave, it was never to keep up the old English mirth, but to hear sermons three hours long, or to proclaim bounties on the heads of wolves and the scalps of Indians. Their festivals were fast days, and their chief pastime the singing of psalms. Woe to the youth or maiden who did but dream of a dance! The selectman nodded to the constable; and there sat the lightheeled reprobate in the stock; or if he danced, it was round the whipping-post, which might be termed the Puritan Maypole." The practices of the Puritan are described as being a horrible parody of those of the Maypole worshippers, a deliberate offense against the spirit of Life. The force of the cunning phrase "to proclaim bounties on the heads of wolves and the scalps of Indians," charged with a sense of the inhumanity that leveled the Indian with the wolf, should not be overlooked.

I need not continue to analyze and quote in detail, I hope, to demonstrate the success of the kind of literary art Hawthorne has here created, but I want to note a few more of his total effects, by way of prelude to his later work. We have seen and felt what the religion of the old order was. We find ourselves then inescapably faced by Hawthorne with the question: And what did the Puritans worship? We are left in no doubt as to Hawthorne's answer: Force. Hawthorne had realized that religion is a matter of symbols, and his choice of appropriate symbols is not at all simple-minded. The Maypole worshipers are not, it turns out, to be accepted without qualification. They have another symbolic quality attached to them, they are "silken"—"Sworn triflers of a life-time, they would not venture among the sober truths of life, not even to be truly blest." Everyone was "gay" at Merry Mount, but what really was "the quality of their mirth"? "Once, it is said, they were seen following a flower-decked corpse, with merriment and festive music, to his grave. But did the dead man laugh?" We have been rounded on as in the passage about the Puritans. Hawthorne is preparing a more complex whole for us, and preparing us to receive it. The term for the Puritans corresponding to "silken" for the settlers is "iron." We find it immediately after the passage quoted above where their practices are described as systematically inhumane. A party comes "toiling through the difficult woods, each with a horse-load of iron armour to burden his footsteps." A little later they are "men of iron," and when they surround and overpower the Maypole-worshippers their leader is revealed as iron all through: "So stern was the energy of his aspect, that the whole man, visage, frame and soul, seemed wrought of iron, gifted with life and thought, yet all of one substance with his headpiece and breast-plate. It was the Puritan of Puritans; it was Endicott himself." He cuts down the Maypole with his sword, which he rests on while deciding the fate of the May Lord and Lady, and "with his own gauntleted hand" he finally crowns them with the wreath of mingled roses from the ruin of the Maypole. The associations of iron are all brought into play, suggesting the rigid system which burdens life, the metal that makes man militant and ultimately inhuman, and it is spiritually the sign of heaviness and gloom, opposed in every way to the associations of lightness—silken, sunny, gay and mirthful, used for the followers of the old way of life. The iron imagery is finally concentrated in the doom brought on New England by the Puritans' victory at Merry Mount: "It was a deed of prophecy. As the moral gloom of the world overpowers systematic gaiety. . . ." The armor in *Endicott of the Red Cross* and *The Scarlet Letter* has more extensive meanings too.

The Puritans' religion is expressed in their rites—acts of persecution, oppression and cruelty. Endicott and his followers pass sentence on "the heathen crew." Their tame bear is to be shot—"I suspect witchcraft in the beast," says the leader, and even the "long glossy curls" on the May Lord's head must be cut. "Crop it forthwith, and that in the true pumpkin-shell fashion"—the brutal denial of personal dignity and natural comeliness is indicated with striking economy. The language of Bunyan is made to sound very differently in these mouths; Hawthorne, a master of language, has many such resources at his command. But Hawthorne's total meaning is very complex and his last word is not by any means a simple condemnation. While the Merry Mount way of life embodies something essential that is lacking in the Puritans', making theirs appear ugly and inhuman, yet Hawthorne's point is that in the New World the old way could be only an imported artifice; New England, he deeply felt, could never be a mere reproduction of the Old. The fairies, as John Wilson says in *The Scarlet Letter*, were left behind in old England with Catholicism. And Hawthorne implies that the outlook of Merry Mount is not consonant with the realities of life in the New World, or the new phase of the world anywhere perhaps. The Puritans may be odious but they have a secret which is a better thing than the religion of the nature and humanity. The May Lord and Lady, at Endicott's command, leave their Paradise—the reference to Adam and Eve driven from the Garden is unmistakable, as others to Milton in this tale—and there is a general suggestion that the "choice" imposed on New England is like that made by Adam and Eve, they sacrifice bliss for something more arduous and better worth having. Hawthorne has no doubt that the May Lord and Lady enter into a finer bond in Christian marriage than they could otherwise have known as symbolic figures in a fertility rite. Nevertheless though their future is "blessed" it is not pleasant or gracious. Hawthorne felt acutely the wrong the Lord Brethren had done to the Blaxtons, typified by the doings of an Endicott. The close parallel between the Merry Mount drama and the corresponding conflict in Milton's poem between the Brothers and the followers of Comus must be intentional—there are explicit references—and intended by Hawthorne as a criticism of Milton's presentment of the case. Virtue and Vice are a simple-minded division in Milton's *Comus,* however his symbolism may be interpreted. In Hawthorne's view that contest was quite other than a matter of Right and Wrong; his Puritans are an ironic comment on Milton's cause and case. Hawthorne's rendering shows two partial truths or qualified goods set in regrettable opposition. What Hawthorne implies is that it was a disaster for New England that they could not be reconciled. Hawthorne is both subtler and wiser than Milton, and his poem, unlike Milton's, is really dramatic and embodies a genuine cultural and spiritual conflict. Milton is a Puritan and Hawthorne is not; to Hawthorne, Milton is a man of iron. Hawthorne is seen explicitly the unwilling heir of the Puritans, and their indignant critic, in a fine passage in *Main Street* which ends "Let us thank God for having given us such ancestors; and let each successive generation thank him not less fervently, for being one step further from them in the march of ages."

Just as the rose, the flower that symbolizes human grace and whose beauty is essentially something cultivated, the product of long training—just as the rose is used from *The Maypole* onwards, so the concept of the iron man becomes basic thereafter. The meaning is expounded in a remarkable section of *Main Street* which concludes: "All was well, so long as their lamps were freshly kindled at the heavenly flame. After a while, however, whether in their time or their children's, these lamps began to burn more dimly, or with a less genuine lustre; and then it might be seen how hard, cold and confined, was their system,—how like an iron cage was that which they called Liberty."

I believe the image was taken by Hawthorne, consciously or

unconsciously, from Bunyan; it may be remembered that in the Interpreter's House Christian is shown a Man in an Iron Cage as an awful warning of what a true Christian should never be. Now Bunyan's Man in an Iron Cage exemplified Despair. I have mentioned also that "Blackstone" recurs in *The Scarlet Letter* in an almost mystically poetic context. In fact, these writings of Hawthorne's, to yield all they offer, must be studied as a whole, as a poet's works are, each illuminating and strengthening the rest. This is not the case with the fictions of any English nineteenth-century novelist. Perhaps this makes my point that Hawthorne needs a quite other approach from the one we commonly make to a novelist. His recurrent drama is a poet's vision of the meaning of his world, and it is communicated by poetic means.

Young Goodman Brown, visibly a much later and more practiced work than the last, is also more powerful and more closely knit than anything else of Hawthorne's with the possible exception of the very complex and ambitious *Major Molineux*. It lends itself to much the same kind of analysis, that is, demands the same approach, as has been already outlined, and is even more unmistakably a prose poem. If its content has reminded literary critics of *Macbeth* and the Walpurgisnacht of *Faust*, that is unfortunate, for the relevant point is that Young Goodman Brown is Everyman in seventeenth-century New England—the title as usual giving the clue. He is the son of the Old Goodman Brown, that is, the Old Adam (or Adam the First as he is called in Bunyan), and recently wedded to Faith. We must note that every word is significant in the opening sentence: "Young Goodman Brown came forth at sunset into the street of Salem Village; but put his head back, after crossing the threshold, to exchange a parting kiss with his young wife." She begs him to "put off his journey until sunrise," but he declares he cannot: "My journey, as thou callest it, forth and back again, must needs be done 'twixt now and sunrise." It is a journey he takes under compulsion, and it should not escape us that she tries to stop him because she is under a similar compulsion to go on a "journey" herself—"*She* talks of dreams, too," Young Goodman Brown reflects as he leaves her. The journey each must take alone, in dread, at night, is the journey away from home and the community, from conscious, everyday social life, to the wilderness where the hidden self satisfies, or is forced to realize, its subconscious fears and promptings in sleep. We take that journey with him into the awful forest. We note the division, which is to be the basis of *The Scarlet Letter*, between the town (where the minister rules) and the forest (where the Black Man reigns). From his pious home and Faith Young Goodman Brown reluctantly wanders back into the desert, meeting as he expects one who "bears a considerable resemblance to him. They might have been taken for father and son." He resists as best he can until he is made to realize to his surprise and horror that his father had gone on that journey before him, and sees many respected neighbours indeed pass him to the trysting-place. At first, confident in the appearance of virtue in the daily life of his fellows, he retorts indignantly: "My father never went into the woods on such an errand, nor his father before him. We have been a race of honest men and good Christians since the days of the martyrs." "We are a people of prayer, and good works to boot, and abide no such wickedness." The sinister likeness of his grandfather is able to convince him otherwise, though "the arguments seemed rather to spring up in the bosom of his auditor than to be suggested by" the Devil. We feel how an accumulation of unconscious doubts about the "saints" precipitates Young Goodman Brown's conviction of universal sinfulness. As he loses his belief in the reality of virtue in others the scene grows increasingly sinister until the road "vanished at length, leaving him in the heart of the dark wilderness, still rushing onward with the instinct that guides mortal man to evil. The whole forest was peopled with frightful sounds—the creaking of the trees, the howling of the wild beasts, and the yell of Indians." We see Hawthorne making timely use of the traditional Puritan association of trees, animals, and Indians as the hostile powers, allies of the fiend.

> But he was himself the chief horror of the scene, and shrank not from its other horrors.
> "Ha! ha! ha!" roared Goodman Brown when the wind laughed at him. "Let us hear which will laugh loudest. Think not to frighten me with your deviltry. Come witch, come wizard, come Indian pow-wow, come devil himself, and here comes Goodman Brown. You may as well fear him as he fear you." In truth, all through the haunted forest there could be nothing more frightful than the figure of Goodman Brown.

The nightmare poetry gathers volume and power as he approaches the flaming center of the forest, but Hawthorne's poetic imagination is as different as possible from Poe's—there is no touch of the Gothic horrors one might anticipate. When Goodman Brown ends his journey he finds his whole world, even the elders and ministers, assembled to worship at the devil's altar; he and his Faith are only the latest to be received into the communion of the lost.

When Young Goodman Brown returns to Salem Village with the morning light, "staring around him like a bewildered man," his eyes have been opened to the true nature of his fellowmen, that is, human nature; he inescapably knows that what he suspected of himself is true of all men. He must live with that knowledge, and he is thenceforward a man of gloom, the Man in the Iron Cage, a Calvinist indeed.

What Hawthorne has given us is not an allegory, and not an ambiguous problem-story (we are not to ask: Was it an actual Satanic experience or only a dream?). Hawthorne has made a dramatic poem of the Calvinist experience in New England. The unfailing tact with which the experience is evoked subjectively, in the most impressive concrete terms, is a subordinate proof of genius. I should prefer to stress the wonderful control of local and total rhythm, which never falters or slackens, and rises from the quiet but impressive opening to its poetic climax in the superb and moving finale, which I should have liked to quote in full. It ends "they carved no hopeful verse upon his tombstone; for his dying hour was gloom."

Hawthorne has imaginatively recreated for the reader that Calvinist sense of sin, that theory which did in actuality shape the early social and spiritual history of New England. But in Hawthorne, by a wonderful feat of transmutation, it has no religious significance, it is as a psychological state that it is explored. Young Goodman Brown's Faith is not faith in Christ but faith in human beings, and losing it he is doomed to isolation forever. *Young Goodman Brown* seems to me very much more impressive than the Walpurgisnacht scene in Joyce's *Ulysses*, which smells of the case-book and the midnight oil. If anyone is inclined to question its claim to be a dramatic poem he might be asked to examine along with it Cowper's acknowledged masterpiece *The Castaway*, comparable in theme but in every other respect so inferior. And I am tempted to ask what advantage has *The Castaway* or even *The Ancient Mariner* over *Young Goodman Brown* by being in verse? In fact, the regularity of verse and stanzas is a disadvantage, imposing monotony and other limitations; either of these poems is less forceful, artistically serious and truly "poetic" than Hawthorne's prose poem. The alleged superiority of poetic form may be specious and there is in fact no sharp distinction between prose and poetry.

In this tale Hawthorne achieved a considerable contribution toward the comprehensive masterpiece he was to produce in *The Scarlet Letter*, for the tale is partially taken up into the later romance.

In his introduction to a volume of tales brought out in 1851 but mostly written much earlier Hawthorne, then in his prime as an artist, with *The Scarlet Letter* a year behind him, confessed that he was "disposed to quarrel with the earlier sketches," most of all "because they come so nearly up to the standard of the best that I can achieve now." As one of the earlier sketches in his collection was *My Kinsman Major Molineux* (1831), he might justly have felt that he was never to achieve anything better.

Ideally it should be preceded by a reading of the three studies collected under the title *Old News*, which give the historical background and are clearly the fruit of work preparatory for *Major Molineux*. This remarkable tale might have been less commonly overlooked or misunderstood if it had had a sub-title, such as Hawthorne often provided by way of a hint. It could do with some such explanatory sub-title as "America Comes of Age." But though if a naturalistic story is looked for the reader would be left merely puzzled, the tale lends itself readily to comprehension as a poetic parable in dramatic form, and the opening paragraph as usual clearly explains the situation and furnishes the required clue. We are in the age which was preparing the colonies for the War of Independence and we are made to take part in a dramatic precipitation of, or prophetic forecast of, the rejection of England that was to occur in fact much later.

The actual tale begins by describing a country-bred youth coming to town, starting with the significant sentence: "It was near nine o'clock of a moonlight evening, when a boat crossed the ferry with a single passenger." The sturdy pious youth Robin, the son of the typical farmer-clergyman, represents the young America; he has *left his home* in the village in the woods and crossing by the *ferry, alone, at nightfall,* reaches the little metropolis of a New England port— that is, the contemporary scene where the historic future will be decided. He arrives poor but hopeful, confidently anticipating help in making his fortune from "my kinsman Major Molineux," the reiteration of the phrase being an important contribution to the total effect. The kinsman is Hawthorne's and ours (if we are Americans) as well as Robin's, and his name suggests both his military and aristocratic status. Robin explains much later in the tale that his father and the Major are brother's sons—that is, one brother had stayed in England and the other left to colonize New England. Their children, the next generation, represented by Robin's father and the Major, had kept on friendly terms and the rich Major, representative in New England of the British civil and military rule and keeping "great pomp," was in a position to patronize his poor country cousin. We do not get this straightforward account in the tale, of course, we have to unravel it for ourselves, for the presentation of the theme is entirely dramatic and we have to identify our consciousness with the protagonist Robin. The essential information is revealed only when we have ourselves experienced for some time the same bewilderment as poor Robin, who cannot understand why his request to be directed to the house of his kinsman is met by the various types of citizen with suspicion, with contempt, with anger, with disgust, with sneers, or with laughter. In fact, Robin has arrived at a critical moment in his kinsman's history. The colonists—with considerable skill and economy Hawthorne represents all ranks and classes of the states in this dream-town—have secretly planned to throw off

British rule, or at any rate to rid themselves of Major Molineux, a symbolic action which, performed in the street outside the church at midnight and before the innocent eyes of the mystified youth, takes the form of something between a pageant and a ritual drama, disguised in the emotional logic of a dream. As a dream it has a far greater emotional pull than actuality could have. Hawthorne never anywhere surpassed this tale (written when he was not more than twenty-seven) in dramatic power, in control of tone, pace, and tension, and in something more wonderful, the creation of a suspension between the fullest consciousness of meaning and the emotional incoherence of dreaming. How this is achieved and for what purpose can be seen only by a careful examination of the last half of the tale, but I will quote as sparingly as possible.

Until this point, precisely the middle of the work, no departure from the everyday normal has been necessary, though we have been wrought to a state of exasperation which is ready for working on. And Hawthorne now introduces another note:

> He now roamed desperately, and at random, through the town, almost ready to believe that a spell was on him, like that by which a wizard of his country had once kept three pursuers wandering, a whole winter night, within twenty paces of the cottage which they sought. The streets lay before him, strange and desolate, and the lights were extinguished in almost every house. Twice, however, little parties of men, among whom Robin distinguished individuals in outlandish attire, came hurrying along; but though on both occasions they paused to address him, such intercourse did not at all enlighten his perplexity. They did but utter a few words in some language of which Robin knew nothing, and perceiving his inability to answer, bestowed a curse upon him in plain English, and hastened away. Finally, the lad determined to knock at the door of every mansion, trusting that perseverance would overcome the fatality that had hitherto thwarted him. Firm in this resolve, he was passing beneath the walls of a church, which formed the corner of two streets, when, as he turned into the shade of its steeple, he encountered a bulky stranger, muffled in a cloak. The man was proceeding with the speed of earnest business, but Robin planted himself full before him, holding the oak cudgel with both hands across his body, as a bar to further passage.
>
> "Halt, honest man, and answer me a question," said he, very resolutely. "Tell me, this instant, whereabouts is the dwelling of my kinsman, Major Molineux!"
>
> . . . The stranger, instead of attempting to force his passage, stepped back into the moonlight, unmuffled his face, and stared full into that of Robin.
>
> "Watch here an hour, and Major Molineux will pass by," said he.
>
> Robin gazed with dismay and astonishment on the unprece-

dented physiognomy of the speaker. The forehead with its double prominence, the broad hooked nose, the shaggy eyebrow, and fiery eyes, were those which he had noticed at the inn, but the man's complexion had undergone a singular, or, more properly, a two-fold change. One side of the face blazed an intense red, while the other was black as midnight, the division line being in the broad bridge of the nose; and a mouth which seemed to extend from ear to ear was black or red, in contrast to the color of the cheek. The effect was as if two individual devils, a fiend of fire and a fiend of darkness, had united themselves to form this infernal visage. The stranger grinned in Robin's face, muffled his parti-colored features, and was out of sight in a moment.

The stranger, whose unearthly appearance we were prepared for by the "individuals in outlandish attire" speaking in a code—for as we realize later they were obviously conspirators demanding from Robin a password he could not furnish, but they help to increase the nightmare atmosphere—is shown by his face to be something more than a man in disguise. The tension is being screwed up to the pitch needed for the approaching climax of the drama: this is not a man like the others but a Janus-like fiend of fire and darkness, that is, we presently learn, "war personified" in its dual aspects of Death and Destruction. But it is not just a personification, it is a symbol with emotional repercussions which passes through a series of suggestive forms. The account of its features at first: "The forehead with its double prominence, the broad hooked nose" etc. suggests Punch and so also the grotesque associations of puppet-show farce. The division of the face into black and red implies the conventional get-up of the jester, and indeed he "grinned in Robin's face" before he "muffled his parti-colored features." At this point Robin, carrying the reader with him, having "consumed a few moments in philosophical spec-ulation upon the species of man who had just left him," is able to "settle this point shrewdly, rationally and satisfactorily." He and we are of course deceived in our complacency. He falls into a drowse by sending his thoughts "to imagine how that evening of ambiguity and weariness had been spent in his father's household." This actually completes his bewilderment—"Am I here or there?" he cries, "But still his mind kept vibrating between fancy and reality."

Now, so prepared, we hear the murmur that becomes a confused medley of voices and shouts as it approaches, turning into "frequent bursts from many instruments of discord, and a wild and confused laughter filled up the intervals." "The antipodes of music" heralds "a mighty stream of people" led by a single horseman whom Robin recognizes as the eerie stranger in a fresh avatar. With the "rough music" that in Old England was traditionally used to drive undesirable characters out of the community, by the red glare of torches and with "War personified" as their leader, the citizens of America, with Indians in their train and cheered on by their women, are symbolically if proleptically casting out the English ruler. The nightmare impression reaches its climax: "In his train were wild figures in the Indian dress, and many fantastic shapes without a model, giving the whole march a visionary air, as if a dream had broken forth from some feverish brain, and were sweeping visibly through the midnight streets. . . . 'The double-faced fellow has his eye upon me' muttered Robin, with an indefinite but uncomfortable idea that he was himself to bear a part in the pageantry."

It seems indeed that the pageant has been brought to this place for Robin's benefit.

> A moment more, and the leader thundered a command to halt: the trumpets vomited a horrid breath, and then held their peace; the shouts and laughter of the people died away, and there remained only a universal hum, allied to silence. Right before Robin's eyes was an uncovered cart. There the torches blazed the brightest, there the moon shone out like day, and there, in tar-and-feathery dignity, sat his kinsman Major Molineux!
>
> He was an elderly man, of large and majestic person, and strong, square features, betokening a steady soul; but steady as it was, his enemies had found means to shake it. His face was pale as death, and far more ghastly; the broad forehead was contracted in his agony, so that his eyebrows formed one grizzled line; his eyes were red and wild, and the foam hung white upon his quivering lip. His whole frame was agitated by a quick and continual tremor, which his pride strove to quell, even in those circumstances of overwhelming humiliation. But perhaps the bitterest pang of all was when his eyes met those of Robin; for he evidently knew him on the instant, as the youth stood witnessing the foul disgrace of a head grown gray in honor. They stared at each other in silence, and Robin's knees shook, and his hair bristled, with a mixture of pity and terror.

The pageant is thus seen to represent a tragedy and is felt by us as such; it arouses in Robin the appropriate blend of emotions— the classical "pity and terror." But Hawthorne has by some inspiration—for how could he have known except intuitively of the origins of tragedy in ritual drama?—gone back to the type of action that fathered Tragedy. Just as the "War personified" suggests an idol or a human representative of the god, so does the other terrible figure "in tar-and-feathery dignity" in the cart. We seem to be spectators at that most primitive of all dramatic representations, the conquest of the old king by the new.

If the story had ended here, on this note, it would have been remarkable enough, but Hawthorne has an almost incredible consummation to follow. I mean incredible in being so subtly achieved with such mastery of tone. From being a spectator at a tragedy, Robin has to fulfill his premonitions of having "to bear a part in the pageantry" himself. He is drawn into the emotional vortex and comes to share the reactions of the participants. He has felt intimately the dreadful degradation of his English kinsman, but now he is seized with the excitement of the victors, his fellow-countrymen, and sees their triumph as his own—"a perception of tremendous ridicule in the whole scene affected him with a sort of mental inebriety." Drunk with success the whole town roars in a frenzy of laughter, and Robin's shout joins theirs and is the loudest. Then in a sudden calm that follows this orgy "the procession resumed its march. On they went, like fiends that throng in mockery around some dead potentate, mighty no more, but majestic still in his agony." We are left in the silent street, brought back into the world of problems in which the tale opened. Robin still has to settle with reality and decide his future, the future of his generation. He asks to be shown the way back to the ferry: "I begin to grow weary of a town life" he says to the townsman who has stayed behind to note his reactions. But his new friend replies: "Some few days hence, if you wish it, I will speed you on your journey. Or, if you prefer to remain with us, perhaps, as you are a shrewd youth, you may rise in the world without the help of your kinsman, Major Molineux."

Hawthorne has been blamed for failing to provide a "solution" and for not being optimistic as a good American should be, but it seems to me that here, as in *The Maypole*, he ends in reasonable, sober hopefulness for the future of life. Provided we recognize the facts and fully comprehend the positions, we can cope with it, if not master it, he implies. Declining to be, perhaps incapable of being, a naturalistic novelist, he was true to his best perceptions of his genius when he did the work of a dramatic poet, the interpreter and radical critic of the society which had produced him and for whose benefit he expressed his insight in a unique literature.

Notes

1. "Poe, Hawthorne, Melville: an Essay in Sociological Criticism," *Partisan Review*, Feb., 1949. This naïve demand should be measured against this passage from *Hawthorne's Last Phase* (E. H. Davidson, 1949): "The rare springtime beauty of the English scene struck him more forcibly than it could the ordinary tourist, for it represented to him the perfect balance between man and nature. This balance was conspicuously absent in the untamed forests of the U. S., where man was busily engaged in subduing nature and dominating a continent. 'It is only an American who can feel it,' Hawthorne wrote."

Fathers, Sons, and the Ambiguities of Revolution in "My Kinsman, Major Molineux"

Peter Shaw°

In one of the first essays to draw modern attention to Hawthorne's "My Kinsman, Major Molineux," Q. D. Leavis pointed out in 1951 that this story of a young man coming to town to find the kinsman who has promised to advance him parallels the relationship between young America and its protecting elder, England. When the boy, Robin, joins in the laughter of a pre-Revolutionary crowd that has tarred and feathered his kinsman, he prefigures America's Revolutionary break from the parent country. Psychological, folklorist, and moral readings have tended to avoid this emphasis while favoring Robin's private experience, about which they differ. Yet Hawthorne's historical parallel, if pursued, enriches each of the warring readings at the same time that it effectually resolves the disagreements among them.[1]

As Leavis and later critics have shown, both the adolescent ritual of coming of age and the crowd's ritual overthrow of authority are rooted in folklore. Hawthorne is said to have "intuited" the motif of the old king replacing the new in Major Molineux's overthrow, a ritual that harks back to the sacrificial origins of tragedy. (Still further behind this event, of course, there lies the Frazerian "primitive Ritual" of the "Scapegoat King.")[2] In fact Hawthorne and his contemporaries were more aware of such origins than has been realized. At the same time, by the nineteenth century the connection between coming of age and revolution had an age-old historical familiarity. In official hagiography and popular terminology alike, at least until the eighteenth-century age of revolutions, the king and his magistrates commonly were conceived of as fathers of their people, while protesters and revolutionists were depicted as unruly, ungrateful children. For hundreds of years governments based their legitimacy on rituals that enacted the king-father analogy and emphasized the identification of all officials with the king as father. This hagiography remained a commonplace of the debates between Englishmen and Americans throughout the Revolutionary period. English and loyalist writers accused the Americans of ingratitude toward the parent country, only to be answered with the argument that the child must come of age and leave its parents.[3] Even as the legitimating rituals of kingship fell into disuse, mobbings of government officials like Major Molineux continued to be understood in their time as symbolic acts of revolt by children against their father.

° Reprinted by permission from *New England Quarterly* 49 (1976): 559–76.

Critical dispute over "My Kinsman, Major Molineux" arises from the problem of interpreting Hawthorne's use of this traditional symbolism of revolt. As critics have grown increasingly sensitive to Hawthorne's disapproval of the crowd that tars and feathers Major Molineux, Robin's identification of himself with that crowd has raised the question of Hawthorne's attitude toward him and, in turn, toward the American Revolution. The political reading, in which Robin prefigures American Independence, is weakened by assuming, partly on the evidence of Hawthorne's later, liberal politics, his approval of Robin and the Revolution. Critics in the 1970s, no doubt as the result of a changed political climate, have been less willing than in the 1950s to assume that the outcome of the Revolution justifies all.[4] The psychological reading, in which Robin expresses his resentment of paternal authority by joining against Molineux, neglects the moral implications of his unprovoked hostility. A mixture of love and hate is expected from the oedipal conflict in a young man, but the psychoanalytic approach, to be sure, goes perhaps too far in treating Robin like a patient for whose actions the analyst bears no responsibility. The moral reading, curiously enough, also founders on neglect of Hawthorne's disapproval of the crowd. Robin's experience is described as eventuating in a growth of awareness, maturity, and moral stature, but little evidence can be found for such development. Robin displays aggressive tendencies throughout, and after acting brutally toward his kinsman, shows no more than a hint of mild remorse. The most that can be said is that Hawthorne grants Robin "intimations of self-knowledge sharp enough to let him begin to comprehend his symbolic fate."[5] Whether or not he does so is left an open question. The confident ascription of moral growth to Robin, therefore, speaks well for his critics but not necessarily for Robin himself.

Hawthorne conveys his attitude toward Robin and the crowd through historical allusions. At the outset he relates that the eighteenth-century governors of Massachusetts Bay had grown unpopular because of "the compliances by which, in softening their instructions from beyond the sea, they had incurred the reprehension of those who gave them." Thus, Americans in the eighteenth century attacked their governors instead of "the kings" who, Hawthorne writes in his opening sentence, began the troubles by usurping the "right of appointing the colonial governors." This displaced aggression is matched by Robin's turning on Major Molineux instead of his own father. In turn, the crowd has substituted Major Molineux for the governor, for Major Molineux's crime apparently amounts to no more than association as a member of the "court party" with one of the unpopular governors. Here Hawthorne not only brings history to bear on Robin's act but through him comments on the morality of history.

In one of the first Stamp Act riots, the crowd attacked just such an innocent victim as Major Molineux in place of the governor himself. Hawthorne points to this particular riot when he recounts the ordeals of Massachusetts governors in the "annals of Massachusetts Bay" from 1688 "till the Revolution." This is a reference to Thomas Hutchinson, whom Hawthorne presently names, and his *The History of the Colony and Province of Massachusetts Bay*. This work, written by the colony's last civilian governor, who was himself driven out of office by the Revolution, describes the riot in question.[6]

At the beginning of the Stamp Act disturbances in August, 1765, the mob broke into the house of Hutchinson, then Lieutenant Governor, and destroyed it. In *Grandfather's Chair*, again drawing on Hutchinson's account, Hawthorne devoted a special section called "the Hutchinson Mob" to this incident. As in "My Kinsman, Major Molineux," his disapproval of the crowd is evident. In a similar atmosphere of sinister festivity it undertakes "mischief and destruction" as its "sport." The crowd is said to consist of "all those idle people about town who are ready for any kind of mischief." After the destruction of Hutchinson's house, Hawthorne writes, "manuscripts, containing secrets of our country's history, which are now lost forever, were scattered to the winds."[7] Among these manuscripts, in fact, was a volume of Hutchinson's *History*, ready for the printer. Actually, a friend was able to gather up the pages of the *History*, which Hutchinson published the following year. This volume, with its preface recounting the near loss of the manuscript, recounts the sufferings of the governors alluded to in the opening paragraph of "My Kinsman, Major Molineux."

By bringing in Hutchinson, Hawthorne suggests the psychological mysteriousness of the phenomenon of displaced aggression. Lieutenant Governor Hutchinson was opposed to the Stamp Act, yet he, and not the governor himself, suffered the fury of the mob. Within a few years he was driven from the colony while being hanged in effigy: truly a scapegoat figure like Major Molineux. Like Molineux's suffering, the "ordeal" of Hutchinson has remained something of an historical puzzle. Hawthorne seems to be suggesting that not political but ritual motives turned the crowd against him. In coming of age, young America, like Robin, was attacking not its real political father, the king, but the Royal Governors, and in Hutchinson's case a further removed figure of authority, the Lieutenant Governor. (The father of a family continued in the eighteenth century to be referred to by the Puritan designation of "governor.")[8] Expanding on the historical anomaly of displacement, Hawthorne employs a kind of symbolism by historical allusion to bring to bear on "My Kinsman, Major Molineux" a number of figures suggesting similar historical anomalies. Originating in folklore, literature, and history, they share with Hutchinson the motif of displaced anger, or else a related reversal of normal role and behavior. The story's allusion to William Molineux, the Revolutionary crowd leader, begins the series of reversals.

Roy Harvey Pearce, who has championed the historical approach to Hawthorne, first identified Major Molineux's namesake as William Molineux, one of the most notorious anti-Tory crowd leaders of the 1770s. Pearce suggests that the humiliation of the fictional Molineux represents Hawthorne's retribution against the excesses of the real one. This reversal of roles is paralleled by the story's double-faced crowd leader, who is illogically dressed as a British soldier though engaged in ousting Major Molineux, himself a British officer and loyalist. Hawthorne emphasizes the doubleness of the crowd leader's facial disguise and links it with ambiguity, leaving the impression that it in some way corresponds to Robin's experience. Through historical allusion it does.

Pearce identifies the crowd leader as "the celebrated Boston mob leader, Joyce Jr." "Joyce Jr." was an assumed name that referred to one of the executioners of King Charles. Cornet (a military rank) George Joyce in 1647 led the king from his palace to his trial and later stood disguised at his execution. Appropriately, the American Revolutionary, Joyce Jr., appeared in British uniform, mounted, disguised, and in charge of tarring and feathering those loyal to the king.[9] In addition to reversing the role of a king's soldier, he turned the crowd's anger from the king himself to one of his representatives. At the same time, his presence at a tar and feathering implied the ultimate crime against the king-father: regicide.

Hawthorne, like the American Revolutionaries of the 1760s and 1770s, seems to have taken a particular interest in Charles's regicides. He again linked them with the Revolution in "The Grey Champion." He may have known that the warrant circulated for their arrest in New England, where they fled after the Restoration, accused them of murdering their "Royal Father."[10]

In any case, the double-faced, militarily clad figure of the crowd leader fits into a series of figures implying doubleness, displacement, and reversed roles. Another of these is the old man who keeps repeating to Robin, "I have authority." One critic recently has pointed out that the old man is the first person whom Robin questions and the one whom he catches sight of at the end standing on a balcony and overlooking the crowd just before Major Molineux appears. Why, this critic asks, if the old man is a conspirator is he represented as a figure of authority and then placed on the balcony of a prominent building that evidently is the governor's house?[11] Is the overthrow of Molineux, one is tempted to ask, really a coup d'état rather than a popular movement?

Further anomalies arise from repeated references to *A Midsummer Night's Dream*. Hawthorne names Pyramus and Thisbe of the play-within-the-play, imitates Shakespeare's use of moonshine to express confusion and mystery, and takes the name of his protagonist from the play's fairy child, Puck, also known as Robin Goodfellow.[12] In addition, his story shares with Shakespeare's play the themes of disguise, fruitless search, and lost ways, all presented in an atmosphere of phantasmagoria and dream, and all connected with the usurpation of authority. In the play the lowest of the dramatis personae, Bully Bottom, unwittingly plays a mock king to the accompaniment of the boy, Robin Goodfellow's, break from authority. The overtones of social upheaval expressed by Hawthorne's mob are present in Shakespeare's "mechanicals," or workingmen, who though they respect authority, act out its overthrow by playing aristocratic roles. Moreover, Bottom's profession of weaver places him with England's most radical group of workers, known from the Middle Ages through the Luddites of the nineteenth century for riotous behavior.[13]

Hawthorne in effect defined his fanciful use of legend and history in "Roger Malvin's Burial," another early tale. There he begins by describing the incident on which his story is based as one of the few in the American tradition "susceptible of the moonlight of romance" and the workings of "imagination." What follows, of course, is a psychological study. In effect, then, Hawthorne modified history and folklore in order to explore individual psychology. In Robin's case the search for Molineux reveals a divided wish to remain dependent on authority and, in its unconscious avoidance of finding him, the wish to break away from that authority. Hawthorne's historical allusions offer political parallels with those divided and displaced emotions, while the *Midsummer Night's Dream* atmosphere provides a fit accompaniment for them. Robin arrives in town at night, questions apparition-like figures about his uncle, falls asleep by moonlight, and wakes to a tar-and-feathering procession which, with its "visionary air, as if a dream had broken forth from some feverish brain," almost seems to issue from his own imagination.

When Robin begins inquiring after his kinsman by speaking to the mysterious, old, gray-haired citizen who angrily rebuffs him with the repeated phrase, "I have authority," he elicits such a reply, of course, because he has spoken his kinsman's name to someone who knows of the conspiracy against the major. But the old man's words also suitably respond to the resentment of authority that is a component of Robin's unconscious ambivalence. Hawthorne implies as much with Robin's manner of asking his question, which he delivers "very loudly." He "laid hold of the skirt of the old man's coat. . . . 'Good evening to you, honored sir,' said he, making a low bow, and still retaining his hold of the skirt." Robin, this is to say, expresses obeisance and dependence by taking hold of the skirts of authority, and hostility by not letting go.

He continues to behave in this way toward figures of authority throughout, culminating in his "mixed pity and terror" at witnessing his kinsman's agony. On the street he fears to ask his question, yet provokes "rebukes for the impertinence of his scrutiny into people's faces." His "instinctive antipathy towards the guardian of midnight order," the watchman, prevents him "from asking his usual question." But at the last minute he shouts "lustily" after him. The second time he encounters the crowd leader, now in disguise and on his way to take charge of the crowd, Robin "resolutely" stands in his way. Later, he is transfixed by the leader's eye. Throughout, Robin suppresses the urge to use his cudgel, which for a moment he uses to bar the crowd leader's way.

The initiation ritual which Robin is undergoing all this time is itself related to his divided emotions. Once again the connections lie in a set of allusions: this time to the ritual of overthrow. When Major Molineux appears in "counterfeited pomp" like "some dead potentate," he evokes the Saturnalia at which the scapegoat king was sacrificed. Hawthorne frequently employed saturnalian festivals in his tales and novels, drawing on contemporary folklore scholarship for his details.[14] The Roman Saturnalia, according to one of his sources, Strutt's *Sports and Pastimes of England,* featured ritual overthrows of authority by licentious crowds with leaders in disguise. It was a period, in Strutt's words, "when the masters waited upon their servants, who were honoured with mock titles, and permitted to assume the state and deportment of their lords."[15] The crowning of a mock king of the Saturnalia is appropriately imitated by tar and feathering, a mock version of a king's anointment at his coronation.

Temporarily ruling over all, the King of the Revels or Lord of Misrule led the processions. Bully Bottom is a mock version of the mock lord of misrule, while Hawthorne's crowd leader is a serious version who recalls the underlying political reality of one regime replacing another. The crowd leader's costume, at the same time as it imitates Cornet Joyce, also mocks Molineux's "military rank." In the meantime the conspirators dress in "outlandish attire," and the old man, knowing about the imminent overthrow of authority, mockingly repeats, "I have authority." Evidently he does have authority, but the joke is that in putting Robin off he is cooperating with the enemies of authority. His knowing but passive role is made clear when he appears at the end in his nightshirt, having been awakened by the throng. Robin's laugh on seeing his kinsman derives from his perception of the crowd's Saturnalian spirit. He hears the old man's laugh, and the laughs of the others whom he has asked about his kinsman, then follows with his own, shouted version. "More than all," Hawthorne writes, "a perception of tremendous ridicule in the whole scene affected him."

According to modern scholarship, the Saturnalia is supposed to have derived from the practice, still observable in some societies, of an unfettered period of celebration at the succession of kingship. The saturnalian King of the Revels, mock killer of the King, derives from a primitive mock king who presided over a festive interregnum until being deposed, often by death, to make way for the legitimate new king.[16] The usurper and usurped, in other words, in effect are related, for each is a king and each is deposed. Robin and Major Molineux are related in this way as well as by blood, as we shall see, and so by allusion, are Major Molineux and William Molineux. These connections do not necessarily suppose an intuited modern understanding on Hawthorne's part. As Shakespeare, in accordance with the understanding of his day, placed his myth and folklore elements in ancient Greece, the setting of *A Midsummer Night's Dream*, so Hawthorne traced his ritual to the Saturnalia in accordance with nineteenth-century theories. But both explored the connections between folkways and history with impressive sophistication. Shakespeare, for example, has perplexed commentators by employing May Day games and observances in *A Midsummer Night's Dream*, yet moving them to midsummer. This enabled him, in the first place, to bring the lovers' games of May Day to his midsummer setting. But it also brought in the revolutionary associations of May Day—something Hawthorne showed his understanding of in his other tale of ritual and (threatened) overthrow of authority, "The May-Pole of Merry Mount."

The English May Day frequently was the occasion of popular disturbances, notably in 1517 when an apprentices' riot led to trials and executions of the rioters. The May games derived from May Day but were played on Sundays as well. Later these games became a focus of Puritan disapproval: their saturnalian atmosphere and symbolism of passage from the old to the new was perceived as a threat to established government.[17] In "The May-Pole of Merry Mount" the saturnalian atmosphere of May Day is unmistakable: there are a Lord of Misrule, "counterfeit" disguises, and a mock crowning. Both "The May-Pole of Merry Mount" and "My Kinsman, Major Molineux" follow Shakespeare in being set at midsummer, the time of solstice that symbolizes passage from the old to the new: old king to new king, old regime to new, end of childhood to start of maturity. Most striking, though, as Strutt reveals, is that the mock king of the revels at the English May Day often was played by another kinsman of Robin: Robin Hood.[18] Robin Hood appeared on May Day not only as mock king but also in a Robin Hood play taken from the saga of Robin Hood and his Merry Men. Afterwards, he and Maid Marian were crowned King and Queen of the May. Thus the same actor played both the usurper and the usurped: the rebel outlaw and the mock King of the Revels. It is no accident that rebel and revel are etymologically identical.

All this is more or less clear in Strutt. But one wonders if Hawthorne intended to suggest a further aspect of the symbolism of the Robin Hood plays. In these plays Robin Hood is bested in a contest which frequently is followed by the famous scene of his bleeding to death from arrow wounds while being watched over by Maid Marian. Modern interpreters see the pattern as an enactment of the defeat and death of the old king, whose blood replenishes the ground, followed by his resurrection as the new king—in this case as King of the May.[19] The relationship by blood of Hawthorne's Robin to the old king figure, Major Molineux, is therefore intensified by allusion to the old and new king figure, Robin Hood.

Hawthorne's allusion to two namesakes for young Robin similarly suggests the pattern of overthrow and succession. Robin Goodfellow is the recalcitrant boy, a defier of authority. He has a reputation for shrewdness, echoed in Robin's "cunning." Robin Hood is the adult rebel of Saturnalian reversals: he takes from the rich and gives to the poor; like Bully Bottom he plays the mock king; and he is King of the Revels. That Hawthorne understood the symbolic possibilities of Robin Hood's marriage to Maid Marian is clear from "The May-Pole of Merry Mount," where the newly crowned Lord and Lady of the May represent the ideal political future of America. With both Robin Goodfellow and Robin Hood the symbolism of rebellion overshadows that of fealty. Yet, young Robin's relationship to one figure that is young and another that is old suggests the continuity of generations.

Clearly no single allusive relative of Robin can define Hawthorne's attitude toward him, especially as each relative is himself defined by his participation in a ritual—either of overthrow, coming of age, or both. Furthermore, the rituals themselves offer further complications. Twice in "My Kinsman, Major Molineux" men in "outlandish attire" stop to "utter a few words in some language of which Robin knew nothing." This recalls the Boston Tea Party, where Masonic passwords were used (at the period Hawthorne was writing, Masonry had resurfaced as an important issue in the 1827 political campaign).[20] On December 17, 1774 members of the St. Andrew Masonic lodge were prominent among those assembled at the Green Dragon tavern, the lodge's regular meeting place, before leaving to dump the tea.[21] More significantly, the regular business of the Masons was conducting the initiations of young men at the end of their apprenticeships. These initiations involved gulling a young man, usually at night, with tricks of disguise and secret passwords, followed by a final, surprising ceremony.

Here and elsewhere Hawthorne links coming of age and revolution through rituals that release the divided emotions expressed so well by Robin's pity and terror and the crowd leader's parti-colored face. In suggesting, through Molineux's aspect of "dead potentate" and through allusion to the dying Robin Hood, that these emotions had their origin in still more primitive ritual, Hawthorne anticipated both Frazer and Freud. Mythographers are well aware that the connections between folk practices and primitive origins were not discovered by Frazer. In Strutt's *Sports and Pastimes of England* Hawthorne had a source that Frazer himself employed—and whose tracings to the primitive he often agreed with. Furthermore, both the seventeenth-century Puritans and eighteenth-century Tories recognized in the Maypole and its successor, the Liberty Pole, folk adaptations of ancient fertility rites. Frazer's contribution was to trace a wide range of religious, folk, and political phenomena to fertility rites. But even in this he was anticipated, as early as the eighteenth century, in Charles François Dupuis's *Origine de Tous les Cultes* (1791). Dupuis gathered the same kind of collection as Strutt and Frazer "to illustrate his underlying proposition that all religions were in their remotest origins fertility cults."[22]

Hawthorne's link between deposition and coming of age especially anticipates Freud's analysis in *Totem and Taboo* (1913) of Frazer's description of scapegoat king rituals. Freud emphasizes the double, seemingly contradictory emotions expressed toward the dying king (and later repeated in the worship of his totem). He suggests that these emanate from youth's oedipal ambiguity toward the father, and he goes on to posit an original father murder that was at once a coming of age for the sons who committed the act, and a succession of political power from one generation to the next. Theodor Reik extended this explanation of the scapegoat ritual to coming of age rituals, which he saw as another kind of enactment of the ambiguous oedipal emotions.

Reik suggested that the adults who arrange the rituals *themselves* feel both "hostility and affection"—toward the younger generation. Out of fear for their own safety they devise forms through which their sons can express their murderous oedipal feelings without acting on them. The fathers direct the youths through their ritual ordeal with a combination of threats, lies, and assurances of protection. The boys, as a result of the form of the initiation, never act on their instinct to kill and castrate their fathers. Instead they themselves undergo symbolic death and resurrection, along with circumcision or its symbolic equivalent. Like them, Hawthorne's Robin encounters both hostility and friendship from his elders (the hostility coming in the form of threats that he will be punished in the stocks for his lack of respect toward authority), along with lies about the meaning of his experience. He falls asleep and awakes—the most common form for ritual imitation of death and rebirth. Finally, in joining against Major Molineux, his "cruel impulses," in Reik's words, "are turned away from their real object, the father, and are directed upon a substitute object outside the tribal organization."[23]

Hawthorne, in linking Robin's displacement of aggression from his father to Major Molineux with the crowd's from the king to Major Molineux, in effect offered a similar psychological interpretation of events like the Hutchinson mob. In so doing he both anticipated and took a step beyond Freud's *Group Psychology and the Analysis of the Ego* (1921), an attempt to account for the behavior of crowds, again in oedipal terms. The mass hysteria and irrationality of crowds Freud called a release of the unconscious, with accompanying regression to the childlike behavior usually remarked by observers and theorists of the crowd. The tendency of crowds to follow a leader slavishly he called submission to a symbolic father. Thus much Hawthorne appears clearly to have anticipated. Robin's childish feelings of aggression toward his father—hinted at throughout in his behavior toward authority—are released in a welling up of the unconscious at the moment he joins the sportive, child-like crowd. The crowd leader in his paternal aspect contributes to this apotheosis. First he is seen to "thunder" his commands. He rides slowly past Robin, turns, and fixes him with a long stare, leaving the youth in a state of obedience that prepares him to follow the crowd.

Hawthorne goes further than Freud by exploring the psychology of a crowd whose subservience to its leader-father has as its chief purpose the overthrow of another figure also symbolizing the father. In doing so Hawthorne shows the crowd as being susceptible, not only to the submissive side of the oedipus complex, but also to its rebelliousness. Or, as a pre-Freudian theorist put it, the crowd may be described as both excessively obedient and excessively rebellious.[24] In a crowd of overthrow, it would appear, these opposed tendencies are divided between the crowd leader and his victim, much on Reik's pattern of redirected oedipal urges in initiation rites. In an initiation rite the youths show exaggerated gratitude to their fathers while they attack animals or human beings who have been substituted for those fathers. In the case of the crowd, the same division of emotions is secured with equally primitive purity (Freud agreed that crowds behave not only like children but like "savages" as well).[25] The crowd displays rigid obedience in following its one symbolic father and implicable cruelty in overthrowing the other.

This polarity between obedience and revolt is evoked at every level of "My Kinsman, Major Molineux." From the beginning Hawthorne establishes a pattern of divided emotions toward paternal authority along with displacement of their aggressive component onto substitute, symbolic figures. The crowds in Huchinson's "Annals" revere the king but drive out his representatives, the governors. Hawthorne's crowd obeys a leader who recalls a revolutionary named Molineux in order to overthrow a king's representative with the same name. The crowd leader resembles Joyce, Jr. who stands both for authority (as one of King Charles's judges) and for regicide. Robin Goodfellow and Robin Hood suggest both obedience (Robin Goodfellow obeys Oberon; Robin Hood repeatedly declares his obeisance to the king), and at the same time revolt. Similarly, Bully Buttom and his fellow workingmen, along with the Masons and the conspirators—all simultaneously obey and overthrow.

The figures who appear in the story are linked to one another through their involvement in the two related rituals of coming of age and saturnalian overthrow of the king-father. At the same time, by propinquity and allusion Robin is linked both to those who experience divided and displaced feelings toward paternal authority, and those who suffer as a result. He is related both to William Molineux and Major Molineux; he is identified with both the crowd and its victim; in his initiation he both suffers from and joins with the crowd; and as namesake of Robin Hood he evokes both the dying and reborn king. Accompanying figures like Joyce, Jr. and Thomas Hutchinson intensify and relate to history the divided and displaced impulses of the story's characters. Others, like Bottom, relate the emotions to ritual. All the while the crowd recalls both history and ritual.

These overlapping patterns of ambivalences have an evident relationship to Hawthorne's attitude toward Robin and the crowd. As in his stories of the Puritans, Hawthorne has translated a moral question into an ambiguous psychological and ritual drama. In "The Gentle Boy" persecution of the Quakers by the Puritans is weighed against the ambiguous mixture of righteousness and masochism in the victims. In "The May-Pole of Merry Mount" persecution of the Merrymounters is weighed against an ambiguous jollity in the victims (one that contains its own measure of intolerance), and also against the future needs of America, which must include the strength of the Puritans as well as the better part of the Merrymount spirit. Finally, in "Endicott and the Red Cross" the persecution of a wide range of dissenters is weighed against the fanaticism of those opposed to the Puritan establishment. In each case the Puritan legacy includes not only intolerance but also glorious revolution: not the Merrymounters, Quakers, or other dissenters overthrew King Charles, but the Puritans.

In "My Kinsman, Major Molineux" the admirable part of the Puritan tradition has in effect moved to the persecuted side. The judicious sentencing of the king in which Cornet Joyce was involved— an event praised by Hawthorne in "The Grey Champion"—has degenerated into the Saturnalia of Joyce, Jr. The honorific gray hair of the revolutionary figures among the Puritans has passed not to the gray, old man of "authority," who is on the Revolutionary side, but to Major Molineux, an admirable figure among the Tories. And now, like the Puritans, whose sin was rigid intolerance, the new party of Revolution has to answer for its crimes.

In *Grandfather's Chair* Hawthorne calls the destruction of Hutchinson's house by a mob "a most unjustifiable act," then adds: "But we must not decide against the justice of the people's cause, merely because an excited mob was guilty of outrageous violence. . . . Afterwards the people grew more calm."[26] With the Molineux mob, however, the people's cause is never mentioned. On the one hand, the crowd is viewed as engaged in ritual behavior. As the boy Robin is being turned into a man, men in the crowd temporarily have become boys, even as a prophecy of the nation's birth is being acted out by both. On the other hand, as in "The May-Pole of Merry Mount," the moral question is tied in with the future of the country, here represented by Robin. He has acted cruelly but joined in what is but "a temporary inflammation of the popular mind." Presumably, his good health, country upbringing, and religious background (we are told that he resists the prostitute by recalling that he is the son of a minister) will see him through the future. Presumably, the same virtues will sustain the new-born nation.

This is not to say that Robin has gained moral insight or that the outcome of the Revolution justifies his joining in the crowd's licentious cruelty. Neither is it to suggest that Hawthorne wavered in his attitude. His disapproval of the crowd is unequivocal, though he conveys the ambiguous meaning of its act of usurpation. His ambiguity may be termed one of knowledge rather than uncertainty: by making ritual connections between coming of age and revolution he provides a clear insight into the essential ambiguities of both. Hawthorne does not excuse the past. Instead he appears to suggest that as the emotions of the actors who overthrew authority were divided, so must be our evaluation of their/our Revolution.

Notes

1. Q. D. Leavis, "Hawthorne As Poet," *Sewanee Review*, LIX, 179–205 (1951). The points at issue among the different approaches are summarized by Alexander W. Allison, who ranges himself on the anti-psychological, anti-political "moral" side of the controversy: "The Literary Contexts of 'My Kinsman, Major Molineux,' " *Nineteenth Century Fiction*, XXIII, 304-305n. (1968).

2. Daniel G. Hoffman, "Yankee Bumpkin and Scapegoat King," in *Form and Fable in American Fiction* (New York, 1961), 118.

3. See Michael Walzer, *Regicide and Revolution* (New York and London, 1974), 1-68. Samuel Adams argued America's coming of age in these terms: Edwin G. Barrows and Michael Wallace, "The American Revolution: The Ideology and Psychology of National Liberation," *Perspectives in American History*, VI, 193 (1972).

4. Following Alexander Allison in their critiques of earlier, political readings are Julian Smith, "Historical Ambiguity in 'My Kinsman, Major Molineux,' " *English Language Notes*, VIII, 115–120 (1970), and Jerry A. Herndon, "Hawthorne's Dream Imagery," *American Literature*, XLVI, 538–545 (1975).

5. See Roy Harvey Pearce, "Robin Molineux on the Analyst's Couch," (1959) rpt. in *Historicism Once More; Problems & Occasions For the American Scholar* (Princeton, N. J., 1969), and "Romance and the Study of History," in Pearce, editor, *Hawthorne Centenary Essays* (Columbus, 1964), 240. The first of these essays is a critique of Simon O. Lesser's "Hawthorne and Anderson, Conscious and Unconscious Perception," in *Fiction and the Unconscious* (Boston, 1957). One psychoanalytic critic goes so far as to say that Robin's failure to come to terms with his experience reveals his coming of age as neurotic rather than the result of normal, oedipal ambivalence. See Louis Paul, "A Psychoanalytic Reading of Hawthorne's 'Major Molineux': The Father Manqué and the Protégé Manqué," *American Imago*, XVIII, 279–288 (1961).

6. Thomas Hutchinson, *The History of the Colony and Province of Massachusetts Bay*, 2, Lawrence Shaw Mayo, editor (Cambridge, Mass., 1936). For additional sources used by Hawthorne see Roy Harvey Pearce," Hawthorne and the Sense of the Past or, the Immortality of Major Molineux" (1954), rpt. in *Historicism Once More*.

7. Hawthorne, *Grandfather's Chair, The Works of Nathaniel Hawthorne* (Salem Edition) (London and New York, 1909), IV, 125, 129.

8. See Bernard Bailyn, *The Ordeal of Thomas Hutchinson* (Cambridge, Mass., 1974). Michael Walzer, "Puritanism as a Revolutionary Ideology," *History and Theory*, III, 85 (1961).

9. Pearce, "Hawthorne and the Sense of the Past," 143. See also Sanford Pinsker, "Hawthorne's 'Double-Faced Fellow,' A Note on 'My Kinsman, Major Molineux,' " *The Nathaniel Hawthorne Journal 1972* (Washington, D. C., NCR/Microcard Editions), 255–256.

In mounting his Joyce, Jr. figure on a white horse Hawthorne strengthens the Biblical apocalyptic impression given by the description of the crowd leader's face. For, the real Joyce, Jr. appeared mounted not on a horse but on an ass. See Albert Matthews, "Joyce Jr. Once More," Colonial Society of Massachusetts Publications 11 (1906–1907) *(Transactions)*, 282.

10. Lemuel A. Welles, *The History of the Regicides in New England* (New York, 1927), 33.

11. Smith, "Historical Ambiguity in . . . 'Molineux,' " 116.

12. See Mario L. D'Avanzo, "The Literary Sources of 'My Kinsman, Major Molineux': Shakespeare, Coleridge, Milton," *Studies in Short Fiction*, X, 121–136 (1973), and Jerry A. Herndon, "Hawthorne's Dream Imagery."

13. Besides the fairy queen's lover, Bottom plays a dying nobleman, Pyramus, though even here, as he puts it, "my chief humour is for a tyrant." Hawthorne makes an additional allusion to *A Midsummer Night's Dream* by imitating its famous definition of the imagination ("as imagination bodies forth / The forms of things unknown, the poet's pen / Turns them to shapes and gives to airy nothing / A local habitation and a name"). In "My Kinsman, Major Molineux": The moon, creating, like the imaginative power, a beautiful strangeness in familiar objects, gave something of romance to a scene that might not have possessed it in the light of day." See the *Boston Gazette*, Sept. 16, 1765 for a report of disturbances among the English weavers that served as a spur to the Stamp Act riots in America to which Hawthorne alludes. The weavers, "for some hundreds of years the largest single group of industrial workers in England," had long been associated with radicalism, the uprising of the Spitalfields silk weavers, 1763–1773, being the immediate example. E. P. Thompson, *The Making of the English Working Class* (New York, 1964), and see chapt. 10.

14. See Norris Yates, "Ritual and Reality: Mask and Dance Motifs in Hawthorne's Fiction," *Philological Quarterly*, XXXIV, 56–70 (1955).

15. Joseph Strutt, *The Sports and Pastimes of the People of England* . . . (1801, rpt. London, 1903, enlarged edition), 344.

16. Elias Canetti, *Crowds and Power* (1960, rpt. New York, 1970), 418–419.

17. See Max Beloff, *Public Order and Popular Disturbances 1660–1714* (London, 1938), 2ff. Edmund F. Slafter, "The Character and History of *The Book of Sports*," Massachusetts Historical Society *Proceedings*, 2nd Ser., XIX, 87–95 (Boston, 1906). See also C. L. Barber, *Shakespeare's Festive Comedy* . . . , Princeton, N. J., 1959, 11–12.

18. Strutt, *Sports and Pastimes*, 161.

19. Lewis Spence, *Myth and Ritual in Dance, Game, and Rhyme* (London, 1947), 32; also 30–37.

20. The anti-Masonry furor began in 1826 and lasted into the 1830s. It was marked by the formation of a national Anti-Masonic political party.

21. Francis S. Drake, *Tea Leaves* . . . (Boston, 1884), LXXXIX. The tavern was also known as "The Arms of Freemasonry." Bernard Fäy, *Revolution and Freemasonry 1680–1800* (Boston, 1935), 240.

22. Frank E. Manuel, *The 18th Century Confronts the Gods* (1959, rpt. New York, 1967), 264. See also John B. Vickery, "The Golden Bough at Merrymount," *Nineteenth-Century Fiction*, XII, 208–209 (1957–1958).

23. Theodor Reik, *Ritual: Psycho-Analytic Studies* (1913, rpt. New York, 1958), 103, 112.

24. Gustave Le Bon, *The Crowd, A Study of the Popular Mind* (1896, rpt. London, 1947).

25. Sigmund Freud, *Group Psychology and the Analysis of the Ego, The Standard Edition of the Complete Psychological Works of Sigmund Freud*, James Strachey *et al.* translators and editors (London, 1955), vol. 18, 85 (for Freud's use of "savages").

26. Hawthorne, *Grandfather's Chair*, 129–130.

The Logic of Compulsion   Frederick Crews°

> "It don't make no difference whether you do right or wrong, a person's conscience ain't got no sense and just goes for him *anyway.*"
> —*Huckleberry Finn*

One further story from Hawthorne's unpublished "Provincial Tales" requires our close interest, both because it has been generally misunderstood and because, once understood, it merits a high place among his fiction. In addition, "Roger Malvin's Burial" offers a classic instance of the way Hawthorne undermines questions of conscious moral choice with demonstrations of psychological necessity. As Harry Levin puts it, "Hawthorne was well aware that the sense of sin is

° Reprinted from *The Sins of the Fathers: Hawthorne's Psychological Themes* (New York: Oxford University Press, 1966), 80–95.

more intimately related to inhibition than to indulgence; that the most exquisite consciences are the ones that suffer most; that guilt is a by-product of that very compunction which aims at goodness and acknowledges higher laws; and that lesser evils seem blacker to the innocent than to the experienced."[1] In previous chapters we have tried to define, not only the customary form that "exquisite conscience" takes in Hawthorne's tales, but also the primitive resentment and ambition that bring such conscience into operation. The plot of "Roger Malvin's Burial" makes sense in no other terms than these—and in these it is precisely, indeed shockingly, logical.

The story goes as follows. Roger Malvin, an old Indian-fighter who has been seriously wounded and finds himself unable to survive the homeward journey through a forest, persuades his young companion, Reuben Bourne, to leave him to die. Reuben will thereby gain a chance to survive, whereas to remain would simply mean two deaths instead of one. After promising to return some day to bury his old friend, Reuben departs and is eventually rescued by a search party. Though he marries Roger's daughter Dorcas, he is unable to explain to her that he left her father alive, preferring to let her imagine that he has already been buried. Reuben's public character and fortunes soon begin to go awry, until finally he is forced to take his wife and adolescent son off into the wilderness to seek a new life. Yet his steps bring him, not to the intended destination, but to the clearing where he left Roger Malvin many years before. There, detecting what might be a deer behind some undergrowth, he fires his musket, only to discover that he has killed his son Cyrus on the very spot where Roger died. The story ends, nonetheless, on an affirmative and extremely pious note: "Then Reuben's heart was stricken, and the tears gushed out like water from a rock. The vow that the wounded youth had made the blighted man had come to redeem. His sin was expiated—the curse was gone from him; and in the hour when he had shed blood dearer to him than his own, a prayer, the first for years, went up to Heaven from the lips of Reuben Bourne."

Such language naturally leads us to interpret "Roger Malvin's Burial" as a parable of atonement, for Reuben's act of manslaughter has melted his heart and enabled him to beg God for forgiveness. But forgiveness for what? It is unclear whether Reuben has atoned merely for not burying Roger or for some other failing, and critics disagree as to what he has done wrong. In Harry Levin's view, Reuben is "innocent" of Roger Malvin's death and only "inadvertently guilty" of his son's. Mark Van Doren, on the other hand, holds Reuben accountable for both the desertion of Roger and the hypocrisy of silence toward Dorcas: "he has committed a sin and he has failed to confess it when he could." A third interpretation is that of Arlin

Turner, who finds that Hawthorne "relieves Reuben Bourne of any guilt for abandoning Malvin" but shows the ill effects of his failure to be honest with Dorcas. The only point of general agreement is that the slaying of Reuben's son Cyrus is accidental. For Van Doren it is "Fate" that engineers the final catastrophe, and that event strikes Levin as "one of those coincidences that seem to lay bare the design of the universe."[2]

All of these opinions, including the unquestioned one about Cyrus's death, miss the essence of Hawthorne's story by not recognizing a difference between the feeling of guilt and the state of being guilty. Turner, to be sure, makes the point that Reuben's guilt is subjective, but in regard to the desertion scene he apparently confuses a moral absolving of Reuben by Hawthorne with an absence of guilty feeling on Reuben's part. We can see, however, in this scene and throughout the story, that Hawthorne is concerned *only* with subjective guilt as Reuben's conscience manufactures it, independently of the moral "sinfulness" or "innocence" of his outward deeds. That this is so at the end of the tale is obvious, for how could we take seriously the religious notion that a man can make his peace with the Christian God by shooting his innocent son? It is clear that Reuben has not performed a Christian expiation but simply rid himself of his burden of guilty feeling. It can be shown, furthermore, that this guilty feeling was never generated by a committed sin or crime in the first place. Once we have recognized this, the task of deciding whether Reuben has been morally absolved becomes pointless, and Reuben's own theory that his steps have been led by "a supernatural power" appears in its true light—as a delusion fostered by, and serving to cloak, a process of unconscious compulsion that is evidenced in great detail.[3]

Everyone agrees that Reuben feels guilty after misleading Dorcas, and it seems quite evident that Reuben's behavior in that scene is governed by an inner discomfort over his having left Roger Malvin behind. But why should Reuben feel this discomfort? The scene of desertion is presented in such a way as to put every justification on Reuben's side; Roger's arguments have persuaded not only Reuben but most of the tale's critics to feel that there is only one reasonable decision to be made. Why, then, does Reuben find it so difficult to explain the true circumstances to Dorcas? The answer seems to be that in some deep way Reuben feels more responsible for Roger's death than he actually is. "By a certain association of ideas," as Hawthorne says of him later, "he at times almost imagined himself a murderer."

How could Reuben feel himself even remotely to be Roger's murderer? If there is no factual basis for the self-accusation, perhaps there is a psychological basis. The charge seems, indeed, to be true in fantasy if not true in fact, for Reuben shows definite signs of looking forward to deserting Roger in spite of his comradely feeling for him. When Roger adduces the point that Dorcas must not be left desolate, Reuben feels reminded "that there were other and less questionable duties than that of sharing the fate of a man whom his death could not benefit. Nor," adds Hawthorne significantly, "can it be affirmed that no selfish feeling strove to enter Reuben's heart, though the consciousness made him more earnestly resist his companion's entreaties." This would seem to be the source of all Reuben's trouble. It is obviously advantageous as well as reasonable for him to go on without Roger, since he faces a prospect of married bliss if he survives. The contrast between Roger's altruism and his own self-seeking motives is painful to his conscience; his personal claims must strive for recognition, and Reuben feels a need to counter-attack them with a redoubled commitment to remain with Roger. "He felt as if it were both sin and folly to think of happiness at such a moment." Thus we see that his feelings of guilt have already set in before he has made a final decision to leave. He feels guilty, not for anything he has done, but for thoughts of happiness—a happiness that will be bought at the price of a man's life.

The more closely we look at the scene of desertion, the more ironical Hawthorne's view of Reuben's mental struggle appears. The mention of Dorcas marks a turning-point between a series of melodramatic, self-sacrificing protestations of faithfulness and a new tone of puzzlement, self-doubt, and finally insincerity. Reuben is no longer really combating Roger's wishes after this point, but posing objections that he knows Roger will easily refute. "How terrible to wait the slow approach of death in this solitude!" But a brave man, answers Roger, knows how to die. "And your daughter,—how shall I dare to meet her eye?" The question is already how *shall* I, not how *would* I! When this too has been answered, Reuben needs only to be assured of the possibility of his returning with a rescue party. "No merely selfish motive, nor even the desolate condition of Dorcas, could have induced him to desert his companion at such a moment—but his wishes seized on the thought that Malvin's life might be preserved, and his sanguine nature heightened almost to certainty the remote possibility of procuring human aid." There follows a grim comedy in which Roger pretends to see a similarity between the present case and another one, twenty years previously, that turned out well, and Reuben fatuously allows himself to be convinced. Hawthorne leaves no doubt that Reuben is semi-deliberately deceiving himself in order to silence his conscience. "This example, powerful in affecting Reuben's decision, was aided, unconsciously to himself, by the hidden strength of many another motive." When he finally does leave, the act is presented as a triumph of these other motives over his human sympathy: "His generous nature would fain have delayed him, at whatever risk, till the dying scene were past; but the desire of existence and the hope of happiness had strengthened in his heart, and he was unable to resist them."

These citations from the story's first scene make it evident that Hawthorne, by having Reuben's self-seeking wishes concur with a morally legitimate but painful decision, has set in bold relief the purely psychological problem of guilt. Unlike his critics, Hawthorne does not dwell on the moral defensibility of Reuben's leaving; rather, he demonstrates how this act appears to Reuben as a fulfillment of his egoistic wishes, so that he is already beginning to punish himself *as if* he had positively brought about Roger's death. As in "Alice Doane's Appeal," Hawthorne has anticipated Freud's discovery that (in Freud's terminology) the superego takes revenge for unfulfilled deathwishes as well as for actual murder.[4] Indeed, Hawthorne's whole rendering of Reuben's mind is based on what we would now call psychoanalytic principles. Some of Reuben's motives, as we have seen, operate "unconsciously to himself," which is to say that they have been repressed; and once this repression has circumvented conscious moral control, Reuben becomes a classic example of the man who, because he can neither overcome his thoughts nor admit them into consciousness, becomes their victim. The real reason for his inability to state the outward facts of the case to Dorcas is that these facts have become associated with the unbearable fantasy that he has murdered his friend. Guilty feeling leads to a hypocrisy, which in turn provides further reinforcement of guilt; "and Reuben, while reason told him that he had done right, experienced in no small degree the mental horrors which punish the perpetrator of undiscovered crime."

One other inconspicuous, but absolutely decisive, element in the scene of desertion remains to be mentioned, namely, that the relationship between Roger and Reuben is that of a father to a son. Roger repeatedly calls him "my boy" and "my son," and at a certain point he turns this language to an argumentative use: "I have loved you like a father, Reuben; and at a time like this I should have something of a father's authority." Reuben's reply is curious: "And because you have been a father to me, should I therefore leave you to perish and to lie unburied in the wilderness?" From a strictly Freudian point of view the answer to this rhetorical question could be *yes;* the "son" feels murderous impulses toward the "father" simply because he *is* the father, i.e., the sexual rival. It is questionable whether Hawthorne's thinking has gone quite this far. Yet it remains true that Reuben, in leaving Roger to die, will get to have Dorcas's affections all to himself, and we cannot say that such a consideration is not among the "many another motive" for his departure. The "father's authority" of which Roger ingenuously speaks is going to be left behind in the forest. In terms of the unconscious role he has assumed in relation to Roger, Reuben must think of himself not simply as a murderer but as a patricide.

This conclusion needs, of course, much further confirmation in order to be persuasive. Yet we may pause here to say that everything we have found in other tales—the violent and sometimes historically unfounded hatred against figures of authority, the crippling sense of guilt for unspecified criminal thoughts, and even a fairly plain fantasy of patricide in "Alice Doane's Appeal"—leads us to believe that Hawthorne was capable of taking the father-son symbolism as a basis for unconscious motivation. Nor can we quite avoid seeing that the complement to particide, namely incest, lurks in the background of "Roger Malvin's Burial." If Roger is to be seen as Reuben's father, Dorcas becomes his sister. Without pressing this argument further, we may observe that Dorcas's later feeling for her son—"my beautiful young hunter!"—does not dispel the characteristic Hawthornian atmosphere of over-intimacy in this tale.

But let us return to less tenuous evidence. Reuben, who henceforth is occupied in "defending himself against an imaginary accusation," gradually turns his interest to his son Cyrus. "The boy was loved by his father with a deep and silent strength, as if whatever was good and happy in his own nature had been transferred to his child, carrying his affections with it. Even Dorcas, though loving and beloved, was far less dear to him; for Reuben's secret thoughts and insulated emotions had gradually made him a selfish man, and he could no longer love deeply except where he saw or imagined some reflection or likeness of his own mind. In Cyrus he recognized what he had himself been in other days. . . ." Reuben has, in a word, projected himself into his son. And what is to be the conclusive deed of "Roger Malvin's Burial"? Reuben, who harbors an accusation of having murdered a "father" and who cannot bring this accusation up to the rational criticism of consciousness, shoots and kills the boy who has come to stand for himself. In killing Cyrus he is destroying the "guilty" side of himself, and hence avenging Roger Malvin's death in an appallingly primitive way. The blood of a "father" rests on the "son," who disburdens himself of it by becoming a father and slaying his son. This is the terrible logic of Hawthorne's tale.

Thus I would maintain, in opposition to the generally held view, that the slaying of Cyrus is not at all the hunting accident it appears to be. It is a sacrificial murder dictated by Reuben's unconscious charge of patricide and by his inability to bring the charge directly against himself. He has become the accusing Roger at the same time that he has projected his own guilty self into Cyrus. These unconscious stratagems are his means of dealing with the contradictory repressed wishes (the desire to atone and the unwillingness to accept blame) that have transformed him into an irritable, moody, and misanthropic man over the course of the years. The killing of Cyrus, by canceling Reuben's imaginary blood-debt, frees his whole mind at last for the task of making peace with God; yet this religious achievement becomes possible, as Hawthorne stresses in the closing sentence, only "in the hour when he had shed blood dearer to him than his own."

There are two main obstacles to the theory that Reuben's shooting his son is intentional. One is that Reuben has no idea that his target is Cyrus instead of a deer; he simply fires at a noise and a motion in the distance. Secondly, there is the possibility that not Reuben but God is responsible for bringing the tale to its catastrophe. The final paragraph, after all, speaks of the lifting of a curse, and Roger Malvin has imposed a religious vow on Reuben to "return to this wild rock, and lay my bones in the grave, and say a prayer over them." Both Roger and Reuben are religious men, and Reuben "trusted that it was Heaven's intent to afford him an opportunity of expiating his sin." Perhaps we are meant to read the story in divine rather than psychological terms.

The answer to this latter point is provided by Hawthorne in a single sentence describing Reuben in the final scene: "Unable to penetrate to the secret place of his soul where his motives lay hidden, he believed that a supernatural voice had called him onward, and that a supernatural power had obstructed his retreat." No one who ponders these words can imagine that Hawthorne's famous ambiguity between natural and supernatural causality is really sustained in "Roger Malvin's Burial." As for the other objection, it is certainly true that Reuben shows no conscious awareness that he is firing at his son. But does this make the act wholly unintentional? Before investigating the actual shooting we must see just what Hawthorne means by intention. His theory is evidently somewhat deeper than that of our law courts, which would surely have acquitted Reuben in a trial for murder. "Roger Malvin's Burial" discriminates from the first between surface intentions and buried ones, between outward tokens of generous concern and inward selfishness, between total ignorance and a knowledge that is temporarily unavailable to consciousness. For this last distinction we may point to the statement that Reuben cannot choose to return and bury Roger because he does not know how to find his way back: "his remembrance of every portion of his travel thence was indistinct, and the latter part had left no impression upon his mind." Yet we have just seen that Reuben will be guided by "his motives," residing in a "secret place of his soul." Furthermore, he has always "had a strange impression that, were he to make the trial, he would be led straight to Malvin's bones." We can only conclude that knowledge of the route he took in that traumatic flight from the deserted comrade has been repressed, not lost; when Reuben finally gives himself over to the guidance of his unconscious he is led infallibly back to the scene.

In order to see the killing of Cyrus in its true light we must scrutinize Reuben's prior behavior. Although Cyrus reminds him again and again that he is taking the family in a different direction from the announced one, Reuben keeps resuming his original course after each correction. His thoughts are obviously dwelling on something other than the relocation of his home. "His quick and wandering glances were sent forward, apparently in search of enemies lurking behind the tree trunks; and, seeing nothing there, he would cast his eyes backwards as if in fear of some pursuer." Reuben would appear to be projecting his self-accusations into multiple exterior threats to himself. The internalized Roger Malvin—the Roger Malvin created by Reuben's unwarranted self-accusation of murder—is evidently redoubling his demand to be avenged as the anniversary of his death draws near. When the fifth day's encampment is made, Dorcas reminds Reuben of the date. " 'The twelfth of May! I should remember it well,' muttered he, while many thoughts occasioned a momentary confusion in his mind. 'Where am I? Whither am I wandering? Where did I leave him?' " Among those "many thoughts" that have suddenly been jolted into consciousness are probably the answers to all three of Reuben's questions. Dorcas has accidentally brought to the surface, though only for a moment, Reuben's feeling that he is on a deliberate mission.

Is this mission simply to bury Roger's bones? Evidently something further is involved, for in reply to Dorcas's next words, praising Reuben for having loyally stayed with Roger to the end, Reuben pleads, "Pray Heaven, Dorcas, . . . pray Heaven that neither of us three dies solitary and lies unburied in this howling wilderness!" And on this foreboding note he hastens away at once. It seems to me obvious that Reuben's terribly sincere "prayer" is a response to his own unconscious urge to commit the sacrificial killing—an urge that has been screwed to the sticking place by Dorcas's unwitting irony. Like all men in the grip of a destructive obsession, Reuben hopes desperately that his own deep wishes will be thwarted; yet he rushes off in the next moment, and a few minutes later Cyrus will be dead.

We have, then, an abundance of evidence to show that one side of Reuben's nature, the compulsive side, has gained mastery over his conscious intentions. The evidence continues to accumulate as the moment of the shooting draws nearer. Reuben is assaulted by "many strange reflections" that keep him from governing his steps in the supposed hunt for a deer; "and, straying onward rather like a sleep walker than a hunter, it was attributable to no care of his own that his devious course kept him in the vicinity of the encampment." No *conscious* care, that is, for Reuben has a very good compulsive reason for his movements. Cyrus has previously set out on another deer hunt, "promising not to quit *the vicinity of the encampment*" (my italics). Surely Hawthorne's repetition of these five words within the space of two pages is meant to strike our attention. Without quite realizing what he is doing, Reuben is stalking his son. His conscious thoughts are straying vaguely over the puzzle of his having reached this spot on this date, and he arrives at a conscious interpretation— explicitly rejected by Hawthorne, as we have already seen—that "it was Heaven's intent to afford him an opportunity of expiating his sin." The consciously accepted "sin" is that of leaving Roger Malvin unburied, but while Reuben busies himself with this lesser anxiety he is going about the business of squaring his deeper unconscious debt. Here is the deed itself: "From these thoughts he was aroused by a rustling in the forest at some distance from the spot to which he had wandered. Perceiving the motion of some object behind a thick veil of undergrowth, he fired, with the instinct of a hunter and the aim of a practised marksman. A low moan, which told his success, and by which even animals can express their dying agony, was unheeded by Reuben Bourne. What were the recollections now breaking upon him?"

These are brilliantly suggestive lines. Reuben is supposedly deer-hunting, but Hawthorne leaves no implication that Reuben thinks he has spotted a deer; he fires at a "rustling" and a "motion." To say that he does this with a hunter's instinct is slyly ironical, for of course a good hunter does not shoot at ambiguous noises, particularly in "the vicinity of the encampment"! The moan that would tell Reuben of his ironic "success," if he were sufficiently in command of himself to heed it, is said to be one "by which *even* animals can express their dying agony"—a hint that animals have not been his primary target. And finally, the question at the end serves to put the blame for Cyrus's death where it properly belongs. The repressed "recollections" of the original scene are now free to become wholly conscious because the guilt-compulsion that protected them has finally completed its work.

If this argument is correct, the various interpretations of "Roger Malvin's Burial" in terms of religious symbolism must be regarded with suspicion. It is true, for example, that three of the four major characters' names are Biblical, but it is doubtful that this entitles us to say that Reuben achieves "salvation" through Cyrus.[5] Even the Abraham-Isaac parallel, which seems more prominent than any other, must be taken in an ironic spirit, for Reuben's "sacrifice" of his son is dictated not by God but by self-loathing. The story's ending is heretical, to put it mildly: Reuben's alleged redemption has been achieved through murder, while the guilt from which he has thereby freed himself stemmed from an imaginary crime.[6] The real murder is unrepented yet—indeed, Reuben shows little concern for his dead son—while the fantasy-murder brings forth tears and prayer.[7] The Biblical allusions suggesting a possible redemption serve the purpose of placing in relief the merely pathological nature of the case at hand. For the idea of divine care is cruelly mocked by a plot in which all exhortations to Heaven spring from self-delusion, and in which the "redeemer" performs his redemptive function by unintentionally stopping a musket ball.

The other symbols in Hawthorne's story ought likewise to be considered in relationship to its essential savagery. The most conspicuous symbol is, of course, the oak sapling upon which Reuben places a blood-stained handkerchief, partly as a signal of rescue for Roger and partly to symbolize his own vow to return. When he does return the tree has grown into "luxuriant life," with "an excess of vegetation" on the trunk, but its "very topmost bough was withered, sapless, and utterly dead." This branch, which is the one that formerly bore the emblem of the vow, falls in fragments upon the *tableau vivant* of the living and dead at the very end. The symbolic meaning is, if anything, too obvious. The sapling is Reuben, whose innocent young life has been "bent" (he bends the sapling downward to affix the handkerchief to it) to a sworn purpose and to a secret self-reproach; Reuben grows as the tree grows, becoming mature in outward respects but blasted at the top, in his soul or mind; and when the withered bough crumbles we are doubtless meant to conclude that the guilt has been canceled and that a possibility now exists for more normal development. I would call particular attention, however, to the *excessive* vegetation and *luxuriant* lower branches. Luxuriance in Hawthorne almost always has something sick about it, and the word "excess" speaks for itself. I would surmise that these aspects of the tree represent the compensatory elements in Reuben's character, the gradual accretion of defenses against the tormenting thoughts that he has been fighting down for years. His peace of mind is partly restored at the end of the tale, but he will never again be the simple person we met in the beginning.

Finally, let us consider the symbolic value of the forest itself. Reuben's initiation into guilt, like Young Goodman Brown's and Arthur Dimmesdale's, occurs in the forest, and it is in the forest that he will bring forth what his guilty feelings have hatched. "He was," as Hawthorne says of Reuben's desire to seek a new home, "to throw sunlight into some deep recess of the forest." The forest is of course his own mind, in which is deeply buried a secret spot, a trauma, to which he will have to return. He thinks he does not know the way back, he resists the opportunity to go, but ultimately he is overruled by the strength of what he has repressed. Self-knowledge is knowledge of what is almost inaccessibly remote, and Reuben will not be free until he has reached this point and released what lies imprisoned here. The tale of compulsion is fittingly climaxed in "a region of which savage beasts and savage men were as yet the sole possessors"— the mental region of Hawthorne's best insight and highest art.

Notes

1. *The Power of Blackness*, p. 40. For another valuable formulation of Hawthorne's reduction of religious problems to psychological ones, see Melvin W. Askew, "Hawthorne, the Fall, and the Psychology of Maturity," *American Literature*, XXXIV (November 1962), 335–43.

2. See *The Power of Blackness*, p. 55; Mark Van Doren, *Nathaniel Hawthorne* (New York, 1949), p. 80; and Arlin Turner, *Nathaniel Hawthorne: An Introduction and Interpretation* (New York, 1961), p. 31.

3. The argument that follows has been anticipated in part by various studies. See Waggoner, *Hawthorne*, pp. 90–98; Richard P. Adams, "Hawthorne's *Provincial Tales*," *New England Quarterly*, XXX (March 1957), 39–57; Louis B. Salomon, "Hawthorne and His Father: A Conjecture," *Literature and Psychology*, XIII (Winter 1963), 12–17; and Agnes McNeill Donohue, " 'From Whose Bourn No Traveler Returns': A Reading of 'Roger Malvin's Burial,' " *Nineteenth-Century Fiction*, XVIII (June 1963), 1–19.

4. I do not mean, however, that Reuben actively wills Roger's death at any point. The link between his prospective happiness and Roger's imminent, already inevitable death is originally a fortuitous irony of circumstance and nothing more. But Reuben's punctilious conscience turns this link into one of causality; he will no longer be able to contemplate his own welfare without imagining, quite falsely, that he has bought it with Roger Malvin's blood.

5. See W. R. Thompson, "The Biblical Sources of Hawthorne's 'Roger Malvin's Burial,' " *PMLA*, LXXVII (March 1962), 92–6. For a detailed reply to Thompson's article see p. 463 of my earlier version of this chapter in *PMLA*, LXXIX (September 1964), 457–65. The fourth principal name, incidentally, appears to be historical rather than Biblical. Two survivors of Lovewell's (or Lovell's) Fight in the Penobscot War, as Hawthorne knew, were Eleanor and David Melvin. See G. Harrison Orians, "The Source of Hawthorne's 'Roger Malvin's Burial,' " *American Literature*, X (November 1938), 313–18, and David S. Lovejoy, "Lovewell's Fight and Hawthorne's 'Roger Malvin's Burial,' " *A Casebook on the Hawthorne Question*, ed. Agnes McNeill Donohue (New York, 1963), pp. 89–92.

6. It is significant that although Reuben consciously thinks that his expiation will consist of burying Roger's bones, the actual release of his guilt-feeling comes about through the killing of Cyrus. There is no mention of burial at the end, yet the "atonement" is indeed complete; it is atonement for the imagined murder of Roger, not for the broken vow to bury him.

7. We can judge the abnormality of Reuben's reaction by contrasting it with that of Dorcas: "With one wild shriek, that seemed to force its way from the sufferer's inmost soul, she sank insensible by the side of her dead boy."

Hawthorne's "Gentle Boy": Lost Mediators in Puritan History
Frederick Newberry[*]

All of Nathaniel Hawthorne's historical tales of seventeenth-century New England are patterned along lines first developed in "The Gentle Boy" (1831). Two significant contests are at issue, both historical and cultural in their implications. The most prominent involves an actual historical struggle between Puritans and their opponents—Merry Mounters, community dissidents, Quakers, or English forces. Because these opponents are by and large presented as extremists, their defeat by the Puritans does not usually lead one to feel much if any regret. They hardly seem any more noble or virtuous than the Puritans who are normally undercut with subtle irony or open denunciation. Generally obscured by the strict ideological conflict between Puritan and non-Puritan factions is the far more important contest between Puritan and non-Puritan absolutism and moderation. Hawthorne insinuates in every tale one or two figures whose function it is to show a possible mediation of the larger historical struggle. Endowed with piety, reason, gentleness, or sympathy, these figures stand in passive or oppressed opposition to the main contenders and, because they lack sufficient strength, come to symbolize recessive forces in New England history. Such positive historical types, with one exception, have no foundation in Hawthorne's historical reading.[1] They are instead characters whom Hawthorne himself must create, perhaps to sustain his hope in a potentially beneficent human community, but also to posit the likelihood that there were once potential alternatives to narrow Puritan rule. Of course, these mediating figures are overpowered or destroyed by Puritan severity and persecution. And with their demise, salutary alternatives in New England history disappear. Their loss is the tragedy of Hawthorne's Puritan drama.

John Endicott represents Hawthorne's archetypal Puritan, bringing together the worst extremes of Puritanism: intolerance, iconoclasm, militancy, and persecution. Endicott's extremism is habitually pitted against less severe Puritans as well as such extreme heretics as the Merry Mount revelers and Quaker fanatics. Whether as a military leader in the 1620s and 1630s, or as governor in the 1650s and 1660s, he defines, as Hawthorne sees it historically, the dominant side of Puritanism. Despite the fact that Endicott sometimes serves as a model in a typological configuration culminating in American independence, he nevertheless remains the arch-villain in Hawthorne's estimation of the devastating cultural and aesthetic results of the

[*] Reprinted by permission from *Studies in Short Fiction* 21 (1984): 363–73.

Puritan experience.[2] In the biographical sketch, "Mrs. Hutchinson" (1830), Endicott "would stand with his drawn sword at the gate of heaven, and resist to the death all pilgrims thither, except they travelled his own path."[3] Endicott's example therefore constitutes the Puritan legacy that Hawthorne studies, argues, and finally deplores— the narrow lines, as Michael Bell argues, along which American character will develop.[4]

"The Gentle Boy" begins a trilogy of tales in which Endicott figures as a rigid Puritan type. He never makes a direct appearance in the story, as he demonstrably does in "The May-Pole of Merry Mount" (1836) and "Endicott and the Red Cross" (1838), but Hawthorne leaves no room for doubt that Endicott's brand of Puritanism has gained the upper hand in New England. The events in the story take place roughly between 1656 and 1664, from the time the Quakers first arrived in Massachusetts Bay to when the Puritans finally bowed to Charles II's pressure and ceased persecuting the Friends in the worst manner.[5] This seven-year period, throughout which Endicott is governor of the colony, comprises the American context of "The Gentle Boy" upon which Hawthorne obviously focuses. In addition, a larger historical context is also included as a background for the Puritan scene, a context encompassing the turbulent years of the English Civil War, the Protectorate, and the Restoration.

Even though Hawthorne pays more specific attention to the Puritan/Quaker conflict in the New World, the English historical background has considerable and heretofore unacknowledged significance for this struggle. The enormous cultural shift brought on by the Civil War, regicide, and Protectorate actually parallels a less noticeable but no less critical shift under way in New England. In both the Old and New Worlds, a radical form of Puritanism ascends to power. Hawthorne, later in his career, specifically points to this cultural shift in New England as a split between first and second generation Puritans. "Mainstreet" (1849) and *The Scarlet Letter* (1850), for example, clearly define this division that Hawthorne begins to suggest as early as "The Gentle Boy." The second generation— wearing "the blackest shade of Puritanism"—succeeds the first with the militant Endicott as its leader.[6] Endicott, of course, succeeds John Winthrop in 1649 as the governor most often elected by the Puritans. By age and experience a member of the first generation, yet often at odds with the milder rule of Winthrop, Endicott perfectly embodies the worst traits of Puritanism generally and thus is the governor most fitting for Hawthorne's view of the notorious second generation. Not coincidentally, the rise in Endicott's political power has an appropriate relation to Cromwell's ascent in England. The regicide of Charles I, which Endicott obliquely forecasts in "Endicott and the Red Cross," is an accomplished fact at the end of *The Scarlet Letter* and within the chronological frame of "The Gentle Boy." England, however, experiences a Restoration after Cromwell dies. Charles II comes to the throne in 1660, reversing the Puritan fortunes of the previous decade. Obviously, nothing analogous to the Restoration can occur in Hawthorne's fictive history of seventeenth-century New England. But it is more than just happenstance, I believe, that Hawthorne notes how the Quaker persecutions do not stop until 1664, approximately the time of Endicott's death. "The Gentle Boy" briefly details a modicum of respite following upon the decree of " 'the king, even Charles' " that Massachusetts Bay observe religious toleration.[7] And yet, before this respite takes effect, the central characters in Hawthorne's tale—Tobias Pearson and Ilbrahim—have been destroyed; and with their destruction a brighter potentiality for New England passes away.

Hawthorne divides the story into five sections. The opening and closing sections provide the historical frame for the inset tale, and they are concentrated on the American foreground. In explicating Pearson's biography in the second section, Hawthorne introduces the larger historical background of England which he takes up again in the final section. Inside the historical frame are the stories of Pearson and Ilbrahim, caught up in the conflict between Puritans and Quakers. The Puritans try to settle the issues at stake only by virtue of their superior militant power. Thus Hawthorne creates dualisms identical to those which will surface again in later historical tales: oppressed versus oppressors, victims versus victimizers.

Along with its pattern of dualisms, "The Gentle Boy" also foreshadows the other historical tales in its very important use of a potential mediator trapped between struggling factions. Ilbrahim, the tale's namesake, represents the innocence of childhood and the basic human need for love and community relations. He does not align himself with either Puritan or Quaker dogma. Instead, he manifests a normal child's desires to have a warm and secure homelife and to enjoy the fellowship of peers. Thus he, along with Pearson, partly symbolizes domestic harmony, perhaps Hawthorne's favorite ideal. The domestic ideal, it's true, is not achieved in the tale. Gentleness and sympathy, which to Hawthorne are inherent in domestic life, are overcome by bigotry and cruelty outside the domestic circle. The community at large is caught up in an ideological war that denies fundamental sympathies and needs. Ilbrahim, a gentle victim of both sides of the battle, might well be likened to a child's version of Roger Williams as he appears in "Endicott and the Red Cross," a Christlike figure, and to Dimmesdale in *The Scarlet Letter*, a man of sympathy and sorrow.[8] Unlike Williams and Dimmesdale, though, Ilbrahim is actually sacrificed; but his death has no salutary influence on either contingent responsible for it—the Puritans or Catherine, the Quaker mother who abandons Ilbrahim for a self-deluding vision of absolute truth.

The direct cause of Ilbrahim's death is Puritan cruelty, and it is within the context of this cruelty and other Puritan excesses that events in "The Gentle Boy" must be analyzed. In the opening historical frame, blame rests solely upon the Puritans for the "indecorous exhibitions" of the Quakers: "persecution . . . was at once their cause and consequence" (69). Hawthorne does not approve of the Quakers' extravagant acts ("abstractly considered," he says, they "well deserved the moderate chastisement of the rod" [p. 69]), but he cannot excuse the Puritans' intolerance for triggering those acts in the first place. Contrary to the views of other readers of the tale,[9] what appears to be a balance between the Puritans and Quakers is really not a balance at all. The Puritans initiate the violence against the Quakers, against Ilbrahim, and even against one of their own— Pearson, whose human sympathy exceeds what is compatible with his denomination's engrained bigotry.

As for the actual execution of two Quakers in 1659, Hawthorne raises no *abstract considerations* to justify the Puritans. "An indelible stain of blood is upon the hands of all who consented to this act," he says (p. 69), anticipating the central legend in *The House of the Seven Gables* twenty years later. But the person most responsible for the executions is "the head of the government," Endicott: "He was a man of narrow mind and imperfect education, and his uncompromising bigotry was made hot and mischievous by violent and hasty passions; he exerted his influence indecorously and unjustifiably to compass the death of the enthusiasts; and his whole conduct, in respect to them, was marked by brutal cruelty" (p. 69).

This judgment of Endicott seems plainly Hawthorne's, and it is buttressed by reference as well to that of the Quakers' as recorded by William Sewall, "the historian of the sect" (p. 69). According to the Quakers and Sewall, Endicott experienced a "loathsome disease, and 'death by rottenness' " for his leading role in the persecutions (p. 70). While this legend expresses only a vindictive wish fulfillment on the Quakers' part, one can imagine how readily Hawthorne fastened upon the outer sign of inner guilt or sin. Later works such as "The Man of Adamant," "Ethan Brand," and *The Scarlet Letter* reveal that visible signs of guilt become a permanent part of the Romancer's imagination.

"The Gentle Boy," however, shows that Hawthorne is less interested in what happens to Endicott than in the excessive form of Puritanism developed in New England coincident with his leadership. The grisly punishments enumerated in "Endicott and the Red Cross," set more than thirty years earlier in history, offer only a mild preview of the persecutions inaugurated by Endicott when he becomes governor and takes charge of the Quaker persecutions.[10] Liberty of conscience, a principle which the early Puritans advocate and for which they partly come to America, is an idea whose meaning is totally lost on Endicott and his followers. They understand the idea only as it applies to their own self-interest, having forgotten or never having learned the purport of their own fruitless efforts to achieve liberty of conscience in England prior to the Civil War. In a blatantly ironic attack, for example, Hawthorne's narrator says in "The Gentle Boy" that the Puritan minister, "in his younger days . . . had practically learned the meaning of persecution, from Archbishop Laud, and he was not now disposed to forget the lesson *against which he had murmured then.* . . . He adverted to the recent measures in the province [penal laws specifically aimed at Quakers], and cautioned his hearers of weaker parts against calling in question the just severity, which God-fearing magistrates had at length been compelled to exercise" (pp. 79–80, emphasis added). Endicott, whom Hawthorne has already indicted, is the leading exponent of these "measures."

History has come full circle in "The Gentle Boy." The Quakers are in the same position the Puritans were in two or three decades earlier: trying to achieve liberty of conscience for themselves and to purify the established church. Only one difference separates them. Whereas New England Puritans had "shunned the cross" of English persecutions and escaped to a "distant wilderness," the Quakers welcome "persecutions as a divine call to the post of danger" (68). Most Puritans in England did not shun the cross of persecution. They remained and eventually took up arms against the King and the English Church. Tobias Pearson is one of those Puritans who remained and fought in the Civil War. His experience in the Old and New Worlds not only illustrates the cycle of history in Hawthorne's tale, but another lost possibility to mediate between contending forces.

Pearson fought "during the first years of the civil war," the narrator says, "as a cornet of dragoons, under Cromwell. But when the ambitious designs of his leader began to develop themselves, he quitted the army of the parliament, and sought a refuge from the strife, *which was no longer holy,* among the people of his persuasion, in the colony of Massachusetts" (p. 76, emphasis added). Apparently, Pearson saw that the Puritans were simply aiming to replace one form of power with another, or that the war would result in the regicide of Charles I, an act not contemplated by Parliament at the outset of the rebellion. He does seem to have realized that Parliament and Cromwell tried to secure more than just liberty of conscience for the Puritan cause. A total break in English traditions was in the making. In any event, the war was not "holy"—an opinion held apparently as much by the narrator as it is by Pearson himself.

It seems certain that Hawthorne drew on Scott's *Woodstock* for

Pearson's relation to Cromwell and for his opinion on the future Protector's ambition. A soldier of Cromwell's named Pearson appears often in this novel. The context of one appearance is Cromwell's raising his voice to deny having any private ambitions in assuming command of the Independent forces against the king.[11] The same Pearson appears again when Cromwell urges him to leap a twelve foot interval atop Woodstock castle. Pearson refuses. Angered, Cromwell then reveals his ambition to hunt down the Crown Prince and thus pave the way for his own assumption of leadership in England: " 'Ah, base and degenerate spirit!' said the General; 'soul of mud and clay, wouldst thou not do it, and much more, for the possession of an empire!—that is, peradventure,' continued he, changing his tone as one who has said too much, 'shouldst thou be called upon to do this, that thereby becoming a great man in the tribes of Israel, thou mightest redeem the captivity of Jerusalem. . . .' "[12] If Hawthorne needed a source for Pearson's view of the "unholy" cause against the King, he would surely have found it in these lines. Additional references to Cromwell's ambition abound, both by Scott's characters and by his narrator.[13]

Pearson's ingenuous motives for leaving Cromwell's army have gained little favor from Hawthorne's critics. His allegedly disingenuous motives for coming to America, however, are usually mentioned.[14] Hawthorne, true enough, allows the barest reason to doubt Pearson's intentions. "A more worldly consideration had *perhaps* an *influence* in drawing him thither; for New England offered advantages to men of unprosperous fortunes, as well as to dissatisfied religionists, and Pearson had hitherto found it difficult to provide for a wife and increasing family. To this *supposed* impurity of motive, the *more bigoted Puritans* were inclined to impute the removal by death of all the children, for whose earthly good the father had been over-thoughtful" (p. 76, emphasis added). This passage quite clearly represents the viewpoint of the Puritans, not of the narrator or of Hawthorne. And it is a viewpoint exposing not only the superstition and bigotry of the Puritans, but their hypocrisy as well. The majority of Puritans themselves came to America with mixed motives. Surely they confirm their own worldly interests when, as the narrator puts it, they "shunned" hardship at home and sought to establish an enclave in the New World. Pearson, on the other hand, did not run away from the persecutions in England; he fought in the Civil War until he found it an anathema to his faith.

Pearson in fact tries to balance the claims of the physical and spiritual realms; but because of the severe conditions of the New World and the absolutist mentality of both the Puritans and the Quakers, he is eventually caught between the two realms and suffers from both. It is certain from the opening scene that he is not the typical iron-willed Puritan (nor suitably iron-clad, even though a soldier) familiar in Hawthorne's other works. As he passes by the gravesite where two Quakers were executed earlier in the day, he hears the wailing of Ilbrahim. Pearson resists "the superstitious fears which belonged to the age," and for the " 'ease of [his] own conscience' " approaches the gravesite and discovers the forlorn child (p. 71).

The subsequent exchange between Pearson and Ilbrahim offers a preview of just how radical the shift in Pearson's attitudes will be in his unsteady balancing act. One has to recall that when the story opens Pearson is one of the elected representatives to the General Court. He therefore was among those Puritan leaders who drew up a series of punitive laws against the Quakers and must therefore in turn bear responsibility for the execution of two Friends at the beginning of the story. This overlooked detail establishes guilt as a powerful motivation behind Pearson's reaction to Ilbrahim's admission, over one of the graves, that the executed man lying beneath the ground was his father: "the Puritan, who laid hold of little Ilbrahim's hand, relinquished it as if he were touching a loathsome reptile" (p. 73). With Pearson's own part in the executions in mind, we more easily understand his sudden change at the gravesite: "his heart stirred with shame and anger against the gratuitous cruelty of the instruments in this persecution" (p. 74). But whether for strictly personal reasons or not, Pearson suddenly discovers that the Puritan campaign against the Quakers is no longer holy, just as the Civil War became unholy for him a decade earlier.

But guilt is not the sole motivation of Pearson's response to Ilbrahim, for the Puritan has a "compassionate heart which not even religious prejudice could harden into stone" (p. 73). Thus he takes Ilbrahim under his protection. As he explains to his wife Dorothy, even " 'the heathen savage would have given [Ilbrahim] to eat of his scanty morsel, and to drink of his birchen cup; but Christian men, alas! had cast him out to die' " (p. 75). Pearson's choice is a natural one, but it is also a Christian one in the best sense. Reenacted here, although not simply, is the parable of the Good Samaritan.[15] But the same "bigoted" Puritans who believe that Pearson's children have died because he had impure motives in emigrating to England fail to acknowledge Tobias and Dorothy's compassion or charity. "Those expounders of the ways of Providence, who had thus judged their brother, and attributed his domestic sorrows to his sin, were not more charitable when they saw him and Dorothy endeavoring to fill up the void in their hearts, by the adoption of an infant of the accursed sect" (p. 76).

The Puritans' ill judgment is influenced more by their belief in the powerful workings of the Devil than by their faith in the benevolent workings of God. Subscribing to the Calvinistic tenet that the natural world is vulnerable to Satan's manipulation, the Puritans mistrust their initial, natural response to Ilbrahim's fine appearance and attribute it instead to the Devil's influence. "Even his beauty . . . and his winning manners, sometimes produced an effect ultimately unfavorable; for the bigots, when the outer surfaces of their iron hearts had been softened and again grew hard, affirmed that no merely natural cause could have so worked upon them" (p. 77). Similarly, in the church scene, when the congregation responds sympathetically to Catherine's anguish, Hawthorne says the Puritans "mistook their involuntary virtue for a sin" (p. 85).

Hawthorne thus contrasts the hearts and minds of the Pearsons with those of the community at large. Imposing limits on religious prejudice and superstition, Tobias and Dorothy do not view the natural world as the Devil's special playground. Throughout the first three sections of the tale, at least, both are models of "rational piety"— a description with which Hawthorne distinguishes Dorothy from Ilbrahim's mother, Dorothy's allegorical foil, who stands for "unbridled fanaticism" (p. 85). The Pearsons occupy a moderating position between the Puritans' absolute reliance on the intellect (the head) and the Quaker's equally absolute reliance on inspiration (abstract feelings), a distortion of the heart. Their moderation is particularly evident in the church scene, Hawthorne's most striking tableau in "The Gentle Boy." Neither Tobias nor Dorothy is associated with the bigoted sermon of the Puritan minister, who lectures on "the danger of pity, in some cases a commendable and Christian virtue, but inapplicable to this pernicious sect [Quakers]" (p. 80). Nor are they associated with Catherine's following sermon, "a flood of malignity which she mistook for inspiration" (p. 82).

Dorothy maintains her "rational piety" throughout the tale, balancing the claims of head and heart. Tobias, however, is unable to sustain this balance and eventually changes from Puritan to Quaker. Hawthorne leads the reader to believe that Pearson's heart is the agent of this transformation. When Tobias explains to Dorothy the circumstances of his finding Ilbrahim, he relates "how his heart had prompted him, like the speaking of an inward voice, to take the little outcast home" (p. 75). The "inward voice" is equivalent to the *inner light* esteemed by the Quakers, and the phrasing seems clearly intended to foreshadow Pearson's change later in the tale. A more explicit foreshadowing of this change comes after the Puritans begin to deride Pearson for adopting Ilbrahim. "These results irritated Pearson's temper for the moment; they entered also into his heart, and became imperceptible but powerful workers toward an end, which his most secret thought had not yet whispered" (p. 77).

It seems very plain, however, that while Pearson's heart is involved in his shift from Puritan to Quaker, the Puritan community sets it in motion. Pearson does not so much seek the Quaker faith as he acquiesces to it in rebellion against the Puritans. In a somewhat obtrusive afterthought in section four, the narrator tries to smooth Pearson's transition by saying that at the opening of the story Pearson was "in a state of religious dulness, yet mentally disquited, and longing for a more fervid faith than he possessed" (p. 94). Ilbrahim serves as the "original instrument" of Pearson's "incipient love for the child's whole sect" (p. 94). Ultimately alienated from and tormented by the community, coupled with his eventual loss of rational objections to Quaker doctrine, Pearson accepts the Friends to a great extent by default as he identifies Ilbrahim's persecutions with his own. His estrangement from the larger community leads him to rely on his individual self, always a dangerous sign in Hawthorne. As with Hester in *The Scarlet Letter*, isolation begets a psychological imbalance in Pearson. He turns his hate upon himself and begins to dwell "too long among visionary thoughts" (p. 95). This mental condition feeds on the Puritan punishments, causing greater isolation from the events of this world and an exaggerated pre-occupation with the self's spiritual existence beyond temporal life.

Despite these unhealthy circumstances identifying his transformation from a respected citizen in the Puritan community to a despised member of the Quakers, Pearson never becomes an extremist like Catherine or the old Quaker introduced in section four. These two deny their essential duty to nature and nature's God, as Hawthorne's narrator seems to see it. Catherine neglects "the holiest trust which can be committed to a woman" (p. 95) when she abandons Ilbrahim in payment to God for her own spiritual rewards. Then too, the old Quaker who visits the Pearsons while Ilbrahim is dying boasts that he once abandoned his dying daughter in response to a revelation to serve God among strangers. In ironic counterpoint, though, Pearson's suffering issues from his taking parental responsibility for Ilbrahim—that is, from his desire to be connected to this world. Catherine and the old Quaker, without recognizing it, rightly suffer for doing wrong. Pearson, by contrast, wrongly suffers for doing right. Although he may be guilty of neglecting "temporal affairs" (p. 95), he never imagines sacrificing Ilbrahim to prove that he can bear the weight of any cross preparatory to martyrdom and salvation. He shudders at the thought of testing his faith by abandoning Ilbrahim on his deathbed, a similar act for which the fanatical old Quaker is still proud (p. 98).

Pearson's story comes to a sudden end at the death of Ilbrahim. Prior to the boy's death, though, Pearson reaches a crisis of faith unresolved by the story. Having been a Puritan and then a Quaker, he is apparently ready to seek another faith or to deny the efficacy of faith altogether. He plainly recognizes the aberrant extremes of Puritanism and Quakerism, and he recoils from both. He therefore serves Hawthorne's purposes very well; for, like Ilbrahim, he is a displaced individual caught up first by one and then another radical force in history. Pearson cannot balance the demands imposed by these forces, just as he cannot balance the conflicting dualisms within himself: the head and heart, the claims of this world and the next. Consequently, as his story ends, he seems utterly defeated.[16]

The home that Pearson hoped to build in the new world finally eludes him.[17] His children are already dead when the tale begins, and Hawthorne pointedly mentions their absence as Pearson brings Ilbrahim into the cottage. With Ilbrahim's arrival, the Pearson cottage once again has all the requirements of a home. Dorothy and Tobias develop an affection for the boy which becomes, "like the memory of their native land, or their mild sorrow for the dead, a piece of the immovable furniture of their hearts" (p. 88). This affection, so often equated by Hawthorne to a nostalgic feeling for "our old home" in England, is in turn paralleled by "the warmth and security of [the cottage's] hearth" (p. 88). But after Ilbrahim is beaten by the Puritan children and Tobias is persecuted by the Puritan fathers, the cottage loses all of its home-feeling. On the dark and stormy night opening section four, "There were no cheerful faces to drive the gloom from his broad hearth" (p. 95). Even though an ample fire is blazing, "the apartment [significantly no longer a "home"] was saddened in its aspect by the absence of much of the homely wealth which had once adorned it; for the exaction of repeated fines, and his own neglect of temporal affairs, had greatly impoverished the owner" (p. 95). Ilbrahim's death then completes Pearson's failure to establish a home in New England.

While the harsh conditions of the new world may be responsible for the deaths of Pearson's children, they have no bearing on the death of Ilbrahim or the utter ruin of Pearson. Just as Puritan persecutions are the "cause and consequence" of Quaker fanaticism, so they are the cause of Ilbrahim's death and Pearson's failure to create a home. That Hawthorne does not favor Quaker extremism is in no way evidence that the contest between Puritans and Quakers is decided in a judgmental draw. The fates of Pearson and Ilbrahim are almost totally determined by the Puritans. And their tragedies are similar: for their gentleness, compassion, and charity, they are scorned and persecuted. Gentleness, as well as moderation, is doomed under the zealous harshness of Puritanism. Pearson began to learn this fact while serving under Cromwell in England and he learned it yet more thoroughly under Endicott in New England. Thus Pearson joins Ilbrahim as potential mediators who, as will be the case with Pearl in

The Scarlet Letter, are completely lost to the New World. Puritan cruelty is inimical to human sympathies of parents and children alike.

Such cruelty, while certainly obvious in the early generation of Puritans, becomes noticeably marked in the next generation—the children with whom Ilbrahim seeks desperately to establish friendly relations. The child bears the scorn of Puritan elders with relative equanimity but loses his will to live when a once-injured child he befriended and entertained with "romances" (p. 91) joins compatriot "fanatics" (p. 92) in unremitting persecution of the little Quaker. The description of the despicable Puritan boy illustrates the story's most telling forecast of the New England future. "The disposition of the boy was sullen and reserved, and the village schoolmaster stigmatized him as obtuse in intellect; although, at a later period of life he evinced ambition and very peculiar talents" (p. 90).[18] The tale concludes with a soporific suggestion that Puritanism became increasingly forbearing after Charles II proclaimed religious toleration, but the reader cannot forget the ominous proclivities of the children who will comprise the next epoch's leaders. During their mature years, they will first enlist in King Philip's War and later condemn their neighbors to die in the Salem Witch trials. Both episodes, on the margin of Hawthorne's concern in subsequent work but deeply important to New England history upon which the Romancer broods, are not significantly different from the Quaker persecutions: they all evince very peculiar talents.

Notes

1. Simon Bradstreet is the exception in "The Gray Champion" (1835). See Frederick Newberry, "Hawthorne's Ironic Criticism of Puritan Rebellion in "The Gray Champion,'" *Studies in Short Fiction*, 13 (1976), 363–70.

2. See for example Michael Davitt Bell, *Hawthorne and the Historical Romance of New England* (Princeton, NJ: Princeton University Press, 1971), pp. 53–60. For the most positive view of Endicott yet written, see Gayle L. Smith, "Transcending the Myth of the Fall in Hawthorne's "The May-Pole of Merry Mount,'" *ESQ*, 29 (1983), 73–80.

3. *The Complete Works of Nathaniel Hawthorne*, ed. George P. Lathrop, Riverside Edition, 12 vols. (Boston: Houghton Mifflin, 1883), XII, 223.

4. Bell, p. 58.

5. For the influence of historical sources on the tale, see G. Harrison Orians, "The Sources and Themes of Hawthorne's 'The Gentle Boy,'" *New England Quarterly*, 14 (1941), 664–78; and Neal F. Doubleday, *Hawthorne's Early Tales* (Durham, NC: Duke University Press, 1972), pp. 159–70.

6. *The Scarlet Letter*, Centenary Edition, ed. William Charvat *et al.* (Columbus: Ohio State University Press, 1963), I, 232.

7. "The Gentle Boy," Centenary Edition, IX, 101. Further references to the story will be cited parenthetically in the text.

8. For discussions of Williams and Dimmesdale as mediators, see Frederick Newberry, "The Demonic in 'Endicott and the Red Cross,' " *Papers on Language and Literature*, 13 (1977), 251–59; and "Tradition and Disinheritance in *The Scarlet Letter*," *ESQ*, 23 (1977), 1–26.

9. For example, see Bell, p. 111; and Seymour L. Gross, "Hawthorne's Revisions of 'The Gentle Boy,' " *American Literature*, 26 (1955), 196–208.

10. In Caleb H. Snow's *History of Boston* (Boston, 1825), p. 141, Hawthorne had a source for the particular severity ushered in by Endicott after he became Governor. Snow says that in the early 1650s, "the scrupulosity of the good people of the colony was at its height. Soon after Mr. Winthrop's death, Mr. Endicott, the most rigid of any of the magistrates, being governour, he joined with the other assistants in an association against the wearing of long hair, as a thing uncivil and unmanly."

11. See *Woodstock* in *Waverley Novels* (Edinburgh: Adam and Charles Black, 1852), pp. 143–44.

12. *Woodstock*, p. 496.

13. *Woodstock*, pp. 117, 198, 498, 504.

14. See Bell, p. 114; and Frederick Crews, *The Sins of the Fathers: Hawthorne's Psychological Themes* (New York: Oxford University Press, 1966), p. 66.

15. Crews says that Pearson is a "peculiarly neurotic Good Samaritan" (p. 67).

16. Roy R. Male deals with Pearson as a sympathetic figure caught between conflicting forces in *Hawthorne's Tragic Vision* (1957; rpt. New York: Norton, 1964), pp. 46–47.

17. I am indebted to Male's discussion of the search-for-home motif in the story, pp. 45–48.

18. Agnes McNeill Donohue, " 'The Fruit of That Forbidden Tree': A Reading of "The Gentle Boy,' " in *A Casebook on the Hawthorne Question*, ed. Agnes McNeill Donohue (New York: Crowell, 1963), pp. 158–70, says that the deformed boy who betrays Ilbrahim has "the characteristics of the devil" (p. 164).

Hawthorne's "The Ambitious Guest" and the Significance of the Willey Disaster

John F. Sears°

On the night of 28 August 1826, numerous avalanches devastated the slopes of the White Mountains, stripping away trees, earth and rock, and leaving deep gashes in the mountainsides that remained visible for years afterward. One of these avalanches wiped out the entire family of Samuel Willey, Jr.: Mr. Willey and his wife, five children between the ages of five and thirteen, a hired man and a boy. The Willeys lived in what is now called Crawford Notch, a wild and lonely spot six miles from the nearest neighbor. They tended a

° Reprinted from *American Literature* 54 (1982): 354–67, by permission of the author. A revised version of the essay appears in the author's *Sacred Places: American Tourist Attractions in the Nineteenth Century* (New York: Oxford University Press, 1989).

small farm and they took in travellers who passed through the Notch on their way to the coast of Maine. On 28 June 1826, the Willeys had been frightened by another avalanche that descended close to their home, and Mr. Willey had taken the precaution of constructing a shelter to which they could flee in case they were threatened again. They apparently tried to reach that shelter on the night of 28 August but they fled right into the path of an oncoming slide. Their house, however, remained unharmed and had they stayed within it, they would all have been saved. One of the avalanches had originated at the top of the mountain above the Willeys' house and descended directly toward it, but just before it reached the house it divided in two, passed by on either side—destroying the stable on its way—and reunited lower down in the valley. The next morning a rescue party found an empty house, with the beds unmade and the family's clothing lying on chairs and on the floor, just as they had left it in their panicked flight. Three of the bodies were never recovered from the wreckage on the valley floor.

Such an event is always the stuff of news, and the Willey Disaster, as it came to be called, received extensive coverage in the New England press at the time.[1] But the nature of the response to the Willey Disaster suggests that it was not just news, but a cultural event. Benjamin Silliman, the leading American scientist of the day, visited the spot and then inserted accounts of the avalanches and the destruction of the Willey family into his *American Journal of Science and Arts;* Lydia H. Sigourney, Grenville Mellen, and other poets wrote poems about the tragic death of the family; and ministers preached sermons on the lessons to be drawn from the incident. Henry C. Pratt, who accompanied Thomas Cole to the White Mountains in 1828, painted a picture of the Willey House that appeared in the first issue of the *Token* (1828); Thomas C. Upham, the Bowdoin philosophy professor, wrote a long letter to the New Hampshire Historical Society on the moral and political significance of the event; and Theodore Dwight, Jr., the travel writer and educator, made the avalanches central to his symbolic account of the New England landscape in his *Scenery and Manners in the United States* (1829). Clearly, the New England imagination had been widely stirred.

The best known record of the Willey Disaster today is Hawthorne's story, "The Ambitious Guest" (1835). Few modern readers, however, are aware that "The Ambitious Guest" was based on an actual occurrence, and even if they are, they bring to the story little or no awareness of the meaning of the event for Hawthorne's contemporaries or of how the preoccupations of the New England culture shaped his tale. The few critics who have written about "The Ambitious Guest" have liked it, but found none of the challenging complexity of Hawthorne's better known tales to unravel.[2] The ironies in the story seem obvious, and most of them are. But if "The Ambitious Guest" is read as an expression of the culture of New England in the 1830s it acquires a deeper significance. It reveals Hawthorne's complex and, in some respects, peculiar acceptance of the values he and his contemporaries paid tribute to.

1

Hawthorne had no doubt read more than one account of the Willey Disaster before he wrote "The Ambitious Guest," and when he visited the scene of the tragedy in 1832 he must have heard the story as local legend, probably from the famous Ethan Crawford who lived near the Notch and acted as White Mountain guide for many of the first visitors to the area.[3] When Hawthorne took up the story, he not only had his own impression of the event to work with, but the knowledge that his audience was thoroughly familiar with it from the numerous accounts that had already been written and from prints showing the scene of the disaster. Even though he does not name the Willeys in the story, any contemporary reader would have known before the end of the first paragraph who the family was and what was about to happen.

Hawthorne would also have known what responsive chords the Willey Disaster had struck in the New England mind. First of all, it presented a problem in the interpretation of the divine meaning of human history and natural phenomena. As one writer put it, the event was "*almost* a miracle," the avalanche circling the house "as if *repelled* by an invisible power."[4] Thus the story appealed strongly to a culture that had been studying the ways of Providence closely for two centuries. Had the Willey Disaster occurred in the seventeenth century it would have found a place in Increase Mather's *An Essay for the Recording of Illustrious Providences* (1684). Hawthorne's audience was trained to ask, what did the destruction of the Willeys illustrate?

The mystery of the event lay in the opportunity the family missed to remain within the magic circle formed by the avalanche around the house. But, if that was not strange enough, the irony of their flight was intensified by an account of their salvation from the avalanche that had threatened them in June. That account was first published on 4 August 1826, then republished after the fatal night of 28 August. In it, Joseph T. Buckingham, editor of the *Boston Courier* and the *New England Galaxy* had written: "The place from which this *slide* or slip was loosened, is directly in the rear of Mr. Willey's house; and were there not a special Providence in the fall of a sparrow, and had not the finger of that Providence traced the direction of the sliding mass, neither he, nor any soul of his family, would ever have told the tale.''[5] Where, then, was the finger of Providence in the later avalanche? Were the Willeys being punished for some transgression? None of the published commentaries on the event even hints that this was the case. On the contrary, the Willeys are presented as exemplary in every respect. Their fate had to be accepted, like Job's, as a mystery beyond the capacity of man to penetrate. Yet God also spoke through the Willey Disaster with perfect clarity. As a minister wrote in a sermon published in the *Christian Spectator* in December 1826, God "repeats again his instructions of old in those terrible acts of his might which the language of his own inspiration best describes. 'Surely the mountain falling cometh to nought, and the rock is moved out of his place. The waters wear the stones; thou washeth away the things which grow out of the dust of the earth; and thou destroyest the hope of man' " (Job 14:18-19).[6]

Hawthorne himself could detect God's voice in the wreckage of an avalanche as well as anyone else in New England. Critics commonly complain of the heavy-handed irony of "The Ambitious Guest": "the ominous note of impending tragedy is too insistently sounded from the beginning," says James R. Mellow in his recent biography of Hawthorne,[7] and for the modern reader, educated in the subtleties of the short story, this is undoubtedly true. But Hawthorne's audience had been reared on the sermon, not the short story. From the jeremiad onward they had been schooled in the ominous. Thus they would have recognized the noisy tread of Fate that resounds through Hawthorne's story as the familiar drumming of the lesson, man is mortal. It is the same lesson that reverberates throughout the sermon on the Willey Disaster published in the *Christian Spectator:* "Let, then, as many of us, as are secretly indulging the thought that we 'shall never be moved,'—that our mortal structure is too strongly built to be dissolved, take a view of the scene among the white summits that skirt yonder horizon, where He who reared those mighty masses, has lately been exerting the terrible energies of his power."[8] And such events not only foreshadowed death, but judgment as well. The "wailing and lamentation" of the wind that announces impending doom at the beginning of Hawthorne's story, culminates in the roaring of the descending avalanche at the end: "the foundations of the earth seemed to be shaken, as if this awful sound were the peal of the last trump."[9]

2

If the intensity of response to the Willey Disaster reflected the puritan tradition of interpreting "Illustrious Providences" and blowing the trumpet of doom, it also expressed the fact that the event satisfied in the most precise way the contemporary demand for a storied landscape. Sarah Josepha Hale, editor of the *American Ladies' Magazine* and later of *Godey's Lady's Book*, wrote in 1835 that the "barrenness" of American scenery, "the vacancy, painfully felt by the traveller of taste and sentiment, arises from the want of intellectual and poetic associations with the scenery he beholds."[10] As wild and romantic as the Notch in the White Mountains was, it needed the tragedy of the Willey family to make its effect on the emotions of the spectator complete. The incident and the story together constituted the ideal subject for a truly American fiction.

Hawthorne would have heard from Thomas C. Upham at Bowdoin and from other literary nationalists of the day that American writers needed to hallow their country's scenery with story and song as Scott and Burns had done in Scotland.[11] Otherwise, her mountains would remain, as Hale put it, "nothing but huge piles of earth and rocks, covered with blighted firs and fern" and her streams continue to be celebrated only for "affording fine fish, good mill-seats or safe navigation."[12] When Hawthorne went to the White Mountains in 1832 he appears to have set out quite consciously to rescue those "huge piles of earth and rocks" from their barrenness, and the work that resulted went far, in fact, to answer the call of his contemporaries for a literature consecrating American scenes. In addition to "The Ambitious Guest," he produced "The Great Carbuncle," a story based on an old legend of the White Mountains, and "Sketches from Memory," an account of his own travels in the region. Later he added "The Great Stone Face." This series did for the White Mountains what Irving's stories had done for the Hudson River, and with a great deal more fidelity to native materials. In reading "The Ambitious Guest," Hawthorne's contemporaries must have felt a twinge of patriotic pride when he says of the family: "Who has not heard their name? The story has been told far and wide, and will forever be a legend of these mountains. Poets have sung their fate" (p. 333). America as well as Scotland had her storied mountains.

3

But it was not just the tragic event attached to a romantic spot that captured the imagination of New England; it was the fact that the avalanches had at last supplied Americans with ruins on a grand scale. On the whole, Americans had to be satisfied with reading about the ruins of the Old World and looking at pictures of them. The passing of the Indian provided only a partial substitute for the vanished civilizations of Pompeii, Egypt, and other ancient places which the discoveries of archeology had recently made famous. Americans also had to depend on the Old World to feed their appetite for catastrophe.

As Curtis Dahl points out, Americans "had developed an almost morbidly avid appetite for the sublime terror of huge devastation." Between 1810 and 1845 American poets, novelists, and painters often chose the destruction of cities, nations, races, or the entire world as the subject of their work.[13] In the avalanches of 1826 and the death of the Willey family Hawthorne's contemporaries found an American version of the destruction of an ancient city, or at least an event that evoked the same associations. The ruins left in the Notch led the author of the sermon in the *Christian Spectator* to thoughts about the mutability of all things and from them back to the ancient sites: "Where now the multitudes which once thronged the busy streets, of Nineveh, Babylon, and Palmyra?"[14]

Another favorite catastrophe among the writers and painters of the period was the Deluge,[15] and here the connection with the avalanches in the White Mountains was not merely through association. It was widely assumed not only that the Notch in the White Mountains had been formed by the Deluge in the first place, but that the powerful forces responsible for that catastrophe had been at work in the 1826 slides. Benjamin Silliman, whose *Outline of the Course of Geological Lectures* (1829) was concerned largely with the Deluge as a natural phenomenon, wrote that the cataclysm in the White Mountains represented "a very striking example of sudden diluvial action, and enables one to form some feeble conception of the universal effects of the vindictive deluge which once swept every mountain, and ravaged every plain and defile."[16] If the events in the White Mountains seemed modest compared, say, to the destruction of Pompeii, they were continuous with an event much more ancient and universal than the ruin of a single city, and one that affected the New World equally with the Old. As the author of the sermon in the *Christian Spectator* said, "There on that *spot* of earth, in that *point* of time, are epitomised the changes of all earth through all time."[17] Hawthorne makes no direct reference to the Deluge in "The Ambitious Guest," but when he wrote, "the foundations of the earth seemed to be shaken," and "Down came the whole side of the mountain, in a cataract of ruin" (pp. 332–33) his contemporaries would have been reminded of the ruin described in Genesis: "all the fountains of the great deep burst forth, and the windows of the heavens were opened" (Genesis 7:11).

4

The curiosity about Providential happenings, the desire to furnish American places with legend, the passion for catastrophe, and the love of ruins, account for much of the literary and artistic interest in the story of the Willey Disaster, but another aspect of the event outranks all the others in importance: the victims of the disaster were the members of an American family. They were not the residents of a decadent Pompeii or Nineveh or one of the sinful families destroyed by the Deluge, but a family in contemporary America whose virtue was emphasized in every version of the tragedy. Their house, which remained standing as an emblem of the Christian and republican values they embodied, was not a castle, the vestige of a feudal society, but a Home.[18] For middle-class Americans in the 1820s and 1830s home was becoming the garden of the gentler emotions. As Nancy F. Cott puts it, home represented "an 'oasis in the desert,' a 'sanctuary' where 'sympathy, honor, virtue are assembled,' where 'disinterested love is ready to sacrifice everything at the altar of affection.' "[19] Thus the poems about the Willeys by Lydia H. Sigourney and Grenville Mellen emphasize the tenderness of the family: Farmer Willey "Shouting his harvest cheerily home!," "the prattling sound / Of children" in their "nest / Of the far Wilderness," both nature and the parents of the children instructing them in a love of God. Even the moss in Sigourney's poem, "The White Mountains. After the descent of the Avalanche in 1826," clings to the granite mountain sides "like the arms / Of some sweet infant, twining the rude neck / Of its proud giant sire, to win his soul / From a stern purpose."[20] And Upham, who visited the Willey household just before the disaster, praises their home as a haven of "order, and peace, and cheerfulness," a domestic version of Winthrop's "city on a hill": "perhaps the moral loveliness, which this hospitable mansion presented, was heightened to the imagination of those, who visited it, by being shut out as it were, from the rest of the world, and blooming in the midst of such vast and terrific solitudes."[21]

Hawthorne himself certainly does everything possible in "The Ambitious Guest" to shape the family into an emblem of warmth and security. The story opens with the family gathered about a roaring fire at their home in the Notch, and it is clear that in raising the age of the eldest Willey daughter to seventeen and adding a grandmother, Hawthorne has sought to round out the family circle. The daughter is "the image of Happiness," the grandmother "the image of Happiness grown old." When Hawthorne says that the family "had found the 'herb, heart's-ease,' in the bleakest spot of all New-England" (p. 324), it recalls Upham's vision of the "moral loveliness" of the Willeys "blooming in the midst of such vast and terrific solitudes." Hawthorne's family, like Upham's, possesses the "warmth and simplicity of feeling, the pervading intelligence of New-England, and a poetry, of native growth, which they had gathered, when they little thought of it, from the mountain-peaks and chasms" (p. 327).

But there is one aspect of the cult of Home that is especially relevant to Hawthorne's story: it celebrated modesty. In Upham's account of the Disaster, the Willey house is situated near "the unambitious Saco," and the families that he extols in his poetry are invariably "humble and secluded." In poems like "The Farmer's Fireside," "The Home in the Mountains," and "The Winter Evening," he praises the independent farmer, "all unnoticed in ambition's strife," who remains "Contented with his little flock of sheep" and refrains from seeking "in glory's paths, her fading wreaths to reap."[22] Such poems draw on the pastoral tradition, but they also reflect the process by which home was becoming idealized as a " 'separate sphere' of comfort and compensation," as Nancy F. Cott puts it. "In the canon of domesticity, the home contrasted to the restless and competitive world. . . ." Upham's farmers, like the women who presided over the middle-class home, were insulated from " 'pecuniary excitement and ambitious competition.' "[23]

It is in response to this image of Home that Hawthorne generates the crucial innovation in his story. Into the garden of felicity steps the snake of restlessness. The wind comes blowing through the Notch with much "wailing and lamentation," the door opens, and in comes a traveller as if he were the messenger of death. The traveller is a young man of "high and abstracted ambition" (p. 327). One could not imagine a more ironic counterpoint to the values embodied in the Willey family.

Thus, when we ask, where did Hawthorne's ambitious guest come from?—he has no precedent in any other version of the Willey story— our first answer is that he is the opposing pole of the contemporary dichotomy between the domestic fireside and the world outside. If, as Barbara Berg says, "The exemplary home was a paradigm of serenity and harmony, a dramatic contrast to its tempestuous surroundings,"[24] then the ambitious guest is the representative of that surrounding field of competition. Hawthorne emphasizes that the family living in the Notch remains in daily contact with the world: "The romantic pass of the Notch is a great artery, through which the lifeblood of internal commerce is continually throbbing, between Maine, on one side, and the Green Mountains and the shores of the St. Lawrence on the other." The family's home serves as an oasis, soothing the loneliness of the traveller and providing the teamster on his way to the market in Portland, not just with food and lodging, but with "a homely kindness, beyond all price" (p. 325).

When the ambitious guest enters he brings with him the striving of the commercial world that streams past the family's door, but in an idealized form. Although he has accomplished nothing in his life so far, nor apparently even chosen a profession, he is obsessed by the desire to achieve a permanent and glorious place in the memory of man. He is willing to live his life in obscurity as long as he acquires this solitary splendor after his death. When he begins to talk about his obsession, he awakens the dormant ambitions of the members of the family. In fact, he might seem to be a projection of their hidden desires, were it not for the fact that their ambitions are of a different kind. Whereas his ambition is vague and centered upon his own glorification, theirs are very specific and involve expressions of kindness between persons. Their ambitions are dreams of closeness, and thus reinforce rather than disrupt the set of values the family embodies. The father dreams of owning a good farm and serving a term or two in the General Court, "And when I should be grown quite an old man, and you and old woman, so as not to be long apart, I might die happy enough in my bed, and leave you all crying around me." He would settle for a slate gravestone with something on it "to let people know, that I lived an honest man and died a Christian." One of the younger children has the most natural and, ironically, wisest wish under the impending circumstances: "I want you and father and grandma'm, and all of us, and the stranger too, to start right away, and go and take a drink out of the basin of the Flume!" The seventeen-year-old girl betrays in a sigh her hidden desire for a lover. And, finally, the old woman expresses a wish that someone hold a mirror in front of her face when she lies dead in her coffin so that "I may take a glimpse at myself, and see whether all's right?" (pp. 329–32).

It is a measure of the warmth and human sympathy expressed in these wishes that during their confession the family and the stranger draw closer together around the fire until its light "caressed them all" (p. 331). But the youth in his self-absorbed fashion persists in reducing their dreams to the same abstraction. To him they all go to prove that his obsession is universally shared. "There now!" he says, ignoring the fact that the father's wish has more to do with living a virtuous life and dying in the bosom of his family than it does with monuments, "it is our nature to desire a monument, be it slate or marble, or a pillar of granite, or a glorious memory in the universal heart of man" (p. 329).

In his single-minded pursuit of his idealistic dream, the ambitious guest reminds us of the high-souled youths of other Hawthorne stories (Owen Warland of "The Artist of the Beautiful," for instance), or even of the archtypal American dreamers, Jay Gatsby and Thomas Sutpen, who are also "ambitious guests," though hardly so modest as the youth in Hawthorne's story. Like the pursuits of those men, the youth's quest is strangely innocent, abstract, and isolating. Normally, the person undertaking such a quest excludes himself from the circle of human sympathy, and this has been true for the youth in "The Ambitious Guest" up until the evening in the Notch. On that evening, however, he finds himself strongly attracted to the family, opens his heart to them in an uncharacteristic way, and flirts with the eldest daughter, which is like flirting with domesticity itself. "It is better to sit here, by this fire . . . and be comfortable and contented, though nobody thinks about us," she says in reply to the young man's fantasies of immortality (p. 328).

The obvious irony of "The Ambitious Guest" is that the family achieve in death the immortality that the youth so passionately wished for. The story of the family "will forever be a legend of these mountains" while his name will remain "utterly unknown" (p. 333). But certainly it is also ironic that just before the members of the family acquire what the youth always wanted, he achieves the human closeness they had always enjoyed, but that he had forgone in the solitude of his quest. Their kindness redeems him from his isolation. When he first arrives he seems melancholy, almost despondent, but the warm sympathy of the family soon cheers him. Without his realizing it, they sustain his spirits as he enters the most desolate passage of his life. As Hawthorne told us at the beginning, that is the function of the family living in the Notch: "The wayfarer, with no companion but his staff, paused here to exchange a word, that the sense of loneliness might not utterly overcome him, ere he could pass through the cleft of the mountain" (p. 325). Was Hawthorne, in the salvation of his hero from loneliness by absorption into the family circle, offering a more subtle justification of the ways of Providence than those suggested by the other commentators on the disaster? If so, he had discovered a Providence perfectly in tune with the contemporary worship of domesticity.

5

One further irony of "The Ambitious Guest," which only a knowledge of the circumstances of Hawthorne's career can bring out, remains to be identified. All of his work before the publication of *Twice-told Tales* in 1837 appeared anonymously. His name was not even publicly connected with his work until a review of *The Token* for 1837 appeared in the *American Monthly Magazine* in October of 1836. The common practice of publishing authors anonymously allowed editors to use a number of pieces by the same author in a single issue and in Hawthorne's case his editors took full advantage of this option. *The Token* for 1837, for example, contained no fewer than eight pieces by Hawthorne. He also seems to have preferred (Mellow says "insisted on") anonymity, even though it prevented the growth of a reputation.[25] In any event, the practice left him in obscurity. When he was working on "The Ambitious Guest" (1835), his expectations for fame must have seemed about as substantial as those of the young man in his story and the fact that he was retelling the tale of the famous Willey Disaster must have struck him as rather sadly comic. He could count on his audience knowing immediately the name of the family in his story without his mentioning it, but he could not expect them to guess the name of the author. While their story would live on, preserved in part by the amber of his art, he, as far as he could tell at the time, would be forgotten.

But this irony is complicated by Hawthorne's ambivalence about his own dreams of glory. In the 1851 Preface to *Twice-told Tales*, when he reviews, in his mocking and self-deprecating way, the obscurity of his early career, he claims that he never had much literary ambition. In fact, he says, the tales were the attempt of "a secluded man . . . to open an intercourse with the world," and when they finally did find readers, they brought him something "far better than fame": "these volumes have opened the way to most agreeable associations, and to the formation of imperishable friendships. . . ."[26] It is difficult to take Hawthorne's disclaimer of ambition with entire seriousness, yet the pattern of values in the 1851 Preface is remarkably familiar. It is as if in his own career, as in "The Ambitious Guest," he viewed ambition suspiciously. He could only justify the effort he put into the writing of his tales by citing the human closeness it eventually brought him. Although he had at last achieved a reputation, and had good prospects of acquiring the lasting fame denied to his ambitious guest, he nevertheless asserted that the most important consequence of his career was that he, too, had been redeemed from isolation.

It would be tempting to think that Hawthorne was aware of the sentimentality of a culture that idealized the gentle values of the home while it acted out an intensely competitive, individualistic ethos, but the ironies in "The Ambitious Guest" are all aimed at the youth, and Hawthorne's denial of his own ambition in the 1851 Preface indicates his willingness to camouflage aggression with sentiment. Nevertheless, he obviously found the story of the Willeys inadequate as it stood. By injecting the figure of the ambitious guest into the tale he casts a more melancholy air over the themes of Providence and ruin and enriches the romantic associations of the wild Notch of the White Mountains. Most important, he introduces a counterpoise to the contentment of the family, thereby recognizing, at least, impulses that the cult of domesticity sought to contain or deny.

Notes

1. Many of the contemporary accounts are reprinted in Kenneth W. Cameron, "The Genesis of Hawthorne's 'The Ambitious Guest,' " *Historiographer of the Episcopal Diocese of Connecticut*, 14 (1955), 2–36. Cameron comments briefly on Hawthorne's use of his sources.

2. Neal Frank Doubleday, for example, writes that it "offers no great difficulty,"

but deserves its popularity with the common reader because of "the centrality of its concern with human experience." See *Hawthorne's Early Tales, A Critical Study* (Durham: Duke Univ. Press, 1972), pp. 144–45.

3. Hawthorne stayed at Crawford's inn. He gives a brief account of his visit to the White Mountains in a letter to his mother dated 16 September 1832. See *The American Notebooks*, ed. Randall Stewart (New Haven: Yale Univ. Press, 1932), p. 283.

4. Benjamin Silliman, "Miscellaneous Notices of Mountain Scenery and of Slides and Avalanches in the White and Green Mountains," *American Journal of Science and Arts*, 15 (1829), 221n.

5. "Excerpts from the Diary of Joseph T. Buckingham," *New England Galaxy*, 4 August 1826; rpt. *Boston Courier*, 9 September 1826; rpt. in large part in *New-Hampshire Journal*, 11 September 1826 and *Essex Register*, 11 September 1826; rpt. in Cameron, "The Genesis of Hawthorne's 'The Ambitious Guest,' " p. 7.

6. J. C. P., "The Late Storm in the White Mountains," *Christian Spectator*, 8 (December, 1826), 626.

7. *Nathaniel Hawthorne In His Times* (Boston: Houghton Mifflin, 1980), p. 52.

8. J. C. P., "The Late Storm," p. 630.

9. "The Ambitious Guest," in *Twice-Told Tales, The Centenary Edition of the Works of Nathaniel Hawthorne*, ed. Fredson Bowers and J. Donald Crowley (Columbus: Ohio State Univ. Press, 1974), IX, 325, 332. Subsequent references to this work will appear in the text.

10. "The Romance of Travelling," in *Traits of American Life* (Philadelphia: E. L. Carey & A. Hart, 1835), p. 189.

11. Upham, who taught both Hawthorne and Longfellow at Bowdoin, was a proponent of the associationist philosophy of Archibald Alison.

12. Hale, *Traits*, p. 189.

13. "The American School of Catastrophe," *American Quarterly*, II (1959), 380. Cameron also mentions the current fascination with ruin.

14. J. C. P., "The Late Storm," p. 331.

15. Dahl mentions John Trumbull, "The Last Family Who Perished from the Deluge" (1838–39) and Paul Allen, "Noah, A Poem" (1821).

16. Silliman, "Miscellaneous Notices," p. 222.

17. J. C. P., "The Late Storm," p. 331.

18. W. H. Bartlett's drawing of the Willey House which appeared in N. P. Willis's *American Scenery* (1840) reflects the importance the structure had assumed as an American ruin with native associations.

19. *The Bonds of Womanhood*, "Woman's Sphere" in New England, 1780–1835 (New Haven: Yale Univ. Press, 1977), p. 64.

20. Mellen, "Buried Valley," in *The Martyr's Triumph; Buried Valley; and Other Poems* (Boston: Lilly, Wait, Colman, and Holden, 1833), p. 277; Sigourney, *Ladies Magazine*, I (1828), 340–41.

21. Letter of Thomas C. Upham to John Farmer, *New Hampshire Historical Society Collections*, 3 (1832), 266–80; rpt. in Cameron, "The Genesis of Hawthorne's 'The Ambitious Guest,' " p. 19.

22. Letter of Upham to Farmer, rpt. in Cameron, p. 18; Upham, *American Cottage Life: A Series of Poems Illustrative of American Scenery, and of the Associations, Feelings, and Employments of the American Cottager and Farmer; Designed to Show the Value of Religion in American Homes* (Boston: American Tract Society, 1862), pp. 13–14.

23. *The Bonds of Womanhood*, pp. 69, 67.

24. *The Remembered Gate: Origins of American Feminism: The Woman and the City, 1800–1860* (New York: Oxford Univ. Press, 1978), p. 66.

25. *Nathaniel Hawthorne*, pp. 46–47, 70.

26. Preface to *Twice-Told Tales, Centenary Edition*, pp. 6–7.

Ironic Unity in Hawthorne's "The Minister's Black Veil"

E. Earle Stibitz°

Because Hawthorne is always very much the same and yet also surprisingly varied, one way of understanding "The Minister's Black Veil," as with any Hawthorne tale, is to read it not only as the unique work of art that it is, but as a tale comparable to others by Hawthorne, viewing it in the context of his essentially consistent thought and art as a whole. Such a reading of "The Minister's Black Veil" yields an unambiguous meaning. Hawthorne, with his usual assumption of the reality of personal evil, presents on one level his fundamental belief in man's proneness to hide or rationalize his most private thoughts or guilt. This is the "parable" (of the subtitle) that the Reverend Mr. Hooper seeks to preach with his wearing of the veil. On another level, Hawthorne reaffirms his equally constant belief that man is often guilty of pridefully and harmfully exalting one idea, frequently a valid truth in itself, to the status of an absolute. This is the sin Hooper commits by his self-righteous and self-deceptive insistence upon wearing the veil.

The second level grows out of the first and remains dependent upon it, a structural pattern repeated in varying ways in each major division of the story. Furthermore, this organic relationship of the two levels is ironic. Hooper in his stubborn use of the veil parable of one sin is unconsciously guilty of a greater one—that of egotistically warping the total meaning of life. This irony is compounded in that Hooper's sin is a hidden one—hidden not only from his fellows but from himself. He thus unintentionally dramatizes the very sin of secrecy that he intentionally sets out to symbolize. The central symbol of the veil keeps pace with this added irony: in addition to standing for man's concealment or hypocrisy and for Hooper's own sin of pride with its isolating effects, it stands also for the hidden quality of the second sin. All told, "The Minister's Black Veil" is less ambiguous and more unified because it is more ironic than has usually been recognized.

° Reprinted with permission from *American Literature* 34, no. 2 (1962): 182–90. © 1962 by Duke University Press.

The interpretations various critics have made of "The Minister's Black Veil," taken as a whole, offer three basic points of view. First is the interpretation that the veil indicates some specific crime by Mr. Hooper. This is Poe's view and is one concurred in by Leland Schubert and in part by R. H. Fogle, who holds that a crime by the minister remains an ambiguous possibility in the story.[1] A second view, and the one most widely held, rejects the idea of personal wrongdoing and sees the veil simply as a device chosen by the minister to dramatize a common human failing: man's refusal to show to anyone his inner heart with its likely load of private guilt. Among the critics that have subscribed to this view are Newton Arvin, Gilbert Voight, Randall Stewart, and Mark Van Doren.[2] Some of the critics who hold generally to this view concern themselves, in addition, with the effect of the veil upon the minister.[3] The third view holds that there is something fundamentally wrong in the minister's wearing of the veil. W. B. Stein is a vigorous exponent of this view, arguing that the story is one of a man of God turned antichrist, especially in Hooper's failure to follow Paul's II Corinthians injunction to ministers to let love be the principle of the relationship with their congregations.[4] Mr. Fogle, basically representative of this view, argues for two meanings.[5] There is the explicit meaning of the veil as a symbol of man's secret sin, with Hooper as Everyman bearing his lonely fate in order to demonstrate a tragic truth; and there is the implicit one of human unbalance, with Hooper's action out of all proportion to need or benefit. The story, says Mr. Fogle, remains ambiguous with the discrepancies in meaning unresolved—albeit an effective lack of resolution. A footnote to Mr. Fogle's argument is Mr. Walsh's comment on the minister's dubious smile, a recurrent element in the story.[6] The smile, always linked with light, though consistently faint, stands in opposition to the veil, always linked with darkness, and produces, says Mr. Walsh, a fundamental ambiguity. Both Mr. Stewart and Mr. Van Doren, in general discussions of Hawthorne's tales, imply that Hooper is perhaps guilty of some spiritually wrong attitude.[7]

That Hooper is in some way in the wrong seems an inescapable conclusion from any careful reading of the story, but some qualification is called for in each of the criticisms presenting this third view. Mr. Stein's low estimate of Hooper must in general be accepted, but because of Hawthorne's humanistic emphasis in this story as well as elsewhere it is very difficult to see Hooper as an antichrist; Mr. Stein makes Hawthorne too orthodox. And the argument for the II Corinthians analogue remains speculative. What Mr. Fogle says about the minister's unbalance is valid, but perhaps less so his judgment about the meaning of the tale as a whole. Against his claim of "discrepancies," of a basic ambiguity, must be asserted the essential unity of the tale. The irony is strongly unifying, not only in tone but also in meaning. Hawthorne here is his usually detached self, but this artistic distance is not noncommittalism. In general too much has been made of Hawthorne's ambiguity in theme. Often he employs ambiguity in details and is ambiguous in total philosophy revealed, but only very rarely does ambiguity qualify a specific theme. Finally, Mr. Walsh's assumption, in his point of ambiguity in the smile-light and veil-dark imagery, that Hawthorne uses light to suggest something spiritually positive, is acceptable. But most readers will not find the smile a true smile or the light clearly light, as the faintness of the whole image makes evident; there is a peculiarly mixed quality about the smile itself—indeed something ironic.

The ironic meaning of "The Minister's Black Veil" is incorporated in and, in part, is created by its vertical or logical structure. Out of the first level of meaning, the calling of attention to the truth of man's proneness to the sin of concealment, rises the second level, the minister's sin in making his veil demonstration all-important; and this second level, with its irony, absorbs the first, creating a dominant theme.[8] An analysis that seeks to offer evidence of this unity of form and meaning can best be presented by following the horizontal or chronological structure of the tale—the successive divisions of its narrative development. Narrative sequence and timing are very important here and have usually been neglected in the religious and philosophical discussions of the story. There are five divisions: (1) the first appearance of Hooper wearing the veil at the Sunday morning service; (2) Hooper's appearances at the funeral and at the wedding on the same Sunday; (3) the unsuccessful effort of a deputation from the congregation, and of Elizabeth, his fiancée, to reason with him about the veil; (4) a summary picture of Hooper's life from the time of these efforts to his death; (5) the deathbed scene. In each of these divisions the two levels of meaning are ironically united to produce a singleness of theme.

At the beginning of the first division the minister is revealed as experiencing a twofold alienation—from man and from God. Because of the strange veil the members of the congregation sense the minister's distance, and he, in turn, sees them darkly. Also the veil comes between him and God as he reads the Scripture and as he prays. That Hooper's estrangement is the first point established in the story suggests the central importance of the minister's second-level sin. In Hawthorne, isolation of one kind or another is consistently presented as the result of sin, and at times as being something very close to sin itself, a sin frequently linked with intellectual or spiritual pride. Here Hooper's alienation argues that the wearing of the veil is in some way profoundly wrong. And under this second level of meaning lies the more briefly developed first level, the veil as the symbol of hidden guilt, which is introduced by the sermon with its condemnation of secret sin.

Not only are the two levels thus established but so also is their ironic relationship. While the one sin is consciously preached (through veil parable and sermon), the second sin is unconsciously embodied (through the minister's egotistic assumptions and actions). Emphasis is upon the minister's pride that leads him to make the truth of man's hypocrisy the only Truth and brings him to force his idea upon the consciousness and conscience of his congregation. For example, though the sermon is supposedly praised as one of the most powerful that the minister has preached, the minister himself is described as creeping upon the members of the congregation behind his awful veil and discovering the hoarded iniquity of each one. In this, Hooper is close to Hawthorne's most damning sin—"the human invasion of the sanctity of the human heart," to use Dimmesdale's description of Chillingworth's sin. That Hooper is acting professionally increases rather than lessens the sin, for as a minister he should have been spiritually more sensitive. Indeed he is like a number of other Hawthorne sinners who ". . . in their attempt to assume the role of God . . . naturally give their allegiance to Satan, and subsequently find themselves contributing to that very imperfection which they had originally wished to eliminate."[9] The irony here is heightened in that the spiritual wrongdoing pictured by the minister in his sermon describes precisely what he is soon guilty of—hiding his sin "from his nearest and dearest, and from his own consciousness."

In the second division, two contrasting yet representative events of life, a funeral and a wedding, dramatize the meaning of the veil on both levels with their continuing ironic tension. At the funeral, the veil for the only time in the story is a truly appropriate emblem. Apart from its somberness it is appropriate (if we accept the idea of the minister's prayer) because the truth of human secretiveness is one that human beings most fully realize when they are confronted with death. Yet even now the incidents that Poe believed linked the minister with the dead girl in some specific crime—for example, his fear that she will see his face—indicate that the wearing of the veil is not entirely right. As often, Hawthorne uses such ambiguous details to enrich the meaning and heighten the tone of the narrative rather than to establish its main direction. These details underscore the meaning already revealed by emphasizing the unnaturalness of Hooper's action, and they heighten the tone by pointing up the ironic discrepancy between the supposedly helpful intent of the minister and the actual spiritual result.

The unbalance of Hooper in his isolation from normal life and love is strongly in evidence at the wedding, where his wearing of the veil brings fear and doubt, a markedly different effect from the feeling of quiet cheerfulness and sympathy he formerly evoked on such occasions. Hooper's use of the veil to instruct his parishioners religiously has resulted in their spiritual impoverishment in that human love has been diminished. To Hawthorne this is a loss of something holy, for throughout his writings the acceptance or rejection of human love usually marks the choice of salvation or damnation. Mr. Hooper faces this choice and is damned by choosing to live by an idea rather than by human love. His unrepentant insistence upon his abstracted idea as central to life violates the warm reality of human existence.

The irony of Hooper's action is humorously symbolized by the prank of the village youngster who in imitation of the minister puts a black handkerchief over his face and so frightens his playmates that he creates a panic in his own mind. The presence of this satiric element, comparable to the dog's chasing its tail in "Ethan Brand," indicates that Hawthorne has a definite point of view and does not intend the story to be ultimately ambiguous. The two levels of meaning are not allowed to stand in uncommitted balance; ironic tension unites them, the first being subsumed into the second.[10]

In the third division, the story comes to its climax with the two futile attempts to break through the wall of isolation that the minister has erected, one attempt by members of the congregation, the other by Elizabeth, his fiancée. Although the two-level irony is present in each of these efforts, the first underscores more the validity of the veil symbol as intended by the minister, the second, the fact of his sin in making the veil idea all important. Even though Mr. Hooper, heretofore, has been almost too amenable to congregational advice, a deputation of parishioners fails in its mission to question him about the veil. Feeling its symbolic truth, the visitors sit speechless before him, aware that his glance goes into their guilty hearts. But as before with the sermon the effect is less than good, for the minister's attitude and action are essentially unkind. It is not the parishioners' guilt alone that alienates them, for we are told that the minister's veil hung down over his heart. Hooper has changed from exhibiting too great submissiveness to displaying an opposite unbalance, the stubbornness of an essentially weak person obsessed with an idea.

In the succeeding scene, Hooper's response to Elizabeth's questions about the veil and his resistance to her pleas to lay it aside constitute a rejection of her love. Her patient efforts to draw him from his vow to wear the veil as a "type and symbol" meet his gentle but insurmountable obstinacy. In Hawthorne, as suggested earlier, the way to salvation is most frequently the acceptance of human love. Hooper fails to take this way. And his reaction to Elizabeth's tears reveals the sharp irony of his attitude, for it is not the hidden-sin meaning of the veil that causes her grief and terror, as he egocentrically thinks, but the rejection of her love and the irredeemable alienation demonstrated by his refusal, even for a moment, to lift the veil.

Hawthorne's description of the minister as gentle, melancholy, and sad and the quiet style of the story throughout tend to hide the fact that we are face to face with an unbalanced and unredeemed sinner. Although Hawthorne does not dwell upon the antecedent cause of Hooper's "fall," some elements of causation are evident and help to illuminate his character and clarify the irony of the tale. The minister is shown as an essentially weak man, poorly prepared by his unmarried solitude, his somewhat morbid temperament, and his professional position to deal in a stable way with an absorbing religious idea that harmonizes with his personal and vocational prejudices. He finds false strength in a kind of fanaticism, which strength destroys him as a balanced human being.

The fourth and penultimate division of the story offers chiefly the results of the events and attitudes already presented, with the ironic pattern of the previous divisions repeated. Here on the dominant second level is the minister's continued isolation, with the veil as a sign of his peculiar sin; on the first level is the account of his work as a minister, with the veil as a valid symbol of the general sin of human duplicity.

Hooper continues to stand abnormally alone in the community. The veil so envelops him with a cloud of sin or sorrow that neither love nor sympathy can reach him, and he fumbles obscurely within his own heart. But the veil also has the supposedly good result of making him an effective minister by enabling him to enter into the dark emotions of agonized sinners. Still this ability is a dubious good, and the terms "efficient" and "awful power," used to describe the minister's spiritual work, are not entirely flattering. Nor is it praise when the author speaks of the terror rather than consolation that Hooper brings to sinners who come to him for help. His awareness of the truth of hidden sin and sorrow ought to enable him not just to enter the lives of his parishioners but to enter comfortingly; however, when with evident irony he egocentrically insists upon the mechanics of the veil, he largely destroys this good potentiality.

The final division of the story, the account of Hooper's death, continues the ironic and unifying relationship of the two levels of meaning. Quantitatively the emphasis is again upon the second level, for of about a thousand words all except a hundred or so are used to picture the minister's intractability in wearing the veil on into death. Organically, this is the emphasis, too, for the irony of his action while depending upon the hidden-sin aspect so absorbs it that the story as it comes to a close is unambiguously one.

Although various persons, including Elizabeth, attend Hooper's dying moments, he is spiritually alone. Hawthorne leaves little doubt that this loneliness is the result of the minister's unbalanced action; an idea has supplanted life and love: "All through life that piece of crape has hung between him and the world; it has separated him from cheerful brotherhood and woman's love, and kept him in that saddest of all prisons, his own heart; and still it lay upon his face, as to deepen the gloom of the darksome Chamber, and shade him from the sunshine of eternity." In these closing moments of his life, his monomania is so powerful that even amid his convulsive struggles and amid the wanderings of his mind he is desperately careful to keep the veil over his face. And it is still upon his face when he is buried, a token of his final lack of repentance.

Particularly demonstrative of the ironic union of the two levels of meaning is Hooper's delayed defense of his wearing the veil by saying that everyone around him has on his own black veil. The veil is no longer merely a symbol of the fact of hidden sin or sorrow, but it is also, more dominantly, a symbol of Mr. Hooper's prideful adherence to a destructive idea—the sin of a spiritual egotism that enables him to see the mote in another's eye and blinds him to the beam in his own. The irony has become even more complex than this, for things have gone full circle, and added to the double symbolism is the fact that the veil now stands for a new *hidden* sin. Actually, by focusing attention, including the minister's own concern, on the general sin of human concealment the veil has made effective the hiding of the more important personal sin. For the reader of Hawthorne's story, of course, the veil is now the means of communicating the total irony of the minister's action and of establishing the single meaning that the author wishes to convey.

Notes

1. Poe's review of Hawthorne's *Twice-Told Tales, The Complete Works of Edgar Allan Poe,* ed. James A. Harrison (New York, 1902), XI, 111; Schubert, *Hawthorne the Artist: Fine Art Devices in Fiction* (Chapel Hill, 1944), p. 165; Fogle, *Hawthorne's Fiction: The Light and the Dark* (Norman, Okla., 1952), p. 36.

2. Arvin, *Hawthorne* (Boston, 1929), p. 60; Stewart, *The American Notebooks by Nathaniel Hawthorne* (New Haven, 1932), p. xlviii; Voigt, "The Meaning of 'The Minister's Black Veil,' " *College English,* XIII, 337–338 (March, 1952); Van Doren, *Nathaniel Hawthorne* (New York, 1949), p. 87.

3. For example, George Edward Woodberry, *Nathaniel Hawthorne* (New York, 1902), p. 145, and R. R. Male, *Hawthorne's Tragic Vision* (Austin, 1957), p. 17, both of whom note the effect of isolation coupled with that of a shared sense of sin.

4. William Bysshe Stein, "The Parable of the Antichrist in 'The Minister's Black Veil,' " *American Literature,* XXVII, 386–392 (Nov., 1955).

5. Fogle, *Hawthorne's Fiction,* Chapter 3.

6. Thomas Walsh, "Hawthorne: Mr. Hooper's 'Affable Weakness,' " *Modern Language Notes,* LXXIV, 404–406 (May, 1959).

7. Stewart, *Nathaniel Hawthorne: A Biography* (New Haven, 1958), pp. 256–258; Van Doren, *The Best of Hawthorne* (New York, 1951), p. 11. The present view of each of these critics represents an alteration of that in an earlier analysis.

8. Robert Stanton points out that Hawthorne in his four major romances used irony almost exclusively to carry a share of the theme ("Dramatic Irony in Hawthorne's Romances," *Modern Language Notes*, LXXI, 420, June, 1956). See also Robert Allen Durr, "Hawthorne's Ironic Mode," *New England Quarterly*, XXX, 486–495 (Dec., 1957); Durr shows, though not in "The Minister's Black Veil," that Hawthorne is most effectively serious when most deliberately ironic.

9. James E. Miller, Jr., "Hawthorne and Melville: The Unpardonable Sin," *PMLA*, LXX, 93 (March, 1955). Miller's catalogue of Hawthorne's unpardonable sinners does not include Hooper.

10. Cf. Chester E. Eisinger's comment: "To unroll a series of antithetical statements and maintain them in balance by the very tension they themselves generate is typical of Hawthorne's complex and suggestive technique" ("Hawthorne as Champion of the Middle Way," *New England Quarterly*, XXVII, 34–35, March, 1954). It is appropriate to mention here that in a brief comment on "The Minister's Black Veil" Mr. Eisinger approaches the idea of the tale as ironic. He states that paradoxically the minister's "idiosyncratic aberration reveals the universal truth" of the ambiguity and the irresistible power of sin (*ibid.*, pp. 28–29).

Women Beware Science: "The Birthmark"

Judith Fetterley*

The scientist Aylmer in Nathaniel Hawthorne's "The Birthmark" . . . is squarely confronted with the realities of marriage, sex, and women. There are compensations, however, for as an adult he has access to a complex set of mechanisms for accomplishing the great American dream of eliminating women. It is testimony at once to Hawthorne's ambivalence, his seeking to cover with one hand what he uncovers with the other, and to the pervasive sexism of our culture that most readers would describe "The Birthmark" as a story of failure rather than as the success story it really is—the demonstration of how to murder your wife and get away with it. It is, of course, possible to read "The Birthmark" as a story of misguided idealism, a tale of the unhappy consequences of man's nevertheless worthy passion for perfecting and transcending nature; and this is the reading usually given it.[1] This reading, however, ignores the significance of the form idealism takes in the story. It is not irrelevant that "The Birthmark" is about a man's desire to perfect his wife, nor is it accidental that the consequence of this idealism is the wife's death. In fact, "The Birthmark" provides a brilliant analysis of the sexual politics of idealization

* Reprinted from *The Resisting Reader: A Feminist Approach to American Fiction* (Bloomington: Indiana University Press, 1978), 22–33.

and a brilliant exposure of the mechanisms whereby hatred can be disguised as love, neurosis can be disguised as science, murder can be disguised as idealization, and success can be disguised as failure. Thus, Hawthorne's insistence in his story on the metaphor of disguise serves as both warning and clue to a feminist reading.

Even a brief outline is suggestive. A man, dedicated to the pursuit of science, puts aside his passion in order to marry a beautiful woman. Shortly after the marriage he discovers that he is deeply troubled by a tiny birthmark on her left cheek. Of negligible importance to him before marriage, the birthmark now assumes the proportions of an obsession. He reads it as a sign of the inevitable imperfection of all things in nature and sees in it a challenge to man's ability to transcend nature. So nearly perfect as she is, he would have her be completely perfect. In pursuit of this lofty aim, he secludes her in chambers that he has converted for the purpose, subjects her to a series of influences, and finally presents her with a potion which, as she drinks it, removes at last the hated birthmark but kills her in the process. At the end of the story Georgiana is both perfect and dead.

One cannot imagine this story in reverse—that is, a woman's discovering an obsessive need to perfect her husband and deciding to perform experiments on him—nor can one imagine the story being about a man's conceiving such an obsession for another man. It is woman, and specifically woman as wife, who elicits the obsession with imperfection and the compulsion to achieve perfection, just as it is man, and specifically man as husband, who is thus obsessed and compelled. In addition, it is clear from the summary that the imagined perfection is purely physical. Aylmer is not concerned with the quality of Georgiana's character or with the state of her soul, for he considers her "fit for heaven without tasting death." Rather, he is absorbed in her physical appearance, and perfection for him is equivalent to physical beauty. Georgiana is an exemplum of woman as beautiful object, reduced to and defined by her body. And finally, the conjunction of perfection and nonexistence . . . develops [the point] that the only good woman is a dead one and that the motive underlying the desire to perfect is the need to eliminate. "The Birthmark" demonstrates the fact that the idealization of women has its source in a profound hostility toward women and that it is at once a disguise for this hostility and the fullest expression of it.

The emotion that generates the drama of "The Birthmark" is revulsion. Aylmer is moved not by the vision of Georgiana's potential perfection but by his horror at her present condition. His revulsion for the birthmark is insistent: he can't bear to see it or touch it; he has nightmares about it; he has to get it out. Until she is "fixed," he can hardly bear the sight of her and must hide her away in secluded chambers which he visits only intermittently, so great is his fear of contamination. Aylmer's compulsion to perfect Georgiana is a result of his horrified perception of what she actually is, and all his lofty talk about wanting her to be perfect so that just this once the potential of Nature will be fulfilled is but a cover for his central emotion of revulsion. But Aylmer is a creature of disguise and illusion. In order to persuade this beautiful woman to become his wife, he "left his laboratory to the care of an assistant, cleared his fine countenance from the furnace smoke, washed the stains of acid from his fingers." Best not to let her know who he really is or what he really feels, lest she might say before the marriage instead of after, "You cannot love what shocks you!" In the chambers where Aylmer secludes Georgiana, "airy figures, absolutely bodiless ideas, and forms of unsubstantial beauty" come disguised as substance in an illusion so nearly perfect as to "warrant the belief that her husband possessed sway over the spiritual world." While Aylmer does not really possess sway over the spiritual world, he certainly controls Georgiana and he does so in great part because of his mastery of the art of illusion.

If the motive force for Aylmer's action in the story is repulsion, it is the birthmark that is the symbolic location of all that repels him. And it is important that the birthmark is just that: a birth *mark*, that is, something physical; and a *birth* mark, that is, something not acquired but inherent, one of Georgiana's givens, in fact equivalent to her.[2] The close connection between Georgiana and her birthmark is continually emphasized. As her emotions change, so does the birthmark, fading or deepening in response to her feelings and providing a precise clue to her state of mind. Similarly, when her senses are aroused, stroked by the influences that pervade her chamber, the birthmark throbs sympathetically. In his efforts to get rid of the birthmark Aylmer has "administered agents powerful enough to do aught except change your entire physical system," and these have failed. The object of Aylmer's obsessive revulsion, then, is Georgiana's "physical system," and what defines this particular system is the fact that it is female. It is Georgiana's female physiology, which is to say her sexuality, that is the object of Aylmer's relentless attack. The link between Georgiana's birthmark and her sexuality is implicit in the birthmark's role as her emotional barometer, but one specific characteristic of the birthmark makes the connection explicit: the hand which shaped Georgiana's birth has left its mark on her in *blood*. The birthmark is redolent with references to the particular nature of female sexuality; we hardly need Aylmer's insistence on seclusion, with its reminiscences of the treatment of women when they are "unclean," to point us in this direction. What repels Aylmer is Georgiana's sexuality; what is imperfect in her is the fact that she is female; and what perfection means is elimination.

In Hawthorne's analysis the idealization of women stems from a vision of them as hideous and unnatural; it is a form of compensation, an attempt to bring them up to the level of nature. To symbolize female physiology as a blemish, a deformity, a birthmark suggests that women are in need of some such redemption. Indeed, "The Birthmark" is a parable of woman's relation to the cult of female beauty, a cult whose political function is to remind women that they are, in their natural state, unacceptable, imperfect, monstrous. Una Stannard in "The Mask of Beauty" has done a brilliant job of analyzing the implications of this cult:

> Every day, in every way, the billion-dollar beauty business tells women they are monsters in disguise. Every ad for bras tells a woman that her breasts need lifting, every ad for padded bras that what she's got isn't big enough, every ad for girdles that her belly sags and her hips are too wide, every ad for high heels that her legs need propping, every ad for cosmetics that her skin is too dry, too oily, too pale, or too ruddy, or her lips are not bright enough, or her lashes not long enough, every ad for deodorants and perfumes that her natural odors all need disguising, every ad for hair dye, curlers, and permanents that the hair she was born with is the wrong color or too straight or too curly, and lately ads for wigs tell her that she would be better off covering up nature's mistake completely. In this culture women are told they are the fair sex, but at the same time that their "beauty" needs lifting, shaping, dyeing, painting, curling, padding. Women are really being told that "the beauty" is a beast.[3]

The dynamics of idealization are beautifully contained in an analogy which Hawthorne, in typical fashion, remarks on casually: "But it would be as reasonable to say that one of those small blue stains which sometimes occur in the purest statuary marble would convert the Eve of Powers to a monster." This comparison, despite its apparent protest against just such a conclusion, implies that where women are concerned it doesn't take much to convert purity into monstrosity; Eve herself is a classic example of the ease with which such a transition can occur. And the transition is easy because the presentation of woman's image in marble is essentially an attempt to disguise and cover a monstrous reality. Thus, the slightest flaw will have an immense effect, for it serves as a reminder of the reality that produces the continual need to cast Eve in the form of purest marble and women in the molds of idealization.

In exploring the sources of men's compulsion to idealize women Hawthorne is writing a story about the sickness of men, not a story about the flawed and imperfect nature of women. There is a hint of the nature of Aylmer's ailment in the description of his relation to "mother" Nature, a suggestion that his revulsion for Georgiana has its root in part in a jealousy of the power which her sexuality represents and a frustration in the face of its inpenetrable mystery. Aylmer's scientific aspirations have as their ultimate goal the desire to create human life, but "the latter pursuit, however, Aylmer had long laid aside in unwilling recognition of the truth—against which all seekers sooner or later stumble—that our great creative Mother, while she amuses us with apparently working in the broadest sunshine, is yet severely careful to keep her own secrets, and, in spite of her pretended openness, shows us nothing but results. She permits us, indeed, to mar, but seldom to mend, and, like a jealous patentee, on no account to make." This passage is striking for its undercurrent of jealousy, hostility, and frustration toward a specifically female force. In the vision of Nature as playing with man, deluding him into thinking he can acquire her power, and then at the last minute closing him off and allowing him only the role of one who mars, Hawthorne provides another version of woman as enemy, the force that interposes between man and the accomplishment of his deepest desires. Yet Hawthorne locates the source of this attitude in man's jealousy of woman's having something he does not and his rage at being excluded from participating in it.

Out of Aylmer's jealousy at feeling less than Nature and thus less than woman—for if Nature is woman, woman is also Nature and has, by virtue of her biology, a power he does not—comes his obsessional program for perfecting Georgiana. Believing he is less, he has to convince himself he is more: "and then, most beloved, what will be my triumph when I shall have corrected what Nature left imperfect in her fairest work! Even Pygmalion, when his sculptured woman assumed life, felt not greater ecstasy than mine will be." What a triumph indeed to upstage and outdo Nature and make himself superior to her. The function of the fantasy that underlies the myth of Pygmalion, as it underlies the myth of Genesis (making Adam, in the words of Mary Daly, "the first among history's unmarried pregnant males"[4]), is obvious from the reality which it seeks to invert. Such myths are powerful image builders, salving man's injured ego by convincing him that he is not only equal to but better than woman, for he creates in spite of, against, and finally better than nature. Yet Aylmer's failure here is as certain as the failure of his other "experiments," for the sickness which he carries within him makes him able only to destroy, not to create.

If Georgiana is envied and hated because she represents what is different from Aylmer and reminds him of what he is not and cannot be, she is feared for her similarity to him and for the fact that she represents aspects of himself that he finds intolerable. Georgiana is as much a reminder to Aylmer of what he is as of what he is not. This apparently contradictory pattern of double-duty is understandable in the light of feminist analyses of female characters in literature, who frequently function this way. Mirrors for men, they serve to indicate the involutions of the male psyche with which literature is primarily concerned, and their characters and identities shift accordingly. They are projections, not people; and thus coherence of characterization is a concept that often makes sense only when applied to the male characters of a particular work. Hawthorne's tale is a classic example of the woman as mirror, for, despite Aylmer's belief that his response to Georgiana is an objective concern for the intellectual and spiritual problem she presents, it is obvious that his reaction to her is intensely subjective. "Shocks you, my husband?" queries Georgiana, thus neatly exposing his mask, for one is not shocked by objective perceptions. Indeed, Aylmer views Georgiana's existence as a personal insult and threat to him, which, of course, it is, because what he sees in her is that part of himself he cannot tolerate. By the desire she elicits in him to marry her and possess her birthmark, she forces him to confront his own earthiness and "imperfection."

But it is precisely to avoid such a confrontation that Aylmer has fled to the kingdom of science, where he can project himself as a "type of the spiritual element." Unlike Georgiana, in whom the physical and the spiritual are completely intertwined, Aylmer is hopelessly alienated from himself. Through the figure of Aminadab, the shaggy creature of clay, Hawthorne presents sharply the image of Aylmer's alienation. Aminadab symbolizes that earthly, physical, erotic self that has been split off from Aylmer, that he refuses to recognize as part of himself, and that has become monstrous and grotesque as a result: "With his vast strength, his shaggy hair, his smoky aspect, and the indescribable earthiness that incrusted him, he seemed to represent man's physical nature; while Aylmer's slender figure, and pale, intellectual face, were no less apt a type of the spiritual element." Aminadab's allegorical function is obvious and so is his connection to Aylmer, for while Aylmer may project himself as objective, intellectual, and scientific and while he may pretend to be totally unrelated to the creature whom he keeps locked up in his dark room to do his dirty work, he cannot function without him. It is Aminadab, after all, who fires the furnace for Aylmer's experiments; physicality provides the energy for Aylmer's "science" just as revulsion generates his investment in idealization. Aylmer is, despite his pretenses to the contrary, a highly emotional man: his scientific interests tend suspiciously toward fires and volcanoes; he is given to intense emotional outbursts; and his obsession with his wife's birthmark is a feeling so profound as to disrupt his entire life. Unable to accept himself for what he is, Aylmer constructs a mythology of science and adopts the character of a scientist to disguise his true nature and to hide his real motives, from himself as well as others. As a consequence, he acquires a way of acting out these motives without in fact having to be aware of them. One might describe "The Birthmark" as an exposé of science because it demonstrates the ease with which science can be invoked to conceal highly subjective motives. "The Birthmark" is an exposure of the realities that underlie the scientist's posture of objectivity and rationality and the claims of science to operate in an amoral and value-free world. Pale Aylmer, the intellectual scientist, is a mask for the brutish, earthy, soot-smeared Aminadab, just as the mythology of scientific research and objectivity finally masks murder, disguising Georgiana's death as just one more experiment that failed.

. . . Hawthorne has not omitted from his treatment of men an image of the consequences of their ailments for the women who are involved with them. The result of Aylmer's massive self-deception is to live in an unreal world, a world filled with illusions, semblances, and appearances, one which admits of no sunlight and makes no contact with anything outside itself and at whose center is a laboratory, the physical correlative of his utter solipsism. Nevertheless, Hawthorne makes it clear that Aylmer has got someone locked up in that laboratory with him. While "The Birthmark" is by no means explicitly feminist, since Hawthorne seems as eager to be misread and to conceal as he is to be read and to reveal, still it is impossible to read his story without being aware that Georgiana is completely in Aylmer's power. For the subject is finally power. Aylmer is able to project himself onto Georgiana and to work out his obsession through her because as woman and as wife she is his possession and in his power; and because as man he has access to the language and structures of that science which provides the mechanisms for such a process and legitimizes it. In addition, since the power of definition and the authority to make those definitions stick is vested in men, Aylmer can endow his illusions with the weight of spiritual aspiration and universal truth.

The implicit feminism in "The Birthmark" is considerable. On one level the story is a study of sexual politics, of the powerlessness of women and of the psychology which results from that powerlessness. Hawthorne dramatizes the fact that woman's identity is a product of men's responses to her: "It must not be concealed, however, that the impression wrought by this fairy sign manual varied exceedingly, according to the difference of temperament in the beholders." To those who love Georgiana, her birthmark is evidence of her beauty; to those who envy or hate her, it is an object of disgust. It is Aylmer's repugnance for the birthmark that makes Georgiana blanch, thus causing the mark to emerge as a sharply-defined blemish against the whiteness of her cheek. Clearly, the birthmark takes on its character from the eye of the beholder. And just as clearly Georgiana's attitude toward her birthmark varies in response to different observers and definers. Her self-image derives from internalizing the attitudes toward her of the man or men around her. Since what surrounds Georgiana is an obsessional attraction expressed as a total revulsion, the result is not surprising: continual self-consciousness that leads to a pervasive sense of shame and a self-hatred that terminates in an utter readiness to be killed. "The Birthmark" demonstrates the consequences to women of being trapped in the laboratory of man's mind, the object of unrelenting scrutiny, examination, and experimentation.

In addition, "The Birthmark" reveals an implicit understanding of the consequences for women of a linguistic system in which the word "man" refers to both male people and all people. Because of the conventions of this system, Aylmer is able to equate his peculiarly male needs with the needs of all human beings, men and women. And since Aylmer can present his compulsion to idealize and perfect Georgiana as a human aspiration, Georgiana is forced to identify with it. Yet to identify with his aspiration is in fact to identify with his hatred of her and his need to eliminate her. Georgiana's situation is a fictional version of the experience that women undergo when they read a story like "Rip Van Winkle." Under the influence of Aylmer's mind, in the laboratory where she is subjected to his subliminal messages, Georgiana is co-opted into a view of herself as flawed and comes to hate herself as an impediment to Aylmer's aspiration; eventually she wishes to be dead rather than to remain alive as an irritant to him and as a reminder of his failure. And as she identifies with him in her attitude toward herself, so she comes to worship him for his hatred of her and for his refusal to tolerate her existence. The process of projection is neatly reversed: he locates in her everything he cannot accept in himself, and she attributes to him all that is good and then worships in him the image of her own humanity.

Through the system of sexual politics that is Aylmer's compensation for growing up, Hawthorne shows how men gain power over women, the power to create and kill, to "mar," "mend," and "make," without ever having to relinquish their image as "nice guys." Under such a system there need be very few power struggles, because women are programmed to deny the validity of their own perceptions and responses and to accept male illusions as truth. Georgiana does faint when she first enters Aylmer's laboratory and sees it for one second with her own eyes; she is also aware that Aylmer is filling her chamber with appearances, not realities; and she is finally aware that his scientific record is in his own terms one of continual failure. Yet so perfect is the program that she comes to respect him even more for these failures and to aspire to be yet another of them.

Hawthorne's unrelenting emphasis on "seems" and his complex use of the metaphors and structures of disguise imply that women are being deceived and destroyed by man's system. And perhaps the most vicious part of this system is its definition of what constitutes nobility in women: "Drink, then, thou lofty creature," exclaims Aylmer with "fervid admiration" as he hands Georgiana the cup that will kill her. Loftiness in women is directly equivalent to the willingness with which they die at the hands of their husbands, and since such loftiness is the only thing about Georgiana which does elicit admiration from Aylmer, it is no wonder she is willing. Georgiana plays well the one role allowed her, yet one might be justified in suggesting that Hawthorne grants her at the end a slight touch of the satisfaction of revenge: " 'My poor Aylmer,' she repeated, with a more than human tenderness, 'you have aimed loftily; you have done nobly. Do not repent that with so high and pure a feeling, you have rejected the best the earth could offer.' " Since dying is the only option, best to make the most of it.

Notes

1. See, for example, Brooks and Warren, *Understanding Fiction* (New York: Appleton-Century-Croft, 1943), pp. 103–106: "We are not, of course, to conceive of Aylmer as a monster, a man who would experiment on his own wife for his own greater glory. Hawthorne does not mean to suggest that Aylmer is depraved and heartless. . . . Aylmer has not realized that perfection is something never achieved on earth and in terms of mortality"; Richard Harter Fogle, *Hawthorne's Fiction: The Light and The Dark*, rev. ed. (Norman, Okla.: University of Oklahoma Press, 1964), pp. 117–31; Robert Heilman, "Hawthorne's 'The Birthmark': Science as Religion," *South Atlantic Quarterly* 48 (1949), 575–83: "Alymer, the overweening scientist, resembles less the villain than the tragic hero: in his catastrophic attempt to improve on human actuality there is not only pride and a deficient sense of reality but also disinterested aspiration"; F.O. Matthiessen, *American Renaissance* (New York: Oxford University Press, 1941), pp. 253–55; Arlin Turner, *Nathaniel Hawthorne* (New York: Holt, Rinehart, and Winston, 1961), pp. 88, 98, 132: "In 'The Birthmark' he applauded Aylmer's noble pursuit of perfection, in contrast to Aminadab's ready acceptance of earthiness, but Aylmer's achievement was tragic failure because he had not realized that perfection is not of this world." The major variation in these readings occurs as a result of the degree to which individual critics see Hawthorne as critical of Aylmer. Still, those who see Hawthorne as critical locate the source of his criticism in Aylmer's idealistic pursuit of perfection—e.g., Millicent Bell, *Hawthorne's View of the Artist* (New York: State University of New York, 1962), pp. 182–85: "Hawthorne, with his powerful Christian sense of the inextricable mixture of evil in the human compound, regards Aylmer as a dangerous perfectibilitarian"; William Bysshe Stein, *Hawthorne's Faust* (Gainesville: University of Florida Press, 1953), pp. 91–92: "Thus the first of Hawthorne's Fausts, in a purely symbolic line of action sacrifices his soul to conquer nature, the universal force of which man is but a tool." Even Simon Lesser, *Fiction and the Unconscious* (1957: rpt. New York: Vintage-Random, 1962), pp. 87–90 and pp. 94–98, who is clearly aware of the sexual implications of the story, subsumes his analysis under the reading of misguided idealism and in so doing provides a fine

instance of phallic criticism in action: "The ultimate purpose of Hawthorne's attempt to present Aylmer in balanced perspective is to quiet our fears so that the wishes which motivate his experiment, which are also urgent, can be given their opportunity. Aylmer's sincerity and idealism give us a sense of kinship with him. We see that the plan takes shape gradually in his mind, almost against his conscious intention. We are reassured by the fact that he loves Georgiana and feels confident that his attempt to remove the birthmark will succeed. Thus at the same time that we recoil we can identify with Aylmer and through him act out some of our secret desires. . . . The story not only gives expression to impulses which are ordinarily repressed; it gives them a sympathetic hearing—an opportunity to show whether they can be gratified without causing trouble or pain. There are obvious gains in being able to conduct tests of this kind with no more danger and no greater expenditure of effort than is involved in reading a story." The one significant dissenting view is offered by Frederick Crews, *The Sins of the Fathers* (New York: Oxford University Press, 1966), whose scattered comments on the story focus on the specific form of Aylmer's idealism and its implications for his secret motives.

2. In the conventional reading of the story Georgiana's birthmark is seen as the symbol of original sin—see, for example, Heilman, p. 579; Bell, p. 185. But what this reading ignores are, of course, the implications of the fact that the symbol of original sin is female and that the story only "works" because men have the power to project that definition onto women.

3. Gornick and Moran, *Woman in Sexist Society*, p. 192.

4. Mary Daly, *Beyond God the Father*, p. 195.

Hawthorne and His Artist   R. A. Yoder°

Critics of American literature may be on the verge of a broad controversy about the nineteenth century. Committed to the idea of an American Renaissance, they are not all committed to the special interpretation of it given by those who may be called the "ironist" school or the school of "blackness": the interpretation that attacks Emerson for his vague Romantic optimism and then goes on to admire the complex subtleties by which Hawthorne and Melville display their wiser, more detached views of life. For Hawthorne, the British critic Martin Green states the case pointedly: "We have had nearly half a century of anti-Emersonianism, and Hawthorne's reputation is one of the major forms it has taken."[1]

It is time, I think, to remember that Melville and to a greater extent Hawthorne had deep roots in the American Romantic tradition. For Hawthorne, these roots are most clearly exposed in a tale written at the midpoint of his career, "The Artist of the Beautiful." The situation for this tale has an analogue, if not a source, in Emerson's essay "The Poet":

° Reprinted from *Studies in Romanticism* 7 (1968): 193–206. Courtesy Trustees of Boston University.

> . . . when the soul of the poet has come to ripeness of thought, she detaches and sends away from it its poems or songs—a fearless, sleepless, deathless progeny, which is not exposed to the accidents of the weary kingdom of time; a fearless, vivacious offspring, clad with wings (such was the virtue of the soul out of which they came) which carry them fast and far, and infix them irrecoverably into the hearts of men. These wings are the beauty of the poet's soul. The songs, thus flying immortal from their mortal parent, are pursued by clamorous flights of censures, which swarm in far greater numbers and threaten to devour them; but these last are not winged. At the end of a very short leap they fall plump down and rot, having received from the souls out of which they came no beautiful wings. But the melodies of the poet ascend and leap and pierce into the deeps of infinite time.[2]

The difference, of course, is that in "The Artist of the Beautiful" Owen Warland's butterfly, detached from its master's soul, perishes in the midst of the Danforths and Hovendens; here the "censures" are victorious, or so it seems to the modern ironist critics, who can then define the tale as "anti-Emersonian." What I suggest is that despite this difference Hawthorne's view of the artist is closer to Emerson's than it is to the critics'; and that the conclusion of this tale is as Romantic as its basic situation because Owen is ultimately the victor.

1

A review of the recent interpretations of "The Artist of the Beautiful" shows the ironists in command, thanks especially to a general theory about Hawthorne elaborated by Frederick Crews in *The Sins of the Fathers* and to Ronald Curran's detailed study of this tale. Both present ingenious arguments and impressive evidence about the story, much of which I would grant; what I question is their general conclusion that Owen Warland's victory must be a hollow one, that the ending of the story must be read ironically. Crews, of course, wants to fit the story into the general pattern of psychoanalytic readings he gives: Owen sublimates his real sexual desires, turning to "the ideal only as a refuge from his weakness of temperament and physique"; Owen is summed up in Crews' earlier remark that for Hawthorne "the idealist is invariably an escapist."[3] Curran, too, stresses Owen's failure: noting that earlier interpretations agreed on Owen's triumph in the end, Curran finds that "emotionally he [Owen] is less than satisfied with his achievement; his sense of victory is less superlative than the narrator describes."[4]

Owen does resemble some of Hawthorne's other artistic or scientific idealists who are unsuccessful in their quests—particularly

Aylmer, also Rappaccini and Giovanni, and the painter of "The Prophetic Pictures."[5] Like Aylmer, Owen is pale and slight of build, perhaps the result of his devotion to the work that Peter Hovenden calls a "flight beyond his usual foolery," an attempt at "the perpetual motion." Drawn into his own world, Owen rejects the strength and power of Robert Danforth's world, and implicitly its sexuality. He expresses "distaste at the stiff and regular processes of ordinary machinery," he "shrinks" before the virile blacksmith, denying a wish for any sort of paternity; he hardly dares to touch old Hovenden's two precious objects, his watch and his daughter Annie, whom Owen idealizes into an inspiring muse. The appropriate underlying source of his energy is hinted at—an interruption of his work would bring "vague and unsatisfied dreams which will leave me spiritless tomorrow." Owen must not allow his sexual libido to spill over, for his pent-up desire is the real source of his artistic-scientific energy.

There is this much irony attached to Owen, but surely there is ironic comment directed at the other characters as well. No one maintains, for example, that Hawthorne shared Peter Hovenden's crassness: "Peter Hovenden shook his head, with the mixture of contempt and indignation which mankind, of whom he was partly a representative, deem themselves entitled to feel towards all simpletons who seek other prizes than the dusty one along the highway. He then took his leave, with an uplifted finger and a sneer upon his face that haunted the artist's dreams for many a night afterwards."[6] And R. H. Fogle rightly emphasizes[7] that the child of Danforth and Annie, who finally smashes the butterfly, is the re-creation of old Hovenden with "the grandsire's sharp and shrewd expression." If Owen resembles Aylmer, Robert Danforth is like Aminadab, but without any wildness or violence. He is domesticated brute strength with a "full, deep, merry voice." And he is simply unaware of any other level of existence—Danforth does not realize the whole meaning of his own exclamation on seeing the butterfly, "Well, that does beat all nature." Annie is like Danforth, kind but imperceptive. She has a certain intuition that rises above the ordinary world, Owen thinks, when he takes seriously her notion that he would spiritualize matter. Later he learns that her intuition is really "a creature of his own," and in the final scene of the story he dissects Annie more shrewdly: "Owen Warland, meanwhile, glanced sidelong at Annie, to discover whether she sympathized in her husband's estimate of the comparative value of the beautiful and the practical. There was, amid all her kindness towards himself, amid all the wonder and admiration with which she contemplated the marvellous work of his hands and incarnation of his idea, a secret scorn—too secret, perhaps, for her own consciousness, and perceptible only to such intuitive discernment as that of the artist" (p. 532). Here Owen is able to separate Annie's personable qualities from her own unconscious scorn for all impractical beauty, and thus he recognizes her as another "representative of the world" (p. 532, cf. p. 515).

Precisely this limitation in Annie is demonstrated when she tries to grasp the little whirligig Owen has been working on:

> "Hold!" exclaimed Owen, "hold!"
>
> Annie had but given the slightest possible touch, with the point of a needle, to the same minute portion of complicated machinery which has been more than once mentioned, when the artist seized her by the wrist with a force that made her scream aloud. She was affrighted at the convulsion of intense rage and anguish that writhed across his features. The next instant he let his head sink upon his hands.
>
> "Go, Annie," murmured he; "I have deceived myself and must suffer for it. I yearned for sympathy, and thought, and fancied, and dreamed that you might give it me; but you lack the talisman, Annie, that should admit you into my secrets. That touch has undone the toil of months and the thought of a lifetime! It was not your fault, Annie; but you have ruined me!"
>
> Poor Owen Warland! He had indeed erred, yet pardonably; for if any human spirit could have sufficiently reverenced the processes so sacred in his eyes, it must have been a woman's. Even Annie Hovenden, possibly, might not have disappointed him had she been enlightened by the deep intelligence of love. (pp. 518–519)

This scene parallels one between Giovanni and Beatrice in "Rappaccini's Daughter" (p. 132), but significantly the roles are reversed. Owen acts Beatrice's part, and if Beatrice was right about Giovanni ("Was there not more poison in thy nature than in mine?" she says, and Crews, for example, supports her judgment[8]), then Owen is even more clearly right about Annie. Annie and Giovanni are both incapable of the deepest love (pp. 123, 133, 519). The analogy suggests further that if Giovanni suffered by repressing physical instincts, so do Annie and her kind—"representatives" of the world or mankind at large—suffer by repressing imagination.

The ordinary domestic life exemplified by the Hovendens and Danforths is not associated with Hawthorne's famous heart, and is not the basic value affirmed in "The Artist of the Beautiful,"[9] for this ordinary world represses rather than warms. Hovenden and Danforth are "steady and matter-of-fact people who hold the opinion that time is not to be trifled with"; they belong to the "order of sagacious understandings who think that life should be regulated, like clockwork, with leaden weights. . . ." For a brief period in the story even Owen joins them: "[Then] the heavy weight upon his spirits kept everything in order, not merely within his own system, but wheresoever the iron accents of the church clock were audible. It was a circumstance, though minute, yet characteristic of his present state, that, when employed to engrave names or initials on silver spoons, he now wrote the requisite letters in the plainest possible style, omitting a variety of fanciful flourishes that had heretofore distinguished his work in this kind" (p. 513).

Here the plain Puritan style signifies the suppression of art; later the "fanciful tracery" of the jewel box and the elaborate beauty of the butterfly invite comparison with the "elaborate embroidery and fantastic flourishes" that Hester Prynne gave to her letter A: they are both revolts against an oppressive order. Indeed, the key-word "gorgeousness" conveys the rich, almost luxuriant sensuousness of both artifacts, just as it conveys the fierce sensuality of Beatrice and her garden in "Rappaccini's Daughter." And the butterfly's "delicate gorgeousness" signals a triumphant combination of spiritual and physical qualities. The butterfly is a triumph, but a triumph subject to time.

However important the analogies from "The Birthmark" or "Rappaccini's Daughter," the obvious difference also must be taken into account: Beatrice dies, and the subject for Aylmer's investigations, his wife Georgiana, dies too. No one dies in "The Artist of the Beautiful"—only the beautiful butterfly is destroyed. The butterfly is, of course, a symbol of the *psyche*, the artist's soul: " '. . . and in the secret of that butterfly, and in its beauty,—which is not merely outward, but deep as its whole system,—is represented the intellect, the imagination, the sensibility, the soul of an Artist of the Beautiful! Yes; I created it. But'—and here his countenance somewhat changed— 'this butterfly is not now to me what it was when I beheld it afar off in the daydreams of my youth' " (p. 531).

Paying full heed to Owen's disclaimer, we should not be misled into identifying the artist with his work of art, with his product, so to speak. Owen had in an earlier mood branded a host of *automata* as "mere impositions."[10] Now he has unquestionably outdone them, but the doing so has made it clear to him that the butterfly which "represents" the artist's soul is not identical with it. At the last, Owen repudiates the butterfly's attempted return to its "master's heart." The conclusion of the story explicitly separates the outward symbol of the artist's soul from the inward experience of it. To read this inward experience as Platonic is, I think, a mistake.[11] The "far other butterfly than this" is not some vision of the Form of butterflies, nor is it the contemplation of a more general, abstract "Beautiful" to which the artist has been led by successive steps in a Platonic ladder. Rather it is Owen's awareness of what he has done and of the fulfillment of himself in that. Owen's "spirit possessed itself," Hawthorne wrote (it did not possess anything outside itself, like the Platonic Form or Idea); Owen has caught hold of himself, we might say, and is fully in control of himself in "the enjoyment of the reality." The experience, the process of creating and understanding, is "the reality" he appreciates and enjoys.

If we now look back over the story, we may see that Hawthorne took great pains to indicate extended passage of time and development in his central character.[12] The problem is stated early: "It is requisite for the ideal artist to possess a force of character that seems hardly compatible with its delicacy" (p. 512). "For a time Owen succumbed to this . . . test," although we soon learn that "the innate tendency of his soul had only been accumulating fresh vigor during its apparent sluggishness." Then he succumbs again, in the winter, to a kind of imaginative hibernation, living a life of good fellowship that approaches debauchery—again ordinary society fails to sustain the heart. In the spring he is reawakened, by a real butterfly, to the "pure, ideal life." And then, for good measure, the whole process is repeated: Owen falls into a "torpid slumber" where the "spirit was not dead or passed away" but "only slept"; and he awakens "as in a former instance" with renewed strength.

Owen's growth is made plausible by this repetition of incident and by the constant reminders of elapsed time (the most pointed reference coming just before the final interview—"so pass we over a long space . . ."). It is symbolized by the winter-spring metaphor associated with cyclical rebirth, in this case rebirth to artistic activity. But the most convincing measure of growth is in character. Toward the end of the story Owen sees Annie for what she really is, separating her kindly attributes from her deeper failings. In the last interview Owen faces the ordinary world with ease—although he is at first "disturbed" by Hovenden's and the child's look, he is never shaken as he had been earlier by the visits of the blacksmith and the old man. He is in command of himself, standing "calmly" and "placidly" even in the catastrophe. Owen realizes, finally, the conditions of the artist's life and willingly accepts the annihilation of his art.

Just before the catastrophe we learn that "Owen, in the later stages of his pursuit, had risen out of the region" where he would have been tortured to discover Annie's secret scorn. He learned "that the reward of all high performance must be sought within itself, or sought in vain." There are two contrasts here: first, between the art-object as a non-utilitarian value and its material worth, a contrast developed in the rest of the paragraph (pp. 532–533); secondly, between "performance" in the sense of the doing and the product, the result of that doing. It is the second contrast that Owen has come to appreciate in the conclusion of the story.

The same contrast is made by Hawthorne as narrator in a long authorial intrusion just before the concluding interview:

So long as we love life for itself, we seldom dread the losing it. When we desire life for the attainment of an object, we recognize the frailty of its texture. . . . [Although those who seek to attain an object in life have faith that they will live to accomplish it, many in fact die before the object is attained.] . . . The prophet dies, and the man of torpid heart and sluggish brain lives on. The poet leaves his song half sung, or finishes it, beyond the scope of mortal ears, in a celestial choir. The painter—as Allston did—leaves half his conception on the canvas to sadden us with its imperfect beauty, and goes to picture forth the whole, if it be no irreverence to say so, in the hues of heaven. But rather such incomplete designs of this life will be perfected nowhere. This so frequent abortion of man's dearest projects must be taken as a proof that the deeds of earth, however etherealized by piety or genius, are without value, except as exercises and manifestations of the spirit. (pp. 526–527)

Not the product—the "object" or "projects" of one's life—but the living of it, in which a man's unique spirit is manifested, is what matters.

The moral of the tale, then, is that art's highest achievement is to make a man of the artist. Hawthorne is saying that the artistic life is worthwhile even if the artist is unproductive or his work is lost; the artist is still a finer person for it. Given this view, one cannot agree with Curran's reading of the conclusion and surely not with Crews' idea that the victory of art coincides with the failure of manhood.

2

Much that surrounds Hawthorne's writing "The Artist of the Beautiful" argues for the interpretation given here. If the key distinction, in simplest terms, is between life and art, then the story could easily have grown out of Hawthorne's own experience during the years at the Old Manse, when he was happy in life and dissatisfied with his art.

The germ of the story may well be an early passage (editorially dated 1840) in the *American Notebooks* proposing for a subject a man who spends his life "in the accomplishment of some mechanical trifle."[13] But the story was probably not written until at least three years later, if the passage referring to Allston's death (p. 526) is any indication of date.[14] Furthermore, an entry in the *Notebooks* during the spring of 1843 suggests that Owen's alternating moods of inspiration and "torpidity" were also Hawthorne's: "If I had wings I would gladly fly; yet would prefer to be wafted along by a breeze, sometimes alighting on a patch of green grass, then gently whirled away to a still sunnier spot. But here I linger upon earth, very happy, it is true, at bottom, but a good deal troubled with the sense of imbecility—one of the dismallest sensations, methinks, that mortal can experience—the consciousness of a blunted pen, benumbed fingers, and a mind no longer capable of a vigorous grasp. My torpidity of intellect makes me irritable."[15] There are a number of such complaints in the notebooks of 1842–45,[16] culminating in the last paragraphs Hawthorne wrote (in 1846) for his introductory essay to *Mosses from an Old Manse:*

> How narrow—how shallow and scanty too—is the stream of thought that has been flowing from my pen, compared with the broad tide of dim emotions, ideas, and associations which swell around me from that portion of my existence! . . . These fitful sketches, with so little of external life about them, yet claiming no profundity of purpose,—so reserved, even while they sometimes seem so frank,—often but half in earnest, and never, even when most so, expressing satisfactorily the thoughts which they profess to image,—such trifles, I truly feel, afford no solid basis for a literary reputation. (pp. 43, 45)

In what is probably the notebook source of this quotation, the emphasis is less on Hawthorne's personal failing and more on the impossibility of adequately representing life in art:

> And now how narrow, scanty, and meagre, is this record of observation, compared with the immensity that was to be observed, within the bounds which I prescribed to myself. How shallow and small a stream of thought, too,—of distinct and expressed thought—compared with the broad tide of dim emotions, ideas, associations, which were flowing through the haunted regions of imagination, intellect, and sentiment, sometimes excited by what was around me, sometimes with no perceptible connection with them. When we see how little we can express, it is a wonder that any man ever takes up a pen a second time.[17]

The project, the object of life, is bound to fail because the beauty of experience can never be captured.

This inevitable failure is a fact of artistic existence: Hawthorne was no doubt thinking of himself confronting it, but two friends might also have served him for prototypes. First, there is the painter Washington Allston, who is mentioned in the story. Allston was also a poet, probably the first American exponent of Coleridge's aesthetic ideas (including the distinction between imagination and mechanical fancy, which figures prominently in the story), and a close friend of Sophia Hawthorne. His early work in England was a success, but on his return to Boston Allston's talent seemed blighted and his career came to be symbolized by "Belshazzar's Feast," the projected masterpiece he left unfinished at his death.[18] The other friend, the poet

William Ellery Channing, is mentioned not in the story but in the introductory "Old Manse."

> So amid sunshine and shadow, rustling leaves and sighing waters, up gushed our talk like the babble of a fountain. The evanescent spray was Ellery's; and his, too, the lumps of golden thought that lay glimmering in the fountain's bed and brightened both our faces by the reflection. Could he have drawn out that virgin gold and stamped it with the mint mark that alone gives currency, the world might have had the profit, and he the fame. My mind was the richer merely by the knowledge that it was there. But the chief profit of those wild days to him and me lay, not in any definite idea, not in any angular or rounded truth, which we dug out of the shapeless mass of problematical stuff, but in the freedom which we thereby won from all custom and conventionalism and fettering influences of man on man. We were so free today that it was impossible to be slaves again to-morrow.[19]

Channing, as the passage indicates, was notorious among Transcendentalists for being unable to fashion his wonderful thoughts into acceptable poetic form.[20] Hawthorne again suggests that the spirit or character of the artist and the value of intimate association with him are greater than his palpable productions.

As for Hawthorne himself, it became for a time the official version of his life that the man was greater than his art: "If he had never written a line, he would still have possessed, as a human being, scarcely less interest and importance than he does now. . . . Some men are swallowed up by their profession, so that nothing is left of them but the profession in human form. But, for men like Hawthorne, the profession is but a means of activity; they use it and are not used by it."[21] This as biography no doubt needed correction, yet the evidence presented by Hawthorne's journals and published autobiographical essays makes me think that in the 1840s Hawthorne would have been content to accept his son's judgment quoted here. By the end of that decade, when Hawthorne again made public reference to his own circumstances in "The Custom-House," the sketch introductory to *The Scarlet Letter*, his ideas about art and life had not changed. He has failed in the great object of his life—at the Manse, to write deep philosophical works or at least a substantial novel; in the Custom-House, "to spiritualize the burden that began to weigh so heavily; to seek, resolutely, the true and indestructible value that lay hidden in the petty wearisome incidents, and ordinary characters."[22] But in this existence devoid of literary interest there is a lesson, one that Hawthorne implies he knew well enough before returning to Salem:

> It is a good lesson—though it may often be a hard one—for a man who has dreamed of literary fame, and of making for himself a rank

among the world's dignitaries by such means, to step aside out of the narrow circle in which his claims are recognized, and to find how utterly devoid of significance, beyond that circle, is all that he achieves, and all he aims at. I know not that I especially needed the lesson, either in the way of warning or rebuke; but, at any rate, I learned it thoroughly; nor it gives me pleasure to reflect, did the truth, as it came home to my perception, ever cost me a pang, or require to be thrown off in a sigh.[23]

By the time he came to the Custom-House Hawthorne had learned the relative unimportance of his "butterflies," and he could face the dreary world, even the torpidity of his own imagination, without wincing. He had learned it, we may guess, because it is the same lesson and strength of character that he gave to Owen Warland in "The Artist of the Beautiful" some six years before.

3

I have tried to show that biography and close reading support each other in the case of Hawthorne's "Artist of the Beautiful." Given the interpretation and assuming that this tale is a major and typical instance of Hawthorne's art, one must seriously doubt Hawthorne's anti-Emersonianism. The tale, according to this interpretation, rests on a distinction important in Emerson's thought—a distinction which Emerson, interestingly enough, applied to Hawthorne long before it became part of the official biography: "Nathaniel Hawthorne's reputation as a writer is a very pleasing fact, because his writing is not good for anything, and this is a tribute to the man."[24] As Hubert Hoeltje warns, we miss the point here if we assume that Emerson thought art aloof from or superior to life: "rather, he belonged in the tradition of Plato and Plotinus and Milton—believing that character is nature in its highest form."[25] In "The Poet" Emerson spoke confidently of the artist's deathless progeny, the works of art themselves. But a more characteristic utterance comes at the end of the essay "Art," where after praising a variety of works and genres, Emerson turns into his peroration:

> Yet when we have said all our fine things about the arts, we must end with a frank confession that the arts, as we know them, are but initial. Our best praise is given to what they aimed and promised, not to the actual result. . . . There is higher work for Art than the arts. They are abortive births of an imperfect or vitiated instinct. Art is the need to create; but in its essence, immense and universal, it is impatient of working with lame or tied hands, and of making cripples and monsters, such as all pictures and statues are. Nothing less than the creation of man and nature is its end.[26]

If the passage from "The Poet" gives us the situation for "The Artist of the Beautiful," this passage provides the conclusion: the perfection of Art is not the work or object, but the man. Owen Warland may fall short of the messianic hero foreshadowed in many of Emerson's conclusions, for although Owen transcends his former self, there is little chance that he will change the world. Still, Owen is perfected within the limits of Hawthorne's own vision of man, which evidently included many of Emerson's aesthetic and moral ideas but not his cosmic optimism.

It might be added that in the 1840s Emerson as well as Hawthorne was convinced that Nature could never be fully explained. As if to acknowledge Hawthorne's later remark that he "admired Emerson as a poet . . . but sought nothing from him as a philosopher," Emerson wrote in his journal of 1839 that the philosopher must become a poet in order to express the "fluxional quantities and values" of experience.[27] Already a poet in Emerson's broad sense, Hawthorne discovered that the artist was limited in exactly the same way, if not to the same degree, as the philosopher: his words could only approximate things, and therefore his work—even his most miraculous butterfly—would always inadequately express his experience.

Finally, I want to suggest that Emerson and Hawthorne shared a method in addition to sharing a number of Romantic suppositions about art. Emerson's method is a loose dialectic, examining his subject first from one side and then from another, forever turning back on himself with qualifying transitions like "but," "yet," or "whilst." He could easily say one thing in one place and the opposite in another, so that he produced no fixed system.[28] Hawthorne's method is a dialectic also, although in a less discursive way: a sketch such as "The Old Manse" is built on a series of contrasting descriptions; and often his fictional narrative is based on what might be called a "some say . . . others say" formula, most explicitly in the commentary on Dimmesdale's death (*The Scarlet Letter*, Chapter 24) or in the conclusion of "Young Goodman Brown."[29] This kind of authorial equivocation is not the kind of irony that takes a definite position behind a mask; nor should it be regarded as anti-Emersonian, for it stems from Emerson's own recognition that life is "a succession of moods or objects" ("Experience") or "a rushing stream that will not stop to be observed" ("The Method of Nature"). Hawthorne borrowed Emerson's image of the stream that cannot be stopped in words, and shared his distrust of conventional theorists—in Hawthorne's words, theorists "whose systems . . . imprisoned them in an iron framework"; his own "fitful sketches," Hawthorne warned the reader of *Mosses*, offered no consistent purpose, only a succession of moods (pp. 41, 45). If the dominant mood of "Rappaccini's Daughter" throws doubtful light on the young idealist Giovanni, the reader may freely apply the psychoanalytic method; but he should not assume, on grounds of consistency alone, that the mood and mechanism are the same for "The Artist of the Beautiful" (just as he should not assume that Emerson's "The Poet" is in the same mood as "Experience"). He may discover, then, that while Hawthorne's reputation depends upon anti-Emersonianism, Emerson is actually a reliable guide in interpreting Hawthorne's work.

Notes

1. Martin Green, *Re-appraisals: Some Commonsense Readings in American Literature* (London, 1963), p. 85. Green is unsympathetic to Hawthorne. Hubert Hoeltje is the one critic who has consistently associated Hawthorne with "Emersonianism," in the biography *Inward Sky: The Mind and Heart of Nathaniel Hawthorne* (Durham, 1962) and in an attack on Melville's interpretation of *Mosses*, "Hawthorne, Melville, and 'Blackness'," *American Literature*, XXXVII (March 1965), 41–51. The problem with Hoeltje, apart from eccentricities of form, is his uncritical acceptance of Hawthorne as an idealist and a follower of Plato and Emerson. See *Inward Sky*, p. 122, the last two paragraphs; the commentary on *Mosses from an Old Manse*, pp. 232–234, 237–238 (Hoeltje contrasts Hawthorne's heart and Socrates' head, but his brief interpretations of the tales are essentially Platonic); and especially the last chapter, pp. 555–561. In short, Hoeltje refutes the ironists only by ignoring them.

2. *Essays: Second Series*; in *The Selected Writings of Ralph Waldo Emerson*, ed. Brooks Atkinson (New York, 1940), p. 330.

3. Frederick Crews, *The Sins of the Fathers: Hawthorne's Psychological Themes* (Oxford, 1966), pp. 167, 98.

4. Ronald Curran, "Irony: Another Thematic Dimension to 'The Artist of the Beautiful,'" *Studies in Romanticism*, VI (Autumn 1966), 34–35, 43. See also L. Hugh Moore, Jr., "Hawthorne's Ideal Artist as Presumptuous Intellectual," *Studies in Short Fiction*, II (Spring 1965), 278–283, and the earlier studies cited by Crews and Curran.

5. See the discussion of character types in *The American Notebooks by Nathaniel Hawthorne*, ed. Randall Stewart (New Haven, 1932), pp. xlv–xlvi; and Crews' delineation of an escapist type, p. 98.

6. *Mosses From an Old Manse, The Complete Works of Nathaniel Hawthorne*, ed. George P. Lathrop (Boston and New York, 1882), II, 515. Hereafter the major references to this volume will be identified simply by the page-number.

7. R. H. Fogle, "The World and the Artist: A Study of Hawthorne's 'The Artist of the Beautiful,'" *Tulane Studies in English*, I (1949), 36.

8. See *Mosses*, p. 147, and Crews, pp. 123–124.

9. Important criticism argues the contrary: Millicent Bell, *Hawthorne's View of the Artist* (New York, 1962), p. 109, says, "Owen's fate indicates that he has chosen to sever himself from the forge and the hearth—twin symbols of the warmth of society—and to pursue the isolate aims of the Head." Crews, p. 170, says, "The victory of pure art coincides with a total failure of manhood and a repudiation of the emotional ties which Hawthorne elsewhere treats as the necessary conditions for sanity."

10. See Curran, pp. 39–42, for sources. Curran sees Owen totally committed to the butterfly, which then becomes a monument to the artist's pride.

11. Crews, p. 169, and Bell, p. 111, both seem to read "the other butterfly" as a Platonic conception and reject it. Curran, pp. 42–43, calls the conclusion ironic

because Hawthorne does not share Owen's pride in his accomplishment (i.e., the butterfly). Daniel Hoffman, "Myth, Romance, and the Childhood of Man," *Hawthorne Centenary Essays*, ed. Roy Harvey Pearce (Columbus, Ohio, 1964), pp. 202–205, sees a dramatization of the myth told by Diotima in the *Symposium*. His conclusion, that Owen's "joy was in the process of creating perfection, not in possessing it" (p. 205), is closer to the view presented here; however, I see Owen growing in character, "on the human side," more than in philosophical knowledge, as Hoffman suggests (p. 204). Hawthorne's use of the word "spirit" in this tale (pp. 527, 536) indicates essential character rather than any transcendent concept. Fogle gives a straightforward Romantic interpretation, but stresses the affirmation of art (p. 40) more than the affirmation of the artist's life.

12. Brief recent studies rightly stress Owen's growth: James W. Gargano, "Hawthorne's 'The Artist of the Beautiful,'" *American Literature*, XXXV (May 1963), 225–230, and Charles Sanders, "A Note on Metamorphosis in Hawthorne's 'The Artist of the Beautiful,'" *Studies in Short Fiction*, IV (Fall 1966), 82–83.

13. See Curran, p. 36, and Stewart, p. xxiv.

14. Allston died July 9, 1843. Stewart, p. lxxxiv, calls attention to notes in Hawthorne's journal probably written soon after Allston's death.

15. Stewart, p. 181.

16. See Stewart, p. 92 (January 1842) and n. 150; p. 185 (June 1843), pp. 189–190 (October 1843); and p. 108 (March 1845).

17. Stewart, p. 105.

18. Van Wyck Brooks' story of Allston in *The Flowering of New England* (New York, 1952), pp. 165–171, is a little unfair. It does not take into account the importance of Allston's conversation in transmitting European ideas and it probably does him injustice as an artist. See E. P. Richardson, *Washington Allston: A Study of the Romantic Artist in America* (Chicago, 1948) for a balancing corrective.

19. *Mosses*, p. 35. The succeeding paragraph is qualified in the Emersonian manner; beginning "And yet," it speaks for the "system" of life at the Manse in contrast to the freedom of the river. However, life at the Manse is definitely not the same system as life at the Danforth hearth in "The Artist of the Beautiful." Danforth life is that of the city or town and is associated with *iron* (pp. 506, 527); life at the Manse is contrasted to the city and to the iron of "a dungeon and a chain" (p. 36).

20. See Emerson's "New Poetry" in *The Dial*, I (October 1840), 220–232, and correspondence between Emerson and Margaret Fuller on Channing's poems, *The Letters of Ralph Waldo Emerson*, ed. Ralph L. Rusk (New York, 1939) II, 226–227, 276, 306. Stewart, p. 312, says that "Hawthorne's opinion of Channing was not nearly so favorable as Sophia's," despite this fishing incident. Perhaps, then, Hawthorne was thinking of the artist in general more than of Channing in particular in the passage quoted.

21. Julian Hawthorne, *Nathaniel Hawthorne and his Wife: A Biography* (Boston, 1885), I, 244.

22. See *Mosses*, p. 13; *The Scarlet Letter*, ed. Scully Bradley, *et al.* (New York, 1962), p. 32.

23. *Scarlet Letter*, p. 24.

24. *Journals of Ralph Waldo Emerson*, eds. E. W. Emerson and W. E. Forbes (Boston and New York, 1909–14), VI, 240. This has always been taken as a derogatory reference to Hawthorne's art; I agree, although it could mean that his art was not "utilitarian."

25. Hoeltje, *Inward Sky*, p. 214. "Character is nature in the highest form" appears in Emerson's "Character," *Essays: Second Series*.

26. *Essays: First Series*, in *Selected Writings*, pp. 311–312. Cf. in "Experience" the passage beginning "The secret of the illusoriness is in the necessity of a succession of moods or objects. . . . We need change of objects. . . . That immobility and absence of elasticity which we find in the arts, we find with more pain in the artist" (pp. 347–348). Whatever is fixed violates Nature, which is fluid. Art, insofar as a work of art is static, can only approximate Nature (as in "The Snow-Storm"); words at best approximate things (*Journals*, III, 492; VI, 274–275). Hence Emerson's essays generally rise to an almost messianic vision, perfecting the man rather than the work of art, as in the conclusion to "The Poet."

27. See *Mosses*, p. 42; *Journals*, V, 189.

28. "Man thinking"—the process of his thought and not so much beliefs or conclusions—is the view of Emerson set out by Stephen E. Whicher, *Freedom and Fate: An Inner Life of Ralph Waldo Emerson* (Philadelphia, 1953), as an antidote to half a century of anti-Emersonianism. See also Whicher's similar comment on Emerson's poetry in his edition, *Selections from Ralph Waldo Emerson* (Cambridge, Mass., 1957), pp. 407–411.

29. Harry Levin makes this observation, though without linking it specifically to Emerson, in *The Power of Blackness* (New York, 1958), pp. 37, 47.

Representative Men ["Ethan Brand"]

Sharon Cameron*

In Hawthorne's sketches human beings fully fleshed out are not simply absent, they are also irrelevant. In distinction from the tales, the sketches characteristically locate the world's conflicts as either internal or external, and do not see the way in which such simplifications wrench human or "complete" beings apart. In "Sights from a Steeple," for example, Paul Pry aspires to be outside himself in sights so distanced from the church tower to whose top he has climbed that they are recognizable only in miniature, in unknown corporeal forms. Oppositely, in "Fancy's Show Box," an everyman named Mr. Smith descends to an imaginative church floor, where he kneels to look inward at existence suddenly shrunk to the size of his own soul. If "Fancy's Show Box" characterizes existence by softening corporeality to spirit made momentarily visible, "Sights from a Steeple" steels the self against such revelations by suggesting it is (others') bodies that must be watched. These simplifications (the reduction of the self to other bodies or the reduction of the self to one's own invisible soul) constitute a more frightening enactment of witchcraft than any Hawthorne directly parodies. In both cases the exorcism of the soul from the body—the making of it immaterial—or the soul's domination and possession of the body pivots on a false understanding of the

* Reprinted from *The Corporeal Self: Allegories of the Body in Melville and Hawthorne* (Baltimore, London: Johns Hopkins University Press, 1981), 88–102.

relation between interior and exterior. That relation, correctly seen, would be acknowledged as threefold rather than as dyadic: existing between the body and the soul, between one self and a human other, between all human selves and the non-human world, which cannot be made integral to either human body or soul.

In "Ethan Brand," the opposite impulses of the two sketches to which I have alluded come together in an acknowledgment of the connection between what lies within the body and what lies outside of it. For in distinction to these two sketches, Hawthorne's tales tend to look like mirrors in which divisions within the self are reflected in divisions between selves, and these divisions are further reflected by the separation between the human self and the disembodied natural world. If "Ethan Brand" is fleshed out, is a tale rather than a sketch, this is because it understands that the body's relation to itself and its relation to the outside world are connected, and because it posits the working out of that connection in the context of a human community (as "Fancy's Show Box" does not) without simultaneously repudiating (as "Sights from a Steeple" does) a soul or heart that is both internal and personal. Yet "Ethan Brand" also addresses the question of what would create such separations, as they are illustrated by the two sketches in which the self exists in isolation, a "haunted chamber" or a "desert," or in which the human community goes about its business, its existence documented by a voice that aspires to characteristics of chillness and obscurity, falsely muting the human to a bodied impersonality. I shall be suggesting that in "Ethan Brand," as in Hawthorne's other tales, characters aspire to be "representative men," to be bodies or souls or other, less frequently dichotomized emblematic parts. I thus invoke Emerson's words, not as he originally coined them—as epitomizing central characteristics to which all men should aspire (characteristics, in other words, that would make men *larger* than ordinary life)—but rather contrarily: "representative" in the sense of "emblematic" or "synecdochic." So reversed, the term designates men who would represent themselves by reducing themselves to discrete bodily parts, who—equated with such parts—would be diminished to their size.

In "Ethan Brand," Bartram, the man with no first name, sits with his son late one night tending a kiln that turns the marble of the white hills to valuable lime. We are told this was Ethan Brand's kiln when he deserted it years ago to look for the Unpardonable Sin. The two sitting together are startled by a laugh "like a wind" (XI:83); laughter, mirthless and terrific, echoes throughout the tale, coming from within the human body yet heard from distances away and having the preternatural power (Bartram says in a joke to little Joe) to "blow the roof of the house off": " 'Oh, some drunken man . . . who dared not laugh loud enough within doors, lest he should blow the roof of the house off. So here he is, shaking his jolly sides, at the foot of Graylock' " (XI:83). Bartram's explanation is meant to calm by making metaphoric a violence Brand will make literal. The terrible mind-noise Bartram designates as laughter of course turns out to be Brand's, and when he appears, Bartram sends Joe to fetch the villagers to listen to Brand's story. Joe comes back with an array of people—Hawthorne illustrating lives and sins alternative to Brand's. In the midst of this menagerie we are shown a stray dog chasing its own tail, a counterpoint to Brand's story as the village people first ask him to recount it and then are rather distracted by the visualization that duplicates in comic (that is, bearable) terms what they have no mind to hear. It is the narrator who delivers the story in full after the villagers have gone home and Joe and Bartram have retired, for we are compelled to listen to the tale from which the others depart. Brand, sickened by his ruminations as they are revealed in the passage below, climbs into the furnace and is found the next day a skeleton, except for the human heart obtruding between his ribs. The heart is nothing to Bartram, as it was once nothing to Brand, so he pokes at the skeleton and reduces it to ashes.

The tale is extraordinary on several independent counts. Perhaps the least of these is the explanation to which the townspeople will not listen and which, when we are told it, seems a stylization—like the sketches of Mr. Smith and Paul Pry—inadequately fleshed out:

> When they had gone, Ethan Brand sat listening to the crackling of the kindled wood . . . deep within his mind, he was reviewing the gradual, but marvellous change, that had been wrought upon him by the search to which he had devoted himself. He remembered how the night-dew had fallen upon him—how the dark forest had whispered to him—how the stars had gleamed upon him—a simple and loving man, watching his fire in the years gone by, and ever musing as it burned. He remembered with what tenderness, with what love and sympathy for mankind, and what pity for human guilt and wo, he had first begun to contemplate those ideas which afterwards became the inspiration of his life; with what reverence he had then looked into the heart of man, viewing it as a temple originally divine, and however desecrated, still to be held sacred by a brother; with what awful fear he had deprecated the success of his pursuit, and prayed that the Unpardonable Sin might never be revealed to him. Then ensued that vast intellectual development, which, in its progress, disturbed the counterpoise between his mind and heart. The Idea that possessed his life had operated as a means of education; it had gone on cultivating his powers to the highest point of which they were susceptible; it had raised him from the level of an unlettered laborer, to stand on a star-light eminence, whither the philosophers of the earth, laden with the lore of universities, might vainly strive to clamber after him. So much for the

intellect! But where was the heart? That, indeed, had withered—
had contracted—had hardened—had perished! It had ceased to
partake of the universal throb . . .

Thus Ethan Brand became a fiend. He began to be so from the
moment that his moral nature had ceased to keep the pace of
improvement with his intellect. And now, as his highest effort and
inevitable development—as the bright and gorgeous flower, and
rich, delicious fruit of his life's labor—he had produced the Unpardonable Sin! (XI:98-99)

The moral's relative insufficiency to explain the power of the tale
provides an inadvertent demonstration of its own central point. Turn
passion for an object into curiosity about its working and you get
the sacrifice that is the tale's ostensible subject—the sacrifice of life
to the idea that would dissect it. This sacrifice is the one made by
Brand. It is the one made *of* Brand, Hawthorne's explanation of what
happens to Brand suffering the same didactic reduction. In addition,
the moral—that Brand loses his heart in the process of intellectualizing
it—is adjacent to aspects of the story (its tableaus and reflections,
to which I shall momentarily turn) for which it fails to account; and
it also curiously contradicts Brand's *defense* of the crime for which
he is ostensibly doing penance. What distinguishes "Ethan Brand" is
the way in which the story told by the explicit moral (as it is advanced
by the passage above and as it is italicized in the emblem of the
heart at the tale's end) comes into relationship with an alternative
and contradictory story, for the illustration of the moral seems not
simply to deflect from that moral but to offer another story entirely.

We are told Brand loses his heart the moment he conceives it
possible to see or study the organ. Yet I would like to suggest that
Brand wishes to look at the heart (as Hawthorne makes us look at
it, makes us momentarily be like Brand) not because seeing it means
understanding it, but rather because seeing it means externalizing it.
" 'Freely, were it to do again, would I incur the guilt,' " Brand says
to the townspeople, " 'Unshrinkingly, I accept the retribution' "
(XI:90). But one half of the story implies that Brand would incur the
guilt so that he could accept the retribution. When Brand climbs
into the furnace, he does not do so out of penance. The defiance of
his explanation makes this sanguine interpretation implausible. Rather,
he subjects himself to fire so that he can make his heart external, so
that he can literally be without it. Thus, despite conventional interpretations—the one proffered by Brand and by the narrator—which
construe Brand's motives (to study the human heart) as innocent,
although the consequences (the losing of the heart) are not, Brand's
defiant explanation suggests that the motives desire the consequence.
The heart is unbearable. Seeing it or studying it is not an end; it is
rather a means for expulsion of the vital organ. These are Brand's

last words: " 'Oh, Mother Earth,' cried he, 'who art no more my Mother, and into whose bosom this frame shall never be resolved! Oh, mankind, whose brotherhood I have cast off, and trampled thy great heart beneath my feet! Oh, stars of Heaven, that shone on me of old, as if to light me onward and upward!—farewell all, and forever! Come, deadly element of Fire—henceforth my familiar friend! Embrace me as I do thee!' " (XI:100). This is Brand turned Ahab, the man who would have no heart, even at that moment when he wishes most succor from the universe. Ahab's appeal in "The Candles" echoes Brand's words: " 'Oh, thou clear spirit, of thy fire thou madest me, and like a true child of fire, I breathe it back to thee. . . . Oh, thou foundling fire . . . again with haughty agony, I read my sire . . . I burn with thee; would fain be welded with thee' " (119:642–43). The desire to be "resolved" into an invisible world bosom, into a "universal throb," and the desire to resolve the self of such a wish by ridding the body of the heart are confused in Brand as they will be confused in Ahab. Brand's description of the stars that are to light him "onward and upward" suggests it is divinity he is after when he embarks upon his search, although if this is a Faust tale, it is personalized by the desire for the "embrace" of the universe as well as by the desire for its power.

Because divinity is unimaginable—because nothing is imaginable—without the body that fleshes thought out, Brand looks for in the world of men what he wishes for from the divine world. Thinking man is made in God's image, Brand knows divinity inheres in man. But when literalizing this idea, when he imagines divinity to have a shape (the shape of the sacred heart) which could first be found in the human body and then separated from it, he is imagining an emblem or a body for what has none. We will be told that "brotherhood," no less than divinity, refuses specific embodiment. Thus, divinity lies outside of the heart as well as within and above it. And while at the beginning of the tale Brand tries to "trample" brotherhood under his feet—this is the tale's verb—at the end of the tale, it is nonetheless visible in the sky: "Stepping from one to another of the clouds that rested on the hills, and thence to the loftier brotherhood that sailed in air, it seemed almost as if a mortal man might thus ascend into the heavenly regions" (XI:101). Brotherhood, like divinity, like all those abstractions in whose name we live, is emphatically dislodged from any specific picture. Yet it is just because he thinks divinity has a body, a shape that could (independently) be known, that Brand imagines particular bodies do not matter. They are containments that must be violated to get to the essence that lies within. Thus, Brand imagines a shape for the divinity that has none, and he simultaneously discounts the shape of the human body as a mere immateriality. For he still cannot understand that the heart can be divine (hence, must not be violated) and that this divinity has no embodiment that can be separated from the human heart. Yet there is no heart outside of the human body or of the world of human selves. The world is too large to be conceived of as an embodiment. It cannot have a heart because it does not have a body. Insofar as Brand *does* understand this, he will have no heart, will—like the world—be an outside with no inside. He will be, as he says, a "frame."

The kiln accommodates this desire. Throughout the tale Brand's contemplation of the fire in the kiln is associated with his search for the human heart. The kiln is personified, and prior to Brand's search it is given daemonic voice: "Ethan Brand," we are told, "had conversed with Satan himself, in the lurid blaze of this very kiln" (XI:89). Such personifications make the kiln into a body. The fire is its heart. In the following comparative (he is here addressing the village people he despises) Brand draws the connection directly: " 'I have looked . . . into many a human heart that was seven times hotter with sinful passions than yonder furnace is with fire' " (XI:90). Brand may in his comparative be acknowledging that his eventual incineration is only a submission of the heart to its own passionate element, which therefore cannot ignite it any more or any differently. At any rate, he is implying that the sight before the eyes (the fire of the kiln) and the sight behind the eyes (the fire of the heart) are identical. In fact, since the Unpardonable Sin is dislodged from any context but that of the human heart, sin and the heart also come into an unspecified equivalence. The search for the Unpardonable Sin is the search for the human heart externalized and made abstract. Brand's central wish, ungratified by the tale, is to abolish the difference between internal and external worlds, to make the fire in the kiln be the fire in the eyes, and this fire a mere reflection of the fire in the human heart. The ultimate goal of this confusion is, as I suggested earlier, to find the world-heart outside the body, which, as Brand specifies in his plea to Mother Earth, will "embrace" him in a literal action we might have mistaken to be a metaphoric one. But since Brand cannot discover the heart outside the body, he will make *his* heart external, and then be consumed by it. Hawthorne describes Brand, an inverted Prometheus, about to leap into the furnace as a "fiend on the verge of plunging into his gulf of intensest torment" (XI:100)—inside and outside effectively confused, forcing the external world to embrace him after all.

The expulsion of the heart from the body is consonant with the other, less palpable expulsion from the body, the ripples of laughter as they echo throughout the tale. We are told that more than anything else laughter "expresse[s] the condition of [Brand's] inward being" (XI:97). We hear the sound initially as it interrupts Bartram's conversation with little Joe. And the same terrible noise that precedes

Brand's arrival also ushers him out of the world: "That night the sound of a fearful peal of laughter rolled heavily through the sleep of the lime-burner and his little son; dim shapes of horror and anguish haunted their dreams, and seemed still present in the rude hovel when they opened their eyes to the daylight" (XI:100).

Laughter is related to the heart first by the way in which the tale makes them coincident, at Brand's appearance and at his death. Second, the two are related as a response is to an idea—in this case Brand's daemonic or despairing response to the (false) idea that the heart could exist outside the body. Finally, laughter is the means through which the heart leaves the body. Laughter is an outburst, with that expression literalized. It repels and displaces what in fact belongs within:

> Laughter, when out of place, mistimed, or bursting forth from a disordered state of feeling, may be the most terrible modulation of the human voice. The laughter of one asleep, even if it be a little child—the madman's laugh—the wild, screaming laugh of a born idiot, are sounds that we sometimes tremble to hear, and would always willingly forget. Poets have imagined no utterance of fiends or hobgoblins so fearfully appropriate as a laugh. And even the obtuse lime-burner felt his nerves shaken, as this strange man looked inward at his own heart, and burst into laughter that rolled away into the night, and was indistinctly reverberated among the hills. (XI:87–88)

Insofar as laughter externalizes (by responding to) what is seen from within, it ousts the interior vision, gets it out of the body. Thus, laughter would expel the mind's visions into the world. Or, as the last sentence of the paragraph suggests, it would leave them where they are while vacating the body to look at it. At the tale's end, very much as at the beginning of Brand's search, Brand does not want his heart back. He rather wants to relinquish it. The devil is in his heart. The devil *is* his heart. Fire, he thinks, if not laughter, will blow the roof off his body, will let the terrible thing out. As his name suggests, Brand does not want to cast sin out of his body. He wants instead to cast his heart out of his body in extension of the crime for which he is ostensibly doing penance. Indeed, while most interpretations of the tale see the shape of the heart left within Brand's body as evidence of Hawthorne's giving Brand back the heart he has come to want, it is in fact as consonant with one aspect of the story to read the conclusion—in which we are told that "within the ribs—strange to say—was the shape of a human heart" (XI:102)—not ironically at all, but as a sign of Hawthorne's refusal to take the heart away from Brand, of his insistence that the heart cannot be—not even conceptually, not even in death—situated anywhere but within.

There is, however, another way of reading the story—the one espoused by the tale's didacticism—which implies that Hawthorne agrees with Brand in the latter's assumption that bodies do not matter. This reading would suggest that bodies must be taken apart because they obscure the heart that lies inside of them. Thus, Brand, looking at the townspeople, dismisses what he sees: " 'Years and years ago, I groped into your hearts' " he says, still misapplying physical idioms to non-physical things, and looking now not at their hearts at all but rather at their degenerate bodies, " 'and found nothing there for my purpose. Get ye gone!' " (XI:93). But they, on the basis of the same external evidence of the body, falsely dismiss Brand: "Finding nothing . . . very remarkable in his aspect—nothing but a sunburnt wayfarer, in plain garb and dusty shoes, who sat looking into the fire," finding nothing remarkable in the external evidence of the searing going on within, "these young people speedily grew tired of observing him" (XI:94). Because the villagers are no more capable of seeing into Brand's heart (however he testifies to the pain of its existence there) than he is capable of looking into their hearts, the story's conventional explanation suggests that bodies are barriers that stand in the way. They must be dismembered or mutilated to get to the essence that lies inside—an idea exactly contrary to the one (that such dismemberment is sin) the story elsewhere advances.

In line with the didactic reading of the tale, we could say that Brand sacrifices his body when he sees that particular bodies make no difference. Like all hearts, they are the same. Thus, for example, Bartram, left alone with Brand, reads the Master Sin in Brand's heart as a mirror for his own: "They were all of one family; they went to and fro between his breast and Ethan Brand's, and carried dark greetings from one to the other" (XI:88). One could say Brand's body remains alive in the physical visage of Bartram—the man who is all body—and in the visage of the little boy—the child who is all heart, and with whom Brand sees "eye to eye." Mutilation (at least in the reading of the story that follows its own didacticism) does not disfigure man by depriving him of parts of his body. It rather shows his essential connection to what lies outside his body. Mutilation shows man that bodies are immaterial.

In this light, of Giles the lawyer (who argues the case for Hawthorne) we are told he is "but the fragment of a human being, a part of one foot having been chopped off by an axe, and an entire hand torn away by the devilish gripe of a steam-engine" (XI:91). We are also told, however, that although "the corporeal hand was gone, a spiritual member remained." The description, of course, refers to the feeling in and of the phantom limb. But in the context of a tale in which—as one directive of the story suggests—characters need to rid themselves of their corporeal bodies in order to become spiritual members, Giles's mutilation redeems him. And indeed throughout the tale, Hawthorne himself seems intent on taking the body apart, or on showing its parts in relief, as if, severed from the body, they would reveal their shared essence. Thus, Joe, looking through the Jew's diorama, has Brand's eyes "fixed upon him" (XI:95). Joe is not simply seen by Brand, as the idiomatic expression suggests. He also sees with eyes so akin to Brand's that for all practical purposes, there is no difference between them—as at certain moments in *Moby-Dick* there is, for all practical purposes, no difference between Pip and Ahab. In fact, the last look we have of Brand, other than the narrator's, is filtered through Joe's vision of him: "As the boy followed his father into the hut, he looked back to the wayfarer, and the tears came into his eyes; for his tender spirit had an intuition of the bleak and terrible loneliness in which this man had enveloped himself" (XI:98). Emphasizing in other terms the desire for synonymy, the narrator tells us that before Brand set out on his journey he had "thrown his dark thoughts into the intense glow of [the] furnace, and melted them, as it were, into the one thought that took possession of his life" (XI:84). The second explanation suggests that this is a tale in which eyes and limbs, or hearts and thoughts, must be taken out of the body, or synecdochically severed from it, in a dismemberment whose purpose is a "melting" of many into one.

The two explanations I have advanced—that the story advances— are at odds on all significant counts. The didactic explanation insists that Brand has to rid himself of the body in order to discover the heart. The undermining explanation insists that the body cannot be gotten rid of; it is heretical to try to do so. The didactic explanation suggests that Brand thrusts himself into the furnace to pay for his crime. The alternative explanation is that he thrusts himself into the furnace to perpetuate his crime. The didactic explanation suggests that Hawthorne gives Brand back his heart. The subversive explanation suggests that Hawthorne never allows him to relinquish it. Yet both explanations concur in faulting the idea that the heart is invisible *because* it is inside the body. Both agree that not being able to see the heart (or the essence that it symbolizes) is rather a consequence of its not being visible anywhere. The heart is not visible inside the self, because one feels rather than sees it there. Nor is the heart visible inside others' bodies, because one cannot see inside others' bodies, at least one cannot literalize that expression. But the heart is not visible outside the body either, for the idea of looking "outside" the self is equivalent to looking *away* from it. Nor is the heart visible in the outsides of others' bodies, if what one expects to see there is something other than the body. Thus, both readings of the tale suggest dissatisfaction with the idea of seeing and with the idea of a dichotomized outside and inside, conventionally defined, although the first reading would express this dissatisfaction by suggesting that outsides (or bodies) cannot be dismissed, and the second reading by insisting that they must be. For we feel rather than see our connection to other beings, and cannot make emblems of, cannot embody what we feel.

In this respect we are all like Giles, missing the palpable embodiments that would both reify (give external shape to) our meanings and simultaneously make them complete. For Giles, the conventional distinction (that one sees what is outside and visible and feels what is inside and invisible) is exactly reversed. As we also are meant to do, Giles feels what is simultaneously outside ("exterior to" as well as "without" or "missing") and invisible. Thus, the initial distinction between outside and inside, as Brand tries to make it (with "outside" construed as the body, "inside" construed as the heart), is corrected by the tale. The correction would go as follows. It would detach the idea of an "inside" from the figure of a human heart and enlarge it one step further to embrace the totality of a single self. Brand—ironizing the point—throws himself into the furnace and shows us how this is done. He becomes the fiery heart. It would now—going one step further—enlarge the idea of an "outside" so that the designation applied not only to the human flesh but to all that lies exterior to it—whether this exterior be designated by the phantom limb to which Giles nonetheless feels himself connected or whether it be designated by the community of human bodies that lies outside the single self to which it nonetheless ought to feel connected. The tale would then advance a final correction, getting "inside" and "outside" right for the first time. At the end of the tale, the whole human community of corporeal beings is itself shown to be the heart that lies in the body of the world. As if to offer us an image (something too amorphous and large to be codified as an emblem) different from the heart limed within Brand's ribs, Hawthorne depicts the sight of the village as the sun lights it up: "The early sunshine was already pouring its gold upon the mountain-tops, and though the valleys were still in shadow, they smiled cheerfully in the promise of the bright day that was hastening onward. The village, completely shut in by hills, which swelled away gently about it, looked as if it had rested peacefully in the hollow of the great hand of Providence" (XI:100–101). The land is like a body in which the human community rests. The land contains the village as the body contains the heart.

If the land is the body and the village is the human heart, then the distinction between inside and outside, as the story has delimited it, is not here corrected; it is actually reversed. Corporeal bodies and palpable dwellings are now conceived of as the land's "inside." The body is the heart. But this heart is the universal one. Hawthorne fleshes the image out: "Every dwelling was distinctly visible; the little spires of the two churches pointed upward, and caught a fore-glim-mering of brightness from the sun-gilt skies upon their gilded weath-ercocks. The tavern was astir, and the figure of the old, smoke-dried stage-agent, cigar in mouth, was seen beneath the stoop. Old Graylock was glorified with a golden cloud upon his head" (XI:101).

This is a vision that does not discriminate—between evil men and good men, between churches and taverns, between the man shapes and the mountain shapes, between similitude and the real thing (the image of the heart in the land's body is, after all, only an analogy), for all are part of the universal pulse. I have said this image is the alternative to the one at the end of the tale. The latter emblem reveals Brand's dead heart within his body. The former reveals the collective heart of the human community in the body of the world. The two images come into fused relationship. While the emblem of the heart limed in Brand's ribs is itself isolated and stresses man's isolation, images like that of the village-heart are plural, intermingled, and scattered throughout the tale. Even in the first description of the kiln, before man enters the picture, we see relationships un-mutilated by the attempts to pry their respective parts into clarity: "There are many such lime-kilns in that tract of country, for the purpose of burning the white marble which composes a large part of the substance of the hills. Some of them, built years ago, and long deserted, with weeds growing in the vacant round of the interior, which is open to the sky, and grass and wild flowers rooting themselves into the chinks of stones" (XI:84). The weeds are inseparable from the interior of the kiln; its vacant enclosures are filled with open sky; the wild flowers are rooted in chinks of stone. All possible discrim-inations are naturally—by nature—muted out of existence.

Similarly, the alternate readings of the story come into confused relationship. It should already have become clear that they are not easy to tell apart. However the tale offers proximate or alternate clues about Brand's motives (hence, about the meaning of his ending), it is crucial to note that both readings converge in their dismissal of the conventional dichotomy between an outside and an inside: in the one case, as I have suggested, by insisting that the heart is in the body (cannot be expelled from it because it cannot be distinguished from it) and in the other case by suggesting that the heart must be expelled, must be housed in the collective body of mankind. Thus, whether the story be understood as a tale about a man who wants to rid himself of his heart—to brand it on the world—or as a story about a man who wants to find the universal heart and who inad-vertently loses his own, either explanation insists this is not a story about simple heartlessness, but rather a story that suggests uncertainty about where the heart resides—on the outside or the inside. The following image would rebuke Ethan Brand, were he alive to see what it represents. It does rebuke the shape of the emblem found between his ribs at the tale's end. In place of that emblem, it acknowledges that the world is larger than morals or emblems, cannot cut itself to human distinction because it will not cut itself to human size:

> Scattered, likewise, over the breasts of the surrounding mountains, there were heaps of hoary mist, in fantastic shapes, some of them far down into the valley, others high up towards the summits, and still others, of the same family of mist or cloud, hovering in the gold radiance of the upper atmosphere. Stepping from one to another of the clouds that rested on the hills, and thence to the loftier brotherhood that sailed in air, it seemed almost as if a mortal man might thus ascend into the heavenly regions. Earth was so mingled with sky that it was a daydream to look at it. (XI:101)

Man cannot fuse with the outside world, cannot become one with it, because the body always intervenes. Yet the natural world embraces the human world. The natural world does to Brand what Brand had wanted to do to *it*. And in encompassing the mortal world, it softens the distinctions it nonetheless insists upon. Brand gives his life, then, for a totality he could have had *in* life but not on human terms. This totality is felt rather than known, seen rather than understood, omnipresent rather than embodied, a mist rather than an emblem. In the specification of the vision as a "daydream" (a word that distills the contradictions of the entire tale) Hawthorne offers us an alternative to the distinctions Brand has tried to make. In fact, the tale offers us alternatives that exactly parallel Brand's: to arrive at a simple meaning by casting out of our minds one half of the story (as Brand tries to cast his heart out of his body), or to acknowledge both sides of the tale and its attendant contradictions, which, like earth and sky, are so mingled as to be inseparable.

The problematic relation between inside and outside (between ostensible oppositions) is insisted upon throughout the tale, mirroring Brand's dilemma. Thus, for example, we are asked to look at the kiln, and at the way in which it casts reflections on the human countenance. But that image is ambiguously complemented by the moonlight in the sky, as it casts reflections on the human countenance. Is this the same light or a different light? What is the relation between the fire in the human heart and the fire in the kiln, or between these and the sky's fire? Hawthorne turns our attention from the story Brand would tell to the stories of the people gathered around him, as the latter stories drown out his words. Do their stories duplicate his own or deviate from it? And what is the relationship between duplication and deviation when it is adjacently conceived? The devil is initially depicted as residing in the furnace, but later he is depicted as residing in the man. Are these conceptions proximate or alternate? Thus, we are made to look within the self for the origin of evil. Brand's story is such a look. But we are alternately asked to look for it in the world, whether that world be depicted by the German Jew's diorama or by the frivolous village people whose lives—compared to Brand's—are as or more pernicious. The displacements to which I refer are made most explicit in the problematic connection between literal ways of understanding the world and metaphoric ways of understanding it. Another way of putting this is to say that Hawthorne's playing off of literality and metaphorization is both at the heart of the tale's conflicts and reveals that heart to insist upon a connection between literality and the outside world, metaphorization and the inside world.

But exterior and literal or interior and metaphoric have neither conventional nor stable associations. We are therefore shown that metaphoric ways of figuring things trivialize what they depict. They distance event from feeling about it by interposing figures of speech between the two, as if hoping that language could empty itself of reality rather than hoping to reflect it. So the German Jew talks about carrying the Unpardonable Sin on his shoulders—the idea of carrying it "on" the body is as close as he wants to come in this debunking of a notion that Brand makes too close for comfort. So Bartram left alone with Brand fears the two will have to deal "heart to heart." But the expression for Bartram's fear wards off the experience unaccommodated by convention by finding the conventional idiom for it. The expression embraces the category to which such dealings would belong. It evades the dealings themselves. In grotesque parody of this subversion, waking the next morning to think that Brand has not tended the fire, Bartram imagines a passion so consuming it could throw a man into the furnace. Hence, Bartram's words do to the thought of Brand what Brand does to himself. But for Bartram, thought bears no relation to the actual world it reflects on. Because he does not understand that words are not literal enactments and yet matter anyway, he also fails to understand how they ever could be literal. Brand's body in the kiln, when Bartram sees it, is as meaningless in reality as the thought that wished to put it there. Bartram's inability to credit his own thought as at all immersed in reality makes him, conversely, unable to let reality—when he sees it—register in thought. In both cases, language intervenes. In the first instance, it takes what we will discover as literal and dismisses it as metaphoric: " 'If I catch the fellow hereabouts again I shall feel like tossing him into the furnace!' " (XI:102). In the second case, Bartram escapes understanding what he has seen by making what is metaphoric literal. " 'Was the fellow's heart made of marble?' " Bartram cries, "perplexed" when he sees that Brand's body, like the marble of the hills has been converted into lime. In each case, experience escapes the meaning that would make sense of it by shifting to another category of discourse, that is, by being displaced. This displacement is analogous to Brand's desire to exteriorize the heart, to shift its location when he cannot bear it to be interior.

Bartram's categorical shifts are possible because he imagines all he thinks and says as a mere manner of speaking. In this respect, we too are like Bartram-Brand. Like Bartram, we normalize the story's violence by categorizing it as an allegory. We then consider allegory as that form of fiction whose literalization has no meaning. Hawthorne will not let us rest long, however, in the satisfactions of such an act, for in the conjunction of the didactic explanation with the explanation that subverts it, he turns a querying of the convention into the tale's subject. At the same time he asks that we examine the alternative to the convention's categorical dismissals. In Ethan Brand's case, the alternative to metaphorizing the world is to understand it literally. Such a reification kills. Metaphorizations of the world, literalizations of the world—these modes of conception, along with the relationship between inside and outside, comprise the tale's subject. Insofar as it enacts a series of displacements about which I have been speaking, these displacements are as if epitomized in the tale's concern with the status of language, or rather its concern with the status of how conception is to "take itself": of whether it is to take itself as embodied in the world (as literal) or as disembodied in the mind (as metaphor). Of course, this way of putting it, which is the tale's way of putting it, is exactly corollary to the problem Ethan Brand ponders. Is the heart "in" the body? Is it in one's own body? Can it be palpably conceived? Would one have to externalize it to so conceive it? Would such externalizations make one heartless? If one looked for the heart outside one's body rather than feeling it within, would this displacement kill? Behind all of these questions is, inescapably, the larger question: why are these alternatives? Hawthorne, like any moralist, answers his own questions. But he answers them indirectly, as he has raised them indirectly. Thus, when Joe and Bartram first hear it, the laugh is "inside" Brand. It sounds "outside," however, "like a wind shaking the boughs of the forest." Even from the first paragraph, inside and outside, literal and metaphoric ways of understanding the world are brought together to be confused. One way of looking at the simile is to see that the laugh does to Brand (to Brand as well as to the listeners) what the wind does to the bough. Forced out of the body, laughter treats the body like a genuine externality, shakes it from outside. The creation of a simile that enacts the spatial displacements that will be the tale's subject cannot be accidental. As if to insist that we question the meaning of what we have heard (is the laugh inside or outside? of what is it made?), Joe, the child whose questions are formed in the image of Brand's, asks, " 'Father, what is that?' " (XI:83).

NEW ESSAYS

Seeing Through "Paul Pry": Hawthorne's Early Sketches and the Problem of Audience

Teresa Toulouse°

Over half of Hawthorne's literary production between 1834 and 1846 consisted of sketches, yet surprisingly little sustained critical attention has been given to his use of this mode.[1] With few exceptions, critics have been content to note that the sketches are more concerned with atmosphere and scene than the tales, that they present personae rather than construct plots, or that, predictably, they manifest Hawthorne's general preoccupation with representing the interplay between fancy and reality.[2] The sketches have attracted interest insofar as these largely self-contained formal and thematic characteristics could be useful in discussions of Hawthorne's later formal and moral preoccupations.

Such approaches to Hawthorne's early sketches, particularly those of the *Twice-told Tales* period, tend to neglect the often problematic relation of the sketches' narrators to their own subject matter.[3] The narrators in fact shape the material of their sketches in ways that reveal troubled desires for, and fears of connection to, an audience. An exploration of the varying strategies by which narrators project a relation to the outer world and, in so doing, project a sense of their readers, both contributes to an understanding of Hawthorne's use of the sketch form and suggests a reason why he abandoned it, despite its relative popularity, and turned to other forms. Such an analysis also indicates that the sketches' strategies of connection and their breakdown are inseparable from the broader cultural conditions under which Hawthorne wrote. The assumptions of Jacksonian America do not serve as a static background against which these sketches must be measured: they become internal to their very working as texts.

1

As early as 1820, the young Hawthorne wrote for his family a series of four short papers, which he called the "Spectator."[4] During

° This essay was written specifically for this volume and is published here for the first time by permission of the author.

the 1830s and 1840s reviewers such as Poe would agree in comparing his newly published writings to Addison and Steel's *Spectator Papers*.[5] Clearly, "Mr. Spectator" serves as a useful prototype; his speculative descendants in Hawthorne should be measured against him in terms of their relationships with the reader.

Albert Furtwangler has argued that the "I" of the *Spectator Papers* presents no distinct persona: he is, rather, an eidolon, an "indistinct image or spectre" that tends to disappear if approached too closely. The vagueness of this figure is a function of the author's sense of the fickle audience whose needs he must continually anticipate. Furtwangler argues that the Spectator's adaptability in this regard makes him at once "a figure to be seen and then seen through."[6] A number of issues significant to Hawthorne's practice are involved in this apparently simple description of the figure's doubleness.

One of the major assumptions in the notion of a character's "transparency" is that an objective shared world is to be seen by all through the lens of this eidolon. The Spectator, however, is not merely seen through; he is also first seen—that is, purposefully distinguished from his readers. In spite of his vagueness and diffuseness, for example, Mr. Spectator is learned and quirky. Immense learning and eccentric silences often serve to separate him from, not to identify him with, his readers. In the tenth paper, the Spectator comes forward to differentiate between those readers who share his beliefs but retain their own individuality and those "Blanks" who become nothing more than what they read.[7] His mocking of these Blanks suggests that similarity of perspective must not be allowed to obliterate individual identity or lead to an equality of those who perceive. Further papers demonstrate that while shared "objective" perspectives exist, so do meaningful social distinctions among perceivers.

Promoting shared perspectives did not, for Addison and Steele, mean promoting shared status or an equality that could overthrow status relations. On the contrary, the *Papers* collectively confirm the value of defining, accepting, and maintaining one's social "role" in an appropriate manner, whatever that role might be. Viewed in this light, the most significant of the Spectator's "objective" speculations would be those that accommodated the greatest number of individual roles and at the same time projected the value of the common social reality (and social hierarchy) in which these roles were played out.[8] Historians have argued that in the late Stuart period, during a time of intense political and social unrest, the *Spectator Papers* did indeed provide a means of calming social tensions by expressing and shaping the attitudes of readers in such a way as to maintain the illusion of a unified and harmonious English audience.[9]

In Washington Irving's Geoffrey Crayon of *The Sketch-Book* and elsewhere, these basic assumptions survive a significant alteration of outward detail. Many scholars have commented on how this figure loses the voice of some unified cultural authority and becomes the eccentric yet lovable antiquarian bachelor, a figure whose appeal is related to his marginality. William Hedges, for example, argues that this narrator's "objectivity" of what he sees has become far less important than his own unique way of seeing: the Spectator looks on as a figure in a scene, while Crayon, like Sterne in *The Sentimental Journey,* makes himself and his feelings the center of scenic interest.[10]

Rather than specifically remarking what will give readers "Pleasure" and "Benefit," as does the Spectator, Crayon makes no explicit nod to an audience. He encourages the audience more indirectly, through his very manner of presenting himself, to enter into the process of feeling as he feels. He presents subjects about which he feels strong, apparently unique emotions that invariably turn out to be conventional. Thus, instead of simply encouraging readers to see through him to some "objective" reality, Crayon clearly desires readers who feel the same as he does about certain subjects, which are in turn important largely because they give rise to shared feelings.

At the very beginning of "The Author's Account of Himself," for example, Crayon attempts to set up a correspondent feeling about traveling to places with "storied associations": "I was always fond of visiting new scenes and observing strange characters and manners."[11] While claiming this feeling as characteristic of himself, he also inscribes precisely what an audience should do as it reads his travel-book. In the body of the sketch, Crayon reveals that he, like the Spectator, becomes the "rambler" he has prepared himself to become, traveling to Europe and particularly to England. But Europe, too, rather than merely proving the ground of his individual experience, also becomes a text: it is, in his words, a perpetual "volume" of "storied associations," not only for Crayon, but also for his own audience to read. The very movement of the verbs here reveals a quiet strategy: they progress from "wander" to "tread" to "meditate" to "escape" as the narrator assumes a reader capable of moving with him from outer events to an inner sharing of feelings about them.[12]

This brief description suggests how Irving, rather than simply presenting the self of his Geoffrey Crayon, also attempts to shape his readers. The individual feelings of Crayon as narrator thus become suspect: not only is he a descendant of the Spectator, but he also stands as an early nineteenth-century variation of a type developed as early as the mid-seventeenth century and largely out of fashion by Irving's time—the so-called man of feeling.[13] Characteristics of the figure are evident in Crayon's attraction to the legions of defeat (dying sailors, dying virgins, failed husbands, embattled artists, kings, and Indian chiefs) as well as in his penchant for shedding a sentimental tear at the gate of every country churchyard. Also evident, however, is Irving's gradual movement away from the purely benevolent aspect of feeling—dominant in the early development of the type—to a more generalized interest in feeling for its own sake. In Irving, whether feeling is directed toward specifically benevolent ends or not, it is still "good," still "pleasurable," to feel. It is not shared action that Crayon envisions, but the inactive warmth of a shared sensibility.

Clearly, the individual feelings of the Crayon figure are tied to his unadmitted role as eidolon. Like the Spectator's speculations, Crayon's strategies for shaping an audience with similar feelings directly points to the broader social dimension of his sensibility. Raymond Williams has placed the term *sensibility* in precisely such a context: "It [sensibility] was more than sensitivity, which can describe a physical or an emotional condition. It was, essentially, a social generalization of certain personal qualities, or, to put it another way, a personal appropriation of certain social qualities. It thus belongs in an important formation which includes TASTE . . . cultivation and discrimination, and, at a different level, CRITICISM & CULTURE in one of its uses, derived from cultivated and cultivation."[14] Geoffrey Crayon's personal feelings, as *The Sketch-Book* continually demonstrates, become social generalizations that readers are encouraged to appropriate as their own. Just as the Spectator's particular views or perspectives become universalized, so also do individual and social sensibilities become interdependent.

Crayon's narrative strategies also support the second part of Williams's definition. People who share his sensibility, it is suggested, have more taste than others; their feelings are cultured and cultivated, and they can make critical distinctions. Thus does sensibility appear to become a measuring stick for social difference: if it creates a bond of shared assumptions, it also projects the existence of those outside the bond.

But this emphasis on distinction must also be qualified. Even though sensibility seems to separate one group from another, Crayon leaves the process of acquiring it (through reading texts such as *The Sketch-Book*, for example) open to all. Irving's effort to "civilize" his democratic countrymen is well known: encouraging a sensibility shared with Europeans becomes one means of doing so. Anyone is free to become part of the distinct group of those sharing in sensibility— though, as in the Spectator's case, such sharing neither encourages identification with the person or thing about which one feels nor, by extension, does it point to some revolutionary leveling of social barriers. Once again, equality of feeling is clearly not identified with social equality.

2

Hawthorne's case proves much more complicated. The narrator-audience relationships enacted in the sketches of the *Twice-told Tales* show that Hawthorne, if initially intending to use the conventional alignments of the sketch, began (perhaps unintentionally) to explore and to challenge them. Many of these sketches present a narrator who threatens, undermines, or changes traditionally accepted relations between being seen and being seen through. Far from consistently projecting some unified audience that participates in a shared play of perspectives or feelings, this narrator invariably belies the assumption that transparency can be achieved or maintained—or, insofar as it is a product of older social assumptions, that it is indeed still desirable.

One of Hawthorne's earliest sketches, "Sights from a Steeple," published in 1830, opens with a revelation of its narrator: "So! I have climbed high, and my reward is small. Here I stand, with wearied knees, earth, indeed, at a dizzy depth below, but heaven far, far beyond me still. O that I could soar up into the very zenith, where man never breathed, nor eagle ever flew, and where the ethereal azure melts away from the eye, and appears only a deepened shade of nothingness! And yet I shiver at that cold and solitary thought!"[15] In contrast to Mr. Spectator and Geoffrey Crayon, this narrator offers no background, places himself in no immediately definable social context, and gives himself no explicit or easily guessed role vis-à-vis his audience. He neither engages in objective speculating nor provides a conventional emotional experience.

His first thought, ending in "a deepened shade of nothingness," obviously frightens him, and he begins to focus on other objects—perhaps, like Geoffrey Crayon, in order to feel other sensations. Unlike Crayon, however, whose fancies invariably prove commonplace, connected to historical or literary sources, and pointed always toward an audience's collaboration in them, the Hawthorne narrator engages in fancies that lead him into unpleasant individual feelings. Turning to the clouds closest to him, for example, he imagines fairies within them who appear only to tempt him and disappear while "longing fancy follows them in vain" (192). In a more telling example, he focuses on another series of clouds and muses: "Every one of those little clouds has been dipped and steeped in radiance, which the slightest pressure might disengage in silvery profusion, like water wrung from a sea-maid's hair. Bright they are as a young man's visions, and like them, would be realized in chillness, obscurity and tears. I will look upon them no more" (192). Each fanciful association leads him toward frightening or painful thoughts of solitude.

Even in those sketches where Hawthorne's subject is more slight—

a meditation on a snowstorm in "Snow-flakes" or a walk with a small child in "Little Annie's Ramble"—the narrator's reveries, beginning in gladness, often become personally disquieting. In "Snow-flakes," he conjures up a conventionally allegorical Winter who, in spite of his ferocity, appears harmless when set in the context of the season's pleasing domestic effects. For one moment, however, another feeling intrudes as frigid Winter overtakes a "homeless wanderer": "There he lies stark and stiff, a human shape of ice, on the spot where Winter overtook him" (347). Whereas this language remains conventional and the sketch almost immediately veers back to homely descriptions, the narrator's concern with dissolution resonates, finding its final realization in his portrait of a winter funeral: "A sable hearse, bestrewn with snow, is bearing a dead man through the storm to his frozen bed" (348). Certainly, such contrasts of mood mark many sketches (including Irving's); here, however, the narrator seems intent on revealing his own morbid concern with death in winter, rather than providing smoothly conventional shifts from one feeling to another.

Such disjunctions, present in "Snow-flakes," are yet more apparent in "Little Annie's Ramble," a sentimental vision of the good effect that children have on adults. In the course of this sketch, the narrator imagines the dancing partners Little Annie might find in the street. Beginning with a focus on the child, he ends with a focus on the sickness and despair of her possible dancing partners: "Some have the gout in their toes, or the rheumatism in their joints; some are stiff with age; some feeble with disease; . . . but many, many have leaden feet, because their hearts are far heavier than lead. It is a sad thought I have chanced upon. . . . For I, too, am a gentleman of sober footsteps . . ." (122–23). While one might expect contact with the child to relieve his distressing associations, it does not. Indeed, by the sketch's conclusion, in direct contrast to its purported moral (the salutary social effects of children), the narrator claims, "But I have gone too far astray for the town crier to call me back!" (129). Clearly, personal associations such as these do not link Hawthorne's narrators to the outer world in expected, conventional ways. Their relation to the "Not Me," as Emerson called the world outside himself, is not easily seen through or shared. Indeed, in spite of their attempts to use conventional subjects and language, Hawthorne's narrators periodically veer to the far pole from Mr. Spectator and Geoffrey Crayon, becoming opaque, not seen through at all.

Neither these sketches nor "Sights from a Steeple" stop at this point, however. Following a pattern used in many sketches, the "Sights" narrator resists the thoughts that leave him solitary and strains to forge links to the external world that will establish his credentials as an eidolon. In the sketch's next section, he looks down rather than up and exercises his powers of association on the landscape and town beneath him. First he offers an unvarnished, almost geometrical description of what he sees, which gradually spirals inward to become another personal dilation on external reality. This time, however, the dilation points in directions other than the terrifyingly isolating. Moving from sea to land to houses to chimneys to the inhabitants within the houses, he comments:

> O that the Limping Devil of Le Sage would perch beside me here, extend his wand over this contiguity of roofs, uncover every chamber, and make me familiar with their inhabitants! The most desirable mode of existence might be that of a spiritualized Paul Pry, hovering invisible round man and woman, witnessing their deeds, searching into their hearts, borrowing brightness from their felicity, and shade from their sorrow, and retaining no emotion peculiar to himself. But none of these things are possible; and if I would know the interior of brick walls, or the mystery of human bosoms, I can but guess. (192)

Tentatively, the narrator describes a more "desirable mode," not only of existing but also of exercising his fancy, than simple and solitary free association with natural objects. Unlike Mr. Spectator, he does not set up a purely speculative relation to what he sees; nor, like Crayon, does he promote connections whereby he can experience feelings about his sights, focusing more on his sensibility than the objects that arouse it. Rather, he appears to call for a new eidolon that can voluntarily lose itself in identifying with what it sees. Momentarily, his Paul Pry becomes less the conventional man of feeling than a representative of Keats's "poetical character," which, to quote Keats, "is not itself—it has no self—it is everything and nothing—It has no character—it enjoys light and shade; it lives in gusto, be it foul or fair, high or low, rich or poor, mean or elevated— It has as much delight in conceiving an Iago as an Imogen. What shocks the virtuous philosopher delights the camelion [sic] Poet."[16]

Paul Pry, too, desires to lose himself in what he sees. Yet in spite of his similarities with Keats, he also displays two important differences. First, he obviously feels skeptical about the process of achieving transparency. He by no means allows himself to enter into the process by which he can become the eidolon he describes—he simply muses on the possibility. In his final disclaimer he at once admits his desire to become seen through and denies the possibility of its happening: "if I would know the interior of brick walls, or the mystery of human bosoms, I can but guess" (192). Second, unlike Keats, who grounds his concept of the poetic character in the possibility of sympathetic identification with that which is seen, Paul Pry finally fears any overwhelming connection to his sights.[17]

In "Night Sketches" the narrator again describes his transparency and then adds an even more self-protective caveat. Creating a context in which he too watches rather than interacts with the outer world, he exclaims: "Onward I go, deriving a sympathetic joy or sorrow from the varied aspect of mortal affairs, even as my figure catches a gleam from the lighted windows, or is blackened by an interval of darkness. Not that mine is altogether a chameleon spirit, with no hue of its own" (431). Here, by coincidence, he uses the same term as Keats—*chameleon*—but then goes on to deny its applicability to himself. The remark only underlines what the sketch makes self-evident. Walking through a rainstorm, the narrator detachedly regards the varying struggles of his fellows and makes absolutely no effort to establish contact or to aid anyone.

Another example from "Sights" suggests a reason for the ambivalence of these narrators toward connection with the outer world. Soon after his comments about Paul Pry, the narrator focuses on a despondent young man. In a series of Keatsian questions, he draws closer to his subject: "Is he in doubt, or in debt? Is he, if the question be allowable, in love? Does he strive to be melancholy and gentlemanlike?—Or, is he merely overcome by the heat?" (193). Like Keats in his odes, the speaker gradually appears to enter into the life of something outside himself; unlike Keats, however, he also maintains an ironic distance from it.[18] The source of the narrator's desire to connect with this young man and his equal fear of doing so seem to lie in an ambivalent response to the young women whom the young man next encounters. Clearly, the narrator's physical distance, as well as his irony, allow him both to fantasize about and to deny a relationship with them. He cannot afford to identify too closely with the despondent young man.

Critics have explained this ambivalence in psychosexual terms: Hawthorne's narrators (and possibly their author) fear connection to an "other" because they may lose their individual identity. Desiring a form of contact that allows them control, they thus become voyeuristic Paul Prys.[19] In a related manner, this anxiety has been translated into evidence for their simultaneous attraction to and distrust of the imagination: fancy provides the illusion of a self with creative freedom, but fanciful associations can also lead to dangerous feelings of self-loss. The difficulties experienced by these narrators, however, point not only to sexual or artistic ambivalence but also to an inability to become conventional eidolons. Their conflicting desire and fear to be seen through reveal their equal incapacity to project a secure sense of their readers.

At only one point in "Sights from a Steeple" does the narrator achieve an integration of self with the outer world, and while this scene suggests the possibility of a new image of his relation to an audience, in the end it too is beset by divisiveness. In his third major attempt to establish contact with the external world, the narrator broadens the scope of his sights, no longer describing his strictly personal fancies, but framing three processions that he sees below him in patently emblematic terms. The first is a group of soldiers; the second is a group of children whose motions mimic those of the soldiers; the third is a funeral, contact with which momentarily unifies the reactions of the disparate processions and the entire town. In this scene, the narrator gropes toward an allegorical awareness in which maturity and youth confront the universal dilemma of age and dissolution. During this passage—and it is the only point in the sketch where he does so—the narrator quietly asks us to share his view.[20] When he notes with relief that the "King of Terrors" can still receive the same age-old human response, the storm threatened at the sketch's beginning starts to break, and the narrator reaches a point of apparent catharsis:

> How various are the situations of the people covered by the roofs beneath me, and how diversified are the events at this moment befalling them! The new-born, the aged, the dying, the strong in life, and the recent dead, are in the chambers of these many mansions. The full of hope, the happy, the miserable, and the desperate, dwell together within the circle of my glance. In some of the houses over which my eyes roam so coldly, guilt is entering into hearts that are still tenanted by a debased and trodden virtue,— guilt is on the very edge of commission, and the impending deed might be averted; guilt is done, and the criminal wonders if it be irrevocable. These are broad thoughts struggling in my mind, and, were I able to give them distinctness, they would make their way in eloquence. Lo! the rain-drops are descending. (196)

In this passage the narrator qualifies the type of nothingness prefigured in his fearful associations at the sketch's opening and the nothingness entailed in becoming Paul Pry. Musing on the fact of nothingness embodied in the funeral procession, he is moved to a sympathy heretofore lacking. An awareness of the shared human reality of death frees him to enter into an imaginative identification with others.

His language, drawing on the images and rhythms of the Bible, takes on a rich emotional cadence far different from the coyness of his discussion of the young man and maidens. He also exhibits an ability to "see" into the houses and hearts beneath him that he had earlier disclaimed. Notably, he does not postulate that guilt "may" be occurring in the town, but emphatically details the process of its coming and enactment: "guilt is entering into hearts that are still tenanted by a debased and trodden virtue,—guilt is on the very edge of commission, and the impending deed might be averted; guilt is done, and the criminal wonders if it be irrevocable." Only an imaginative sympathy for the criminal's state could account for the certainty with which he speaks. For one brief moment, he acknowledges his capacity to become the "Iago or an Imogen" described in Keats's definition.

This new ability to identify with his sights is briefly borne out in the descriptions that follow. The narrator no longer satirizes the old merchant who is the father of the maidens, but notes that the man is limping, a victim of the gout. The merchant-father angrily separates the youth from his daughters, but not before the narrator remarks a "backward glance of mirth" thrown to the "disconsolate lover" by his sweetheart, betokening their future contact. Finally, he offers a wonderful description of the chambermaids "shrinking away from the quick fiery glare" of the lightning as they hasten to close the windows. His ability to note such details has been heightened by his newfound desire to identify with what he sees.

Nevertheless, not only in the light of the ambivalent scenes preceding this catharsis but also in the light of what follows it, we must question the narrator's newfound capacity to connect. At the end of "Sights," the narrator stands once more alone, confronting the natural world of the sketch's beginning, not the town, which has grown as solitary as a "city of the dead." He presents himself as fearful of the storm he is "powerless to direct or quell," yet at the same time implies that he is its prophet, descending "with the blue lightning wrinkling on my brow, and the thunder muttering its first awful syllables in my ear." At the next moment, however, this sense of Mosaic dignity dissipates as the "giant of the storm" becomes tritely personified, "striding in robes of mist" over the "little hills," and the sky grows "gloomy as an author's prospects" (198). The self-conscious pun on *prospects* indicates that the narrator has lost his capacity to identify with his sights. Once more, he stands above and outside the world beneath him, and once again, his way of seeing reflects back on himself. His use of conventional language and imagery at this point does not make him any more seen through than he was at the sketch's beginning. If the entire sketch had employed conventional scenes framed in conventional language, perhaps he could have been seen through in conventional ways. Here at the end, however, his use of phrases like "gloomy as an author's prospects" only points up his distinction from, not his transparency to, his readers.

Nowhere does this narrator's use of convention draw more attention to itself than in his concluding image of the rainbow, invariably an emblem of linkage and reconciliation. While the Spectator or Geoffrey Crayon could have used the image in ways that assumed a unified response, its use here points more to the narrator's own struggle to gain a final conventional control over the materials of his sketch. The rainbow becomes a deus ex machina, lowered on the sketch's disparate sights. Clearly, however, the narrator has not demonstrated that these sights possess any shared meaning: all he has shown is that his own particular ways of seeing them and of thereby relating himself to a world and to an audience remain fragmented and inconclusive.

Many narrators of the *Twice-told Tales* attempt to unify problematic materials by turning to images that ornament ending morals. In "Sunday at Home," for example, the narrator lives next door to the town church and experiences religious feelings simply by watching churchgoers and listening to the service from his own room. Feeling loneliness, he dispels it by spying on, not mingling with, the townspeople. As in other sketches, he also engages in light fantasies about young maidens, irony toward young gentlemen, and a distanced pity for older folk, and admits that he tends to use the sermon merely as the occasion for his own free association. At the sketch's conclusion, he makes no comment about his curious status as observer rather than churchgoer, but turns to a conventional image that can, in retrospect, organize the sketch's varied contents: "Oh! but the church is a symbol of religion. May its site . . . be kept holy forever, a spot of solitude and peace, amid the trouble and vanity of our week-day world! There is a moral, and a religion too, even in the silent walls. And, may the steeple still point heavenward, and be decked with the hallowed sunshine of the Sabbath morn!" (26). Given his distance from the church and his less than religious meditations within the body of the sketch, it seems clear that this image, like the rainbow, does not really correspond to the content of the sketch but is used, once again, in an attempt to give the narrator's material and his sense of his readers some conventional unity.

Likewise, in "Chippings with a Chisel," the narrator observes a sculptor of gravestones and his various customers in great detail, with his usual distance and his usual polite irony. At the sketch's end, however, he himself refuses to choose a stone and moralizes on his refusal: "Every grave-stone that you ever made is the visible symbol of a mistaken system. Our thoughts should soar upward with the butterfly—not linger with the exuviae that confined him. In truth and reason, neither those whom we call the living, and still less the departed, have any thing to do with the grave" (418). In spite of the clever reversal, this kind of ending is conventionally religious. What proves far more curious about "Chippings" is the narrator's failure to conclude the sketch at this point. Instead, he offers another ending that nearly overturns the moral just proclaimed.

The rainbow, the sabbath sunshine, and the butterfly are all images tacked onto disparate views of the outside world. They exemplify their narrators' attempts to unify these materials (and thereby to project a shared response to them) by ending on an uplifting, quasi-religious note. In "Chippings with a Chisel," the narrator himself seems to question this strategy: "yet, with my gain of wisdom, I had likewise gained perplexity; for there was a strange doubt in my mind, whether the dark shadowing of this life, the sorrows and regrets, have not as much real comfort in them—leaving religious influences out of the question—as what we term life's joys" (418). Not only does he leave "religious influences out of the question," he also, by offering an alternate conclusion, leaves this sketch far more open-ended and fragmented than its fellows. As a result, the narrator's sense of his audience, as suggested by his relation to his materials, becomes more patently insecure and indeterminate by the end of this sketch than it does in the others. The sketch seems almost intentionally to display a sense of the disparities rather than the unities involved in seeing and feeling.

3

The narrator of "Sights," and many of the narrators of the sketches in *Twice-told Tales*, cannot be seen through in ways assumed by Mr. Spectator or, despite his affinities with the Hawthorne narrator, by Geoffrey Crayon. As we have noted, this narrator's problematic personal responses invariably color speculations on an "objective" reality, and his feelings regarding the external world are rarely (and certainly not consistently) the products of a sensibility reflecting a secure sense of an audience. When he does use conventional scenes and language, he generally sets them in a context so unremittingly self-centered that with one possible exception, conventions too are shown up as artifices used only to support the preeminence of his personal views.

Thus, although this narrator and his fellows may attempt to represent the objective or shared views or feelings that can make them seen through, they also reveal the difficulties involved in creating illusions of connection to the Not Me. Swinging between a fear of connection and a longing for it, these narrators demonstrate both the ambivalence and the artifice involved in becoming eidolons. In using such a narrator, Hawthorne comes not only to question the eidolons of Addison, Steele, and Irving, but also subtly to undercut romantic presuppositions about the possibility of sympathetic identification. The sketches of the *Twice-told Tales* reveal a Hawthorne who examines the eidolon-audience relationship from all sides and then, in effect, turns it on its head. His narrator is Furtwangler's "vague, indistinct spectre" concretized, exposed in his narcissism, in his doubts, and in his ambivalent response to being seen through.

When Hawthorne's so-called eidolons are viewed in a broader context, however, one must ask whether they alone should be blamed for their ambivalent self-enclosure. In their inability to achieve some consistent means of linking the solitary seer to his sights, these narrators do not simply reveal an uncertain sense of their audience; they also suggest a sense that some audience may resist their attempts at relation. In short, these narrators may not want to see as they do, yet they may be trapped in their ways of seeing. Incapable of projecting a vision of a unified audience, all they can see is themselves. This problem—the Hawthorne narrator's self-entrapment and his inability to be seen through by a unified group of responders—suggests that the cultural and social preconditions for such an audience do not exist.

The sketches of the *Twice-told Tales* period point to the conclusion that the sketch as a form can simply not cohere as it did for Hawthorne's predecessors. The sketch can no longer presume to mirror and to mold either shared perspectives or shared feelings, because external factors are pressing against it, helping at once to undermine and to re-form it. In the longing of Hawthorne's narrators to project a unified audience, and in their fear of doing so, we can trace manifestations of a cultural anxiety central to the rhetoric of Jacksonian democracy in the 1820s, 1830s, and beyond. Viewed in the light of the complex conflation of ideas, values, and feelings that informed this rhetoric, the troubled eidolons of these sketches become less the unique and alienated Hawthornean artists of most critics than the image of a dilemma shared by their countrymen.

In a recent study of the period, John McWilliams, drawing on Tocqueville and others, underscores the concept that "all Americans would be individuals, yet all would be the same." For McWilliams, the psychosocial ramifications of this belief meant that "the democratic American must be a solipsist who creates the world in his own self-image by projecting his self onto the world." The chilling term he often uses to describe this world is "the void."[21]

McWilliams provides an apt analogy to several of the stances taken by the "Sights" narrator. In his effort to connect to the outer world, this narrator, through free association, projects himself onto what he sees. Projecting himself onto Nature, however, leads him to deadening feelings of solitude and nothingness that turn him from natural to social contemplation. But free association about others also leads to a fear of self-loss that must be controlled by physical distance and irony. When he does make momentary identification with the feelings of others during the funeral scene, the projection remains optative rather than fully realized. His desires to become "eloquent" about social relationships are situated in an ending in which the community has disappeared and over which he takes a solitary and artificial control. In "Sights from a Steeple," the individual Me attempts to dominate an outer world, a Not Me, perceived more as void than as substance.

But *free association* contains a pun. If it describes individual fantasy, it also describes democratic political philosophy. To Tocqueville's astonishment, the American freedom of self-projection, rather than leading to social anarchy, leads instead to an obsession with similarity. This similarity can be understood in two ways. On the positive side, the quest for a self that is representative of others could provide a way out of the void of self-enclosure. More negatively, however, the quest could also lead to a deadening conformity—entrapment in a world where all are deemed equal and are equally leveled. Here Tocqueville foresees the "tyranny of the majority," which Marvin Meyers has called the hallmark of an unacknowledged "soft totalitarianism."[22] In America, the Not Me can indeed come to dominate a Me that exists only as it is seen through. If the narrator fears closeness with Nature because it may come to annihilate him rather than submit to his control, he also fears closeness with others because, given the social ideology of the period, they too may void his individuality. "Sights" prefigures the famous dilemma of the aging Clifford Pyncheon in *The House of the Seven Gables*, poised on a windowsill, desiring to make the jump—a suicidal jump—into contact with the Fourth of July crowd in the street below.

Such supposedly extrinsic cultural issues are part and parcel of the intrinsic workings of these sketches. They also help us understand the difficulty of setting up any consistent eidolon-audience relationship in America in the 1830s. It cannot be done in the terms earlier established by Addison, Steele, Irving, or, indeed, John Keats. Each of these writers can construct successful eidolons because each assumes the existence of a concrete social reality and a stable history. Each can project a balance between being seen and being seen through because this balance is grounded in a belief in the value of social hierarchy.[23] If even a Keats voluntarily yields up his identity, there remains a secure sense of self and world to which he can return. He does not need to create this world: he can assume it as a historical and social given. In contrast, as both contemporaneous and modern scholars have realized, Americans in the nineteenth century felt themselves "deprived of institutions and hierarchies that gave men of the old world their identity."[24] While democratic institutions could offer images of possibility or progress or endless self-making, they could not project a stable image of a self created, completed, and living among other completed selves. Unable to project a fixed image of the "free" individual, they were equally incapable of defining the individual's association with an outer world seen as equally in flux.

In his reworking of the sketch form throughout the 1830s, Hawthorne came to test a variety of relationships possible between eidolon and audience and found each of them somehow wanting. His turn away from the sketch to the autobiographical prefaces and to the longer romances indicates that he became interested not in perfecting the presentation of some "successful" mode of blending narrator and reader, but in examining the assumptions and confusions involved in seeking and projecting this blending in the first place.[25] Unlike the earlier sketchers we have noted, he came to make the original problem—not some conventional, momentary, well-structured solution—the subject of his fiction. Confronting the puzzling sameness and multiplicity of his American readers, the task of Hawthorne the romancer became not to resolve discrepancies between viewer and viewed, eidolon and audience, being seen and being seen through, but to represent the psychological and social complexities involved in defining and sustaining personal and communal relationships in a fluid, democratic world.

Notes

1. See, for example, Nina Baym, *The Shape of Hawthorne's Career* (Ithaca, N.Y.: Cornell University Press, 1978), 58.

2. See William Hedges's discussion of sketching in *Washington Irving: An American Study, 1802–1832* (Baltimore: Johns Hopkins Press, 1965), 146–48. Hedges makes use of F. L. Pattee, *The Development of the American Short Story* (New York: New York University Press, 1923), and Ray B. West, *The Short Story in America* (Chicago: University of Chicago Press, 1952). See also Nina Baym's discussion of the sketches, especially pp. 50–52 and 58–64.

3. Baym's study and two more recent essays do address these narrators' relationship to an audience, but in a different manner and with different conclusions from those presented here. Baym reads the early tales and sketches as constricted by Hawthorne's own sense of an audience's moralistic expectations. I am concerned less with Hawthorne's ostensible intentions than with the fragmented image of an audience projected by his narrators. Closer to my reading is that of Dana Brand. In "The Panoramic Spectator in America: A Rereading of Some of Hawthorne's Sketches," *American Transcendental Quarterly* 62 (1986): 5–17, Brand argues that Hawthorne's early narrators, especially the narrator of "Sights from a Steeple," are failed European flaneurs—distanced observers of "the mystery of cities" (p. 7). On the one hand, the sketches portray Hawthorne's ambivalence about the capacity of the artist-flaneur to look into the houses and hearts of those whom he watches. On the other hand, Hawthorne's narrators lack the dense cosmopolitan subject matter and the sophisticated audience that would allow them to become true flaneurs. While Hawthorne may thus covertly criticize the flaneurs, Brand argues that he is also drawn to the richness of the European city life they portray and is correspondingly frustrated with the "thinness" of American life and the lack of sophistication of American readers. For Jeffrey Richards, whose "Hawthorne's Posturing Observer: The Case of 'Sights from a Steeple,' " also appears in *American Transcendental Quarterly* 62 (1986): 35–41, Hawthorne's narrator exposes the artifice of romantic art and its artificer by demonstrating that all the sketch's events and images are simply rhetorical constructs. The sketch, more generally, unmasks all fiction as a "stage-trick." I find myself closer to Brand's conclusions than to Richards', although I arrive at them in a different way. In response to Richards, I would argue

that while "Sights from a Steeple" does present an ambivalence about fiction making, it does so in the broader cultural context of an uncertainty about audience in America. Richards' focus is more ahistorical than mine.

4. For comments about the early "Spectator" essays, see William Charvat et al., eds., *The Centenary Edition of the Works of Nathaniel Hawthorne* (Columbus: Ohio State University Press, 1962–), 9:485.

5. See Thomas J. Rountree, ed., *Critics on Hawthorne* (Coral Gables, Florida: University of Miami Press, 1972), 11. Rountree reprints Poe's 1842 review of the *Twice-told Tales*, in which Poe notes that "the Spectator, Mr. Irving and Mr. Hawthorne" share a "tranquil and subdued manner," but that Hawthorne is far more "original" and suggestive.

6. Albert J. Furtwangler, "The Making of Mr. Spectator," *Modern Language Quarterly* 38 (1977): 21–22.

7. See Donald F. Bond, ed., *The Spectator* (Oxford: Clarendon Press, 1965), 1:46. Mr. Spectator notes that "there is another set of Men that I must likewise lay a claim to, whom I have lately called the Blanks of society, as being altogether unfurnish'd with ideas, till the Business and Conversation of the Day has supplied them." According to Mr. Spectator, since these Blanks "lie at the Mercy of the first Man they meet," they should read his paper before they leave the house.

8. The issue of role playing and its social significance is addressed in Michael G. Ketchum's valuable study *Transparent Designs: Reading, Performance, and Form in the Spectator Papers* (Athens: University of Georgia Press, 1985), 11–26 and passim.

9. See especially Peter Gay, "The Spectator as Actor: Addison in Perspective," *Encounter* 29 (1967): 27–32.

10. Hedges, *Washington Irving*, 146–51.

11. Haskell Springer, ed., *The Complete Works of Washington Irving: The Sketch-Book of Geoffrey Crayon, Gent.* (Boston: Twayne, 1978), 8.

12. "I longed to wander over the scenes of renowned achievement—to tread as it were in the footsteps of antiquity—to loiter about the ruined castle—to meditate on the falling tower—to escape in short, from the commonplace realities of the present, and lose myself among the shadowy grandeurs of the past" (Springer, ed., *Complete Works of Washington Irving: The Sketch-Book . . . .* , 9).

13. For a fine discussion of this figure, see R. S. Crane, "Suggestions towards a Genealogy of the 'Man of Feeling,' " in *The Idea of the Humanities* (Chicago: University of Chicago Press, 1967), 1:188–213. See especially Crane's discussion of the movement from benevolence as feeling to benevolent feelings as "natural" (197–213).

14. Raymond Williams, *Keywords* (New York: Oxford University Press, 1976), 236.

15. Quoted from William Charvat et al., eds., *The Centenary Edition of the Works of Nathaniel Hawthorne* (Columbus: Ohio State University Press, 1962–), 9:191, hereafter cited parenthetically in the text.

16. Letter of 27 October 1818, quoted in W. J. Bate, ed., *Criticism: The Major Texts* (New York: Harcourt Brace Jovanovich, 1970), 349.

17. Note Brand's comment that considering the context in which Hawthorne writes, "the narrator's inability to offer an illusion of spectatorial omniscience is significant" ("The Panoramic Spectator," 10). Brand refers to the context of the flaneur; I refer this "inability" to Hawthorne's broader romantic critical milieu.

18. Compare, for example, these lines from "Ode on a Grecian Urn": "What men or gods are these? What maidens loth? / What mad pursuit? What struggles to escape? / What pipes and timbrels? What wild ecstasy?" See David Perkins, ed., *English Romantic Writers* (New York: Harcourt, Brace and World, 1967), 1186.

19. See, for example, Frederick Crews, *The Sins of the Fathers: Hawthorne's Psychological Themes* (New York: Oxford University Press, 1966), 158–70.

20. "But, leaving these, let us turn to the third procession, which, though sadder in outward show, may excite identical reflections in the thoughtful mind" (*Centenary Edition*, 9:195).

21. John P. McWilliams, Jr., *Hawthorne, Melville, and the American Character: A Looking Glass Business* (Cambridge: Cambridge University Press, 1984), 6, 9, 23.

22. Marvin Meyers, *The Jacksonian Persuasion: Politics and Belief* (Stanford: Stanford University Press, 1957), 39.

23. Such is obviously far more the case for the English writers. I am talking more about Irving's public pose than I am about his private insecurities. For background on the latter and the part they played in Irving's development as a writer, see Jeffrey Rubin-Dorsky, "Washington Irving and the Genesis of the Fictional Sketch," *Early American Literature* 21 (1986/87): 226–47.

24. McWilliams, *Hawthorne, Melville, and the American Character*, 8.

25. Space prohibits a full discussion of this claim. I am well aware that Hawthorne turned to a different kind of sketching in *Mosses from an Old Manse* (1846). Nina Baym has argued that the sketches and tales of this volume largely display a self-assured narrator speaking to a well-defined audience: the democratic readers of *The Democratic Review* (Baym, *The Shape of Hawthorne's Career*, 99–102). Yet she also admits that this secure speaker could have really masked an insecure Hawthorne who was simply "trying out a new authorial stance" while retaining the old ambivalence about his audience. I would argue that this earlier stance, if it seems covert in the Old Manse tales and sketches, is emphatically present in the introduction to the collection, "The Old Manse," and later in "The Custom-House," where Hawthorne presents himself (not a narrator) as an eidolon. The point is that there is no real break in his concern about the relation of being seen to being seen through. *Mosses* is thus not as discontinuous with the *Twice-told Tales* as it might seem.

Pretty in Pink: "Young Goodman Brown" and New-World Dreams

Jerome Loving*

> We are told, in effect, that this is an imaginary garden with a real toad in it, and that we are not to let the imaginariness of the garden blind us to the reality of the toad.[1]

In her study of the use of dreams in Hawthorne's fiction, Rita K. Gollin observes that the author's "dream visions come at the end of the long line that goes from the Bible through medieval dream allegories, *Pilgrim's Progress*, and beyond, but they succeed most where their debt is least, where the dreamer confronts apparitions of his own repressed guilt."[2] Whereas Spenser's *Faerie Queene*, said

* This essay was written specifically for this volume and is published here for the first time by permission of the author.

to be the first book Hawthorne purchased with his own money, is framed by nothing more than the interior wall of the dream, and whereas Dante's *The Divine Comedy*, another allegory whose influence on Hawthorne is readily suggested, begins in "the dark wood of life," Hawthorne's dreamers are always waking up to the "truth" of the allegory. They are seldom if ever secure in the dream (with the Fall behind them) but are orphaned by it in a reality waiting to happen. This is clearly the fate of Goodman Brown, who withdraws from the dream, destined "to penetrate, in every bosom, the deep mystery of sin." Critics have questioned whether Brown's experience was intended to be a dream instead of a clairvoyant vision, but we know Brown dreams from the author's rhetorical tease at the end of the story. "Had Goodman Brown fallen asleep in the forest, and only dreamed a wild dream of a witch-meeting?" he asks. The answer is fairly revealing: "Be it so, if you will. But, alas! *it was a dream* of evil omen" (my emphasis).[3] Brown's beginnings as a dreamer are different from those in Spenser and Dante because he enters the dream from a literal dark wood, where the actual fear of hostile Indians and the superstitious one of "the devil himself" combine to conjure up "the figure of a man, in a grave and decent attire, seated at the foot of an old tree." By *figure* Hawthorne originally intended *apparition*, which is the word he used in the first published versions of the story.[4] Hence, we know exactly where the "actual" ends and the "imaginary" begins. The dream makes up the better part of the tale and concludes when Brown calls out to his wife of three months to "Look up to heaven, and resist the Wicked One!" Subsequently, he staggers "against the [previously 'blazing'] rock and [feels] it chill and damp, while a hanging twig, that had been all on fire, besprinkles his cheek with the coldest dew." Brown wakes up from the imaginary forest to find himself again in an actual one—from which he emerges a changed and gloomy man whose dream-induced experience has real consequences.

What, then, are we to conclude about this imaginary garden with a real toad in it? The vision Brown receives at the initiation ceremony in the dream is that "Evil is the nature of Mankind"; yet we know from a broader view of Hawthorne's work that he found a world of good-and-evil.[5] We also know from the author's statements in "The Custom-House Sketch" and other prefaces that he chose the "neutral territory" of the romance for his literary investigations—"somewhere between the real world and fairy-land, where the Actual and the Imaginary may meet, and each imbue itself with the nature of the other." In such a dreamlike environment, Hawthorne explored the psychological terrain of his characters and dramatized the role of guilt in human motivation. Furthermore, this "neutral territory" enabled him—as countless graduate students have been told—to investigate the burden of the past upon the present. In "Roger Malvin's Burial," for example, Reuben Bourne assumes the guilt for an imaginary crime,[6] but one that becomes real as a "cover-up." I employ the term, with all its connotations of the Watergate and Iran-Contra affairs, because concealment of the past is apparently a more serious and compelling sin than the one being concealed in what Terence Martin has called the "negative structures" of the American imagination—the desire to wipe the slate clean of Old-World imperfection and to adorn the mantle of New World saints in the historical context of puritan ideology.[7] However, Reuben's dream—like those induced by the more recent Washington scandals—produces a vision that is exalted to a nightmare.

Whereas the past becomes a bad dream in "Roger Malvin's Burial," the process is reversed in "Young Goodman Brown." The protagonist emerges from the forest with the knowledge that his neighbors, and most likely his wife as well, have signed the devil's book. His evidence is admittedly spectral, as David Levin has argued.[8] Like the accusers in the Salem witchcraft hysteria of 1692, Brown believes, at the very least, that he has seen the shape of those he tacitly accuses of having kept company with the devil. It was on this basis that Hawthorne's great-great-grandfather, a magistrate in Salem Village, received the first warrants in the witchcraft trials that ultimately sent to the gallows nineteen men and women and two dogs.[9] For Brown, it is the same dreamy evidence that produces nightmarish "facts." Symbolic of the puritan fear of the Fall in the New World, Brown sees the past in "a dream of evil omen." Regarding his dream more scientifically, we might assume that it combined actual facts from the past and present to produce a fictional past. In this view, Brown has done something wrong, perhaps committed adultery, and the dream functions as a transfer mechanism for his guilt. The problem with this reading, however, is that, in "Young Goodman Brown," this New-World pilgrim—like the historical ones he represents in the tale—has no visible past in sin.[10] His story, unlike Dimmesdale's in *The Scarlet Letter*, does not even begin in medias res. The past Brown sees in the forest is imaginary, yet its result is actual.

Of course, we can hardly imagine the reality of Dimmesdale's past in the dark wood of Hester. It seems too imaginary, given the minister's demeanor in the novel, and yet we have the corporeal Pearl. Actually, she is also fantastic—the product of Hawthorne's blending of the imaginary and the real. She exists under a spell of guilt that is broken only when Dimmesdale makes a public confession in which he admits to having had sex with Hester but denounces the act as fornication. In the lunar light of the forest, it had "a consecration of its own," but in the harsh light of Election Day, it is—as Dimmesdale tells Hester—"The Law we broke." It is another bad dream come true, this consecration of evil. "Hush, Hester, hush!" he says. "The sin here so awfully revealed!—let these alone be in thy thoughts." Similarly, after three months of lovemaking, Brown chastizes Faith to look up to heaven. I would argue that both Dimmesdale and Brown deny the significance of their sexual past and thus commit a version of Hawthorne's "unpardonable sin" in their teleological rejection of the idea that "evil"—the sexual act—"is the nature of mankind." In rejecting it, they deny their connection with the Old World and, hence, the necessity of their inevitable fall in the New World.

Although Brown believes at the beginning of the story that he has done nothing wrong—indeed, has "Faith" in the power of sex to keep him young enough to resist the evil that characterizes the misdeeds of his race—he is nevertheless vaguely troubled and anxious over "this one night" away from his wife. For her part, it is the night "of all nights in the year!" that she most needs her husband. Their nervous parting in the sunset—on a night very much resembling Halloween today—is not unlike those contrived scenes in horror movies that prepare the viewer for a plotless series of violent events intended not only to frighten but also to titillate a little. The violence in "Young Goodman Brown" is psychological, but the titillation is real enough. For what we have in this tale is a New-World garden and an Old-World toad. In the fiction or dream that follows, Brown loses his faith in himself as one of the sexual elect. His vision of a past yet to occur binds him to the crimes of the Old World and to the fathers of the New, who have given up their youthful notions of "safe" sex. Although unlike Dimmesdale, Brown consummates his physical relationship within the bonds of marriage (and puritan ideology), there is something almost too corporeal about (his) Faith, as if her pink ribbons signify a sensuality with a consecration of its own. Pretty in pink, she sends Brown into the same dark wood that consumes Dimmesdale.

Neither Brown nor Dimmesdale can ultimately accept the implications of his sexuality in the hopeful context of American ideology. In Dimmesdale's case, it is partly a matter of priestly celibacy (or more intensified puritan idealism) that prevents his development into a sexual "elder"; in Brown's, it is sheer sexual adolescence (or personal idealism) that keeps him from confronting the contradictory conditions of his existence. Both characters suffer from an inflated sense of self, but Brown's crisis is more acute because he has not violated any visible laws—has not, like Dimmesdale, committed adultery. If he has, or if his wife or neighbors have, the evidence is merely spectral. Hawthorne begins both tales in the middle of the story. Whereas we enter Dimmesdale's story after the fact, we enter Brown's before what has already happened. For what Brown discovers in his dream is the same inescapable past that Hawthorne could not talk about, for various reasons, in *The Scarlet Letter*. In other words, every imaginary garden or utopian dream is animated by a reality that ultimately cannot be covered up. Try as he might, in the forest, to ignore the spectral evidence of his universal past, Brown wakes up to discover that he had already fallen by the time his fiction (or Hawthorne's story) began. He encounters his past in the middle of the story proper, and in this sense we should consider "Young Goodman Brown" to be a possibly more tantalizing, if not a more penetrating, analysis of guilt than *The Scarlet Letter*. For Brown's connection with the "crime" is purely psychological: there is no corporeal Pearl to haunt him, only the specters of a past that never (yet) actually happened. It is all a dream, but its effect on him makes the "crime" as real as Dimmesdale's. As Everyman, he cannot escape the fate of his fathers in the matter of sex—whose price is the loss of innocence as a son.

It is important to note that the unmysterious stranger in the forest resembles not only Brown but also his deceased father. Hawthorne tells us that the two "might have been taken for father and son." More significant, they are alike "more in expression than features." They have the same tale to tell, that of the solipsistic motive in "love," which is sexual survival. Brown's faith that his sex both renews his youth and keeps him from the sins of the (Old World) father dissolves—ironically, on the Eve of All Saints—in a vision of the inevitable evil, in which the female is an object of lust rather than of love (now revealed as the delusion that one woman is different from another). "Bring forth the converts!" the father figure commands in this dream full of fathers. They all participate in the orgy of the past that becomes Brown's sexual present (and future). Brown's grandfather, as Daniel Hoffman suspects, has had illicit relations with Goody Cloyse.[11] This is the same grandfather who sadistically enjoyed, as the devil tells Brown, having lashed a half-naked "Quaker woman so smartly through the streets." Brown's father vented his sexual rage in the violent destruction of an Indian Village during King Philip's War, but it is also his father who beckons him to advance toward the concupiscent congregation, while a figure resembling his mother throws out her hand "to warn him back." Brown's sexually dead fathers and ravished mothers and maidens come together in a dream that will inevitably come true: " 'Was it his mother?' But he had no power to retreat one step, nor to resist, even in thought, when the minister and good old Deacon Gookin seized his arms, and led him to the blazing rock. Thither came also the slender form of a veiled female, led between Goody Cloyse, that pious teacher of catechism, and Martha Carrier, who had received the devil's promise to be queen of hell. . . . And there stood the proselytes, beneath the canopy of fire."

Considering the censorious reaction to *Sister Carrie* more than half a century later, we have to wonder how Hawthorne got away with his sexual themes in "Young Goodman Brown" and *The Scarlet Letter*. It is tempting to say that Carrie went to bed with a drummer and thus gave herself for commerce, whereas Hester and Faith fell in love with druids in the sense that both Hawthorne characters are high priests of their idealism about sex. Although Dreiser's heroine had emerged from the Henry Adams stereotype of "the monthly-magazine-made" female who was supposedly sexless and thus acted on her own, Hawthorne's heroines are merely acted upon and are thus reflections of their partner's libidinous images—which in the dream-vision of the dark wood return them to that first imaginary garden with a real toad in it. Brown loses faith in conventional morality and finds himself naked in his worst fears about sex: that it connects him as one of the fathers instead of as a son, and with mothers instead of lovers. In his case and in this sense, his sexual activity is as fatal as Dimmesdale's tryst in the forest, from which the minister also emerges a dazed and changed man. Frankly, Brown deflowers his own faith in himself as a goodman in the New World without a past. He trusts (and hence tests) his wife for one night without him and discovers her at the center of an ancient ceremony involving the misdeeds of the past. Of course, that he is never quite sure of her actual presence (only that of "a veiled female") places the burden of the past squarely on his shoulders.

John Updike, as surely a descendant of Hawthorne in the tradition of a Protestant literature in America as Brown is heir to what is discovered in the forest, enjoys a latitude of sexual themes that neither Hawthorne nor Dreiser ever could have imagined in America. Yet in *Roger's Version,* a novel that retells in modern terms the story of *The Scarlet Letter,* the latter-day Chillingworth comes to the realization that "the best sex is head sex—sex kept safe in the head." It is safe because it preserves the fantasy that kept Goodman Brown young. Before he had Faith, he *had* faith in the power of the future, but ever afterward the sexual act becomes allegorized into a dreamlike ceremony about a past that is perennial. "Out Puritan heritage," exclaims Updike's protagonist, a divinity school professor in a university and an urban area that clearly simulate the historically hung-over Harvard and Boston. "How did those old Israelites get their hooks into us so deeply, sticking us with their frightful black Bible and its imprecations while their modern descendants treat the matter as a family joke, filling their own lives with violin music and clear-eyed, Godless science?"[12] In this context, every American reader of "Young Goodman Brown" is a typological Jew, and a wandering one who, feeling as lost in the puritan legacy as Brown is in the allegory of his dream, is compelled to preface his explication with a plot summary. After determining what happens in the story, we do indeed attempt to dismiss Brown's sexual dilemma as "a family joke," something out of the superstitious adolescence of our existence. But Hawthorne, with his allegorical legerdemain, tricks us into reading the story in terms of the original family plot—in which Adam's confusion cannot be summarized away.

Like Whitman's Adamic dreamer in "Song of Myself," Brown is "both in and out of the game."[13] And he takes the reader with him until the Actual and the Imaginary "imbue" themselves with each other to produce a "theme state" that transcends this story about a puritan who falls asleep in the forest. Quoting Croce, Jorge Luis Borges suggests that allegory "is a tiresome pleonasm, a collection of useless repetitions which shows us (for example) Dante led by Virgil and Beatrice and then explains to us . . . that Dante is the soul, Virgil is philosophy or reason . . . and Beatrice is theology or grace." In this definition, allegory seems a masquerade—an "aesthetic sport" that reduces life to a lesson instead of a labyrinth. But like Poe, who once chastized Hawthorne for his overfondness of allegory,[14] Borges is aware of the linguistic potential of allegory. Despite its ostensible simplicity, it can, like myth or fable, "somehow correspond to the ungraspable reality."[15] Clearly ungraspable in Hawthorne's imaginary garden is the role and function of Brown's Beatrice, for the "vita nuova" she offers her husband is not only an admixture of the real and the imaginary but of the past and the present.

By naming her Faith, Hawthorne toys with the beatific vision that Dante is supposed to have received in the *Vita nuova* through the appearance of Beatrice, the ennobling female who leads him up the Ladder of Love to paradise. Dante, who is beyond sex in the Old World of the Fall, is secure in the dark wood of his lover's allegory. But Brown, whose common name suggests his earthly entrance into the allegory, is cast back upon himself. Sex to this puritan proves to be not an elixir but a solipsism that throws him back to Salem Village, where the reverenced elders—those who have been held up to the youth of the town as having used their sexuality responsibly or not at all—are exposed: "how hoary-bearded elders of the church have whispered wanton words to the young maids of their households; how many a woman, eager for a widow's weeds, has given her husband a drink at bed-time, and let him sleep his last sleep in her bosom." The debauchery that Brown uncovers in his dream of Faith's angelic character, however, is not limited to his parents' generation but extends right down to the one that still claims a sexuality that is beatific: "how beardless youths have made haste to inherit their father's wealth; and how fair damsels—blush not, sweet ones!—have dug little graves in the garden, and bidden me, the sole guest, to an infant's funeral."

At this juncture—or in the bathetic pronouncements that immediately follow—the story almost resembles the Halloween horror film of today. "By sympathy of your human hearts for sin," the devil tells his assembly, you shall "exult to behold the whole earth one stain of guilt, one mighty blood spot." Such sensationalism, which suggests the puritan fantasy about America as the devil's last stronghold and his last chance before the millennium, strains even allegorical credibility. Like the horror film, its denouement is so denuded of ambiguity as to make a mockery of all that comes before it and of Brown as he wakes up to reality. What saves the tale from Hollywood is that although the contrived horror is the product of a dream, it nevertheless has real consequences for Brown. For like little Ilbrahim in "The Gentle Boy," he finds himself in a "practical allegory" in which exaggeration is reduced to fit the scope of reality. "The two females," Hawthorne writes of Dorothy and the boy's mother, "as they held each a hand of Ilbrahim, formed a practical allegory; it was rational piety and unbridled fanaticism contending for the empire of a young heart." Like the Quaker boy, Brown is pulled hither and thither between the real and imaginary worlds of his being. It is, as Roy R. Male suggests, Brown's involvement with the ambiguity of good and evil in the carnal knowledge of his wife: "For Faith and her pink ribbons, so pure in the sunlight, are fiendish at night."[16]

Ilbrahim is ultimately defeated by the practicality of his allegory, which insists that the physical world of "rational piety" (or puritan hegemony) must win out over Quaker idealism. In the same way, Brown must return to Salem Village divested of his faith in sex and go through the perfunctory motions of husband, father, and citizen. Or else, like Dimmesdale, he has gone too deeply into the metaphor of his sexuality, traversed the limits of human curiosity about its restorative power, and thus can never recover from the facts his allegory reveals. For Dimmesdale, sex had been safe in the moonlight of the forest and horrifying in the daylight of the village, but for both men it is the allegory with practical consequences that defeats them. In complaining about allegory in Hawthorne, Henry James wrote that it "is quite one of the lighter exercises of the imagination,"[17] but Poe was closer to the mark when he protested in his review of Hawthorne that "if allegory ever establishes a fact, it is by dint of overturning a fiction."[18] Brown's dream about sex in the New World, his puritan faith in its ecstatic utility, ultimately threatens the fiction of his existence as a goodman by devolving into a nightmare that exposes him as possibly being one with his libidinous fathers—whose deeds of the past lie in wait for him as surely as his suppressed dream of the past emerges in the middle of his "story."

"Young Goodman Brown," Hawthorne's story during the bachelorhood of his writing career, may also be his cautionary statement about the sexual idealism his own age encouraged. The sanctification of sex led to the same kind of allegorization of which he was supposedly so fond. As a fiction in the New World, this "aesthetic sport" was too remote from the raw reality of the American experience— which, lacking a visible past, had thus far resisted aesthetic iconization. Dante, as he learns in canto 27 of the *Inferno*, can never return to the Old World of mortality. And neither can Spenser's Red Cross Knight, who disappears after Book II of that allegory. Both visions are founded upon a Christianity exalted in European art and history, whereas Hawthorne's allegory takes place without such cultural artifacts, in the wilderness of the New World, where the Fall of Man is yet to happen. Here the dream is a jeremiad about to come true. Hawthorne's subject is America's subconscious sense of sin in the wake of a "virgin birth" that came about in the old way. Brown leaves his wife "a blessed angel on earth" to discover her past in the pink ribbon that flutters down before him in the forest. In the moonlight of his fears about Faith's innocence, he imagines her sexual communion with a figure who resembles not only himself but the fathers who fathered him. What he cannot accept, or completely believe, is the easy confluence of the past and present, or how the evil of the Old World and the good of the New "each imbue itself with the nature of the other." Thus, he returns to his wife "a distrustful, if not desperate man" who will nevertheless continue to have sex with her and sire "a goodly procession" of children and grandchildren.

Searching in the 1950s for a moral in the story, Professor Adams, (from whom I take my epigraph) argues that Brown should have acknowledged the reality of the toad in his imaginary garden and gotten on with the business of living in an imperfect world: "Because he refuses to do so he fails to reach maturity, which is a condition of being able to move in any direction one wishes and of being willing to take the consequences of whatever moves one makes." He calls this a state of freedom with responsibility, but that alliance is precisely the "neutral territory" that poses the central problem for Brown. Writing in the memory of World War II (and its movies of "happy" horrors) and before the impending disaster of Vietnam, a critic could perhaps treat Hawthorne's most enigmatic short story so didactically. Brown discovers in the tale that his sobriquet of Goodman is only half deserved, but Adams suggests that Brown should respond to his flaws with stoicism and thus proceed as the victor of his own world war (between the New and the Old). Fearing that his readers will have a "strong moral objection" to the advice that Brown absorb, if not forget, the evil he finds in himself, Adams preempts the criticism by curiously observing that the objection would be erroneously based on the "assumption that Brown is a real person, with a real choice between real courses of action. That is not the fact."[19]

Brown is not real, of course, but his allegory—or Hawthorne's—is, as an ironic emblem of New-World idealism. Like the letter *A*, it shimmers with alternate meanings, with the elements of the Imaginary and the Actual, to suggest the impending disaster. Brown is not at all sure what he has observed between the time he leaves his Faith and returns to her, but he now suspects that nature projects something more than specters and something less than ideological "facts." Freedom with responsibility requires a drama with a beginning, or the Fall, in the middle:

> On the Sabbath-day, when the congregation were singing a holy psalm, he could not listen, because an anthem of sin rushed loudly upon his ear, and drowned all the blessed strain. When the minister spoke from the pulpit, with power and fervid eloquence, and, with his hand on the open Bible, of the sacred truths of our religion, and of saint-like lives and triumphant deaths, and of future bliss or misery unutterable, then did Goodman Brown turn pale, dreading, lest the roof should thunder down upon the gray blasphemer and his hearers. Often, awakening suddenly at midnight, he shrank from the bosom of Faith, and at morning or eventide, when the family knelt at prayer, he scowled, and muttered to himself, and gazed sternly at his wife, and turned away.

Rather than reach maturity, as Adams suggests, Brown (or Hawthorne) realizes that to subscribe to a concept of benign development is to continue inexorably to delude oneself about freedom in the face of inevitable change. Brown does mature in the sense that he returns to the life following his dream-vision, but not as *Young* Goodman Brown, whose Faith—as he tells the devil at the outset of his dream—had kept him back awhile.

Whereas Dimmesdale finally insists on his destiny as a "complete" goodman and so dies out of his fiction as well as his fatherhood, Brown lives with the possibility that his dream in the dark wood is no more spectral than the ideological world to which he returns. A year after "Young Goodman Brown" was published, Ralph Waldo Emerson affirmed in *Nature* the transcendentalist belief that natural facts were signs of spiritual facts. To Brown, however, they become signs of spectral facts—evidence of a past that America had forgotten before it was over. For in the Dantesque version of the American odyssey, there is an Indian behind every tree and the devil in the best of us. In this context, Hawthorne's story, like the puritan America it represents, is an allegory waiting to happen. And when it does, its drama reveals not the millennium but the Salem witchcraft trials, in which the specters of the puritan imagination turn up in the middle of the story. In *The Scarlet Letter* the allegory of the dark wood might finally give way to puritan (and American) ideology, but "Young Goodman Brown" is more problematic because its dreamer wakes up to natural facts that may not mean any more than the nocturnal ones. In Dimmesdale, the later version of Brown, the older Hawthorne could safely moralize (as Adams does in Brown's case) that the minister, despite his maze, ought to have been truer to his "neutral" character. But the young Hawthorne, like Young Goodman Brown, who ages significantly in the story, is not so Emersonian as to suppose the worst might be spectral evidence of the ideological best. Hawthorne was content with—or resigned to—the mixture of good and evil, but to suggest the dangers of tilting this delicate balance, he allows his protagonist his adaptation of the Emersonian formula with regard to natural facts. As a result, there is in "Young Goodman Brown," as there is in such stories as "The Minister's Black Veil," "Roger Malvin's Burial," and "Rappaccini's Daughter," a fatal suspension of trust in appearances. Beatrice in "Rappaccini's Daughter," for example, looks spiritually pure but is chemically toxic. Like Dante's Beatrice, she is a nature of the "neutral territory"; yet in the *Vita nuova* her paradox proves to be spiritually elevating. In Giovanni's case, Beatrice's sexual function is so bewildering that he comes to question the terms of its ecstasy. Her bower looks like "the Eden of the present," but who is the father figure who cultivates it?

Lured into the garden by Rappaccini's ploy as much as Brown is tempted by his father to know more about his Faith, Giovanni suspends his faith in Beatrice's angelic appearance and ultimately loses his identity as a goodman. He flees from the "natural fact" that the sexual act imbues good with evil, or freedom with responsibility, and he is thus destined to live out his days in the "Eden of the present," where the flowers are poisoned by the past. Ever afterwards, experience (as Baglioni, another father figure, already knows) is best described in the manner of the scent given off by those flowers: "faint, but delicious; and yet, after all, by no means agreeable." More precise (and prescient) is their next victim, Giovanni, who initially denies the fact of the poison, saying that "odors, being a sort of element combined of the sensual and the spiritual, are apt to deceive us." The deception, however, derives from his attempt to spiritualize the sensual, to allegorize away its deadly temporality. Like Brown, he insists upon a New-World Beatrice who will take him to heaven without dying. He seeks not love but a sexual experience that will redeem him from the Old World of death and the old men he is doomed to follow. Giovanni wakes up from the allegorical endeavor with Beatrice's father, and Brown wakes up from his dream to father "a goodly procession" of children.

It may be said, without altering Hawthorne's theme in "Young Goodman Brown," that we can write no hopeful verse upon Brown's *tome*, for "his dying hour" is inscribed in his most lifelike experience. The "book" of Brown begins in the middle of the story because Hawthorne knew that the sense of life is always belated. Faith, we are told at the end of this tale of human frailty, "almost kissed her husband" upon his return from the vision in the forest. She does not because it is too late. Brown has lost his Faith in the dream that always anticipates something more than pink ribbons. Hawthorne placed great value in dreams, especially during the period in which "Young Goodman Brown" was composed, but he also feared that dreaming might consume him as a writer[20]—as it does Brown, who in the last analysis falls victim to his New-World imagination. "By some witchcraft," Hawthorne told Henry Wadsworth Longfellow in 1837, describing the previous decade of his life, "I have been carried apart from the main current of life, and find it impossible to get back again. . . . I have not lived, but only dreamed of living."[21] That musing, of course, yielded "a goodly procession" of dreamers, or *Wake*fields, who refuse to accept the Old World of freedom with responsibility. Goodman Brown enters the "Eden of the present" to discover in this twice-told tale about sexual knowledge and puritan ideology that the seasonal bloom of his Faith requires his gradual extinction. "Often, awakening at night," Hawthorne concludes, "he shrank from the bosom of Faith." What Brown has discerned in the sleeping figure of his wife is the specter of his own concupiscence, which rages against the fact that in the very next sentence of Hawthorne's story he will become "a hoary corpse." He outlives his first story, so to speak, to embrace the practical consequences of the second—an allegory that retells his tale according to Roger's version.

Notes

1. My epigraph is taken from the late Richard P. Adams ("Hawthorne's Provincial Tales," *New England Quarterly* 30 [March 1957]: 50), who examines "Young Goodman Brown" in the context of the "Provincial Tales," stories written about 1828 or 1829 and published separately between 1832 and 1836. They include "The Gentle Boy," "Roger Malvin's Burial," "My Kinsman, Major Molineux," "The Gray Champion," "The May-Pole of Merry Mount," and "Young Goodman Brown." As a group they represented Hawthorne's third unsuccessful attempt to bring his work thematically before the public, and their theme—as Adams and others see it—is the passage from nubility to nobility, or from adolescence to psychosexual maturity. Hawthorne's other attempts at book publication prior to the "Provincial Tales" were a cluster of stories

under the title "Seven Tales of My Native Land" and the subsequently suppressed *Fanshawe* (1828).

2. Rita K. Gollin, *Nathaniel Hawthorne and the Truth of Dreams* (Baton Rouge: Louisiana State University Press, 1979), 18.

3. My primary sources in Hawthorne are Roy Harvey Pearce, ed., *Nathaniel Hawthorne: Tales and Sketches* (New York: Library of America, 1982), and Millicent Bell, ed., *Nathaniel Hawthorne: Novels* (New York: Library of America, 1983).

4. David Levin, "Shadows of Doubt: Specter Evidence in Hawthorne's 'Young Goodman Brown,' " *American Literature* 34 (November 1962): 344–52; 346n. *Apparition* was changed to *figure* in Hawthorne's final revision of *Mosses from an Old Manse*.

5. See, for example, Hubert H. Hoeltje, "Hawthorne, Melville, and 'Blackness,' " *American Literature* 37 (March 1965): 41–51.

6. Frederick C. Crews, *The Sins of the Fathers: Hawthorne's Psychological Themes* (New York: Oxford University Press, 1966), 80–82.

7. Terence Martin, "Negative Structures in American Literature," *American Literature* 57 (March 1985): 1–22. One of the most extravagant series of negatives used to define America comes, as Martin notes, from Sylvester Judd's *Margaret* (1845): "We have no monarchical supremacy, no hereditary prerogatives, no patent nobility, no kings, . . . We have no resorts for pilgrims, no shrines for the devout . . . no traditions, legends, fables, and *scarcely a history*" (my emphasis).

8. Levin, "Shadows of Doubt," passim.

9. David Levin, *What Happened in Salem? Documents Pertaining to the Seventeenth-Century Witchcraft Trials*, 2d ed. (New York: Harcourt Brace Jovanovich, 1960), xi.

10. For a more literal reading of the historical context of the tale, see Michael J. Colacurcio, "Visible Sanctity and Specter Evidence: The Moral World of Hawthorne's 'Young Goodman Brown,' " *Essex Institute Historical Collections* 110 (1974), 259–99. Colacurcio argues that Brown's background as a recent convert under the rules of "the Half-Way Covenant" is "implied by the setting and compressed context." However, the reading that Brown is "but three months married" to Faith and thus guilty of "the 'unpardonable sin' of presumption" that he is one of the elect also serves my thesis that in Hawthorne's story Brown begins—as a result of the efficacy of his conversion—as one who has no credible past in the Old World.

11. Daniel Hoffman, *Form and Fable in American Fiction* (New York: Oxford University Press, 1961), 163.

12. John Updike, *Roger's Version* (New York: Alfred A. Knopf, 1986), 190, 275.

13. Harold W. Blodgett and Sculley Bradley, eds., *Leaves of Grass* (New York: W. W. Norton, 1973), 32.

14. T. O. Mabbott, ed., *Selected Poetry and Prose of Poe* (New York: The Modern Library, 1951), 378.

15. Jorge Luis Borges, *Other Inquisitions, 1937–1952*, trans. Ruth L. C. Simms (Austin: University of Texas Press, 1964), 49–50.

16. Roy R. Male, *Hawthorne's Tragic Vision*, 2d ed. (New York: W. W. Norton, 1964), 77.

17. Henry James, *Hawthorne* (New York: Harper & Bros., 1879), 61.

18. Mabbott, *Selected Poetry and Prose of Poe*, 378.

19. Adams, "Hawthorne's Provincial Tales," 56.

20. Gollin, *Hawthorne and the Truth of Dreams*, 45.

21. Quoted from Thomas Woodson, et al., eds., *Nathaniel Hawthorne: The Letters, 1813–1843.* (Columbus: Ohio University Press, 1984), 251.

Hawthorne's Gothic Tales   Allan Lloyd-Smith*

The Gothic genre inclines towards the sensational: offering exaggeration, superstition, fancy dress, folktale and legend, sadomasochism, exacerbated social relations, decadent family ties, concealment, pursuit, entrapment, abuse, and—perhaps above all else—paranoia. These are not the materials generally associated with Hawthorne; indeed, he always used them in quotation, as it were, with a degree of skepticism or even distaste. But then the Gothic was always already in quotation marks: it did not require Thomas Peacock's *Nightmare Abbey* or Jane Austen's *Northanger Abbey* to send it up. In fact, parody of the Gothic is virtually impossible. Who could exceed the tale of the Bleeding Nun in Maturin's *Melmoth,* or outdo *The Monk*?[1] There is, however, also a more genteel Gothic, in which lurid demonism and sexual depravity are hinted at rather than spelled out. Ann Radcliffe developed the form in this direction and generated its large, polite audience. In this mode there is a double displacement: the Gothic is performance (in quotation), acknowledged as an illusion that depends upon outworn superstition and literary models—but it relies upon innuendo and the presenting to the surface only the more acceptable frontage of such disreputable elements as sadomasochistic abuse. This double displacement was congenial both to Hawthorne's literary circumstances and to his personal preoccupations.

For Americans, the Gothic form had to be treated circumspectly. Washington Irving made a reputation by holding up tales like "The Adventure of the German Student" to an elegant and ironic recognition of implausibility: "I had it from the best authority," the narrator declares. "The student told it me himself. I saw him in a madhouse in Paris." And previously, Charles Brockden Brown elaborated a similar point by making Wieland's collapse into madness follow on his reading the latest book from Germany, which was, "according to custom, . . . minute and diffuse, and dictated by an adventurous and lawless fancy." Edgar Allan Poe's "Ligeia" perpetrated a similar undermining of its own necessary illusion: "I cannot, for my soul, remember how, when, or even precisely where, I first became acquainted with the lady Ligeia. . . . Yet I believe that I met her first and most frequently in some large old decaying city near the Rhine." In an aggressively Common-Sense tradition, and coming for the most part relatively late to the form, American writers indulged the passion for the Gothic that had sent several of them along the path to becoming authors (witness Hawthorne's early *Fanshawe,* Brown's later disavowal of his Gothic fictions, Poe's Byronic posturing), but with a sense that

* This essay was written specifically for this volume and is published here for the first time by permission of the author.

if fiction might be unbecoming in the new American society, Gothic fiction must be doubly so.[2] On the other hand, the massive popularity of Gothic fictions that can be deduced from lending-library lists and booksellers' advertisements suggests that the genre had an energy not to be suppressed by academic or clerical fulminations.

The contradiction between an official climate of opposition to imaginative fictions and an actual preponderance of taste in that direction still causes critics to perform uncomfortable gyrations. Donald Ringe, for example, in *American Gothic* (1982), comments that the same refrain occurs for decades in both fiction and criticism: "the rationalistic foundations of American thought are a serious hindrance not only to the writing but also to the enjoyment of fiction." But then he finds that American readers seem to have read tales of ghosts and specters with delight, and concludes "That all of them [American writers] introduce the marvelous into their novels and tales clearly indicates the strength of popular demand and the felt need of the writers to allow some play for the imagination in their fiction."[3] With popular demand so strong, and the desire of the writers to allow the imagination its due so confident as to bring the marvelous into constant exercise, how seriously can we take the assumed consensus from the pulpit and the lectern? In fact, the early nineteenth century was the great age of the marvelous in fiction, in America as in Britain and the rest of Europe, and so it is inaccurate to assert that "Writers of fiction were faced, therefore, with two equally unsatisfactory courses of action: to give full play to the imagination and write a fiction that, on its very basis, was necessarily suspect, or to concentrate on the unimaginative commonplaces of actuality."[4] This was no more a necessary choice then than ever, and misrepresents as mechanical the writers' selection of particular fictional modes.

It is also insufficiently noticed, when Nathaniel Hawthorne's own adherence to Common-Sense views (through his Bowdoin education at the hands of Thomas Upham) is brought into the question, that the ultimate thrust of the Common-Sense philosophy that dominated American thought may not have been exclusively to foster materialist interpretations of reality. What the usual interpretation misses is a considerable investment of the Common-Sense thinkers in the supernatural. Their philosophy, although Lockean in its inspiration, was developed specifically, even propagandistically, to counter such materialist readings of Locke as Condillac's, as well as to oppose both idealism of the Berkeleyan sort and the skepticism of Hume. Although materialist in their insistence on immediate cognition of a world of sense objects independent of the mind, the Common-Sense thinkers assumed an innate ability apart from experience when they proposed a universal moral sense, and they also posited some avenue to transcendent perception in the will, which was then seen as the most mysterious aspect of mind.[5] In accepting that a major area of intellectual conflict lay in the struggle between the Common-Sense philosophers and more Kantian romantic thinkers, we should not ignore the differences between the former and the materialists, especially not when considering the question of the Gothic supernatural.

The American literary inheritance was almost excessively supernaturalist in foundation. The tradition of puritan typology, offering readings of the world in terms of religious analogies and precursors, is a familiar example. The European Gothic genre was deeply rooted in protestant ideology, and it is immediately apparent that much of Hawthorne's gothicism derives not only from the protestant tradition that informs horror fiction but more specifically from the fierce self-scrutiny and polarizing of good and evil inherent in American puritanism. The lurid, demonic gothicism of "Young Goodman Brown" or "Ethan Brand," but equally the Edenic gothicism of "Rappaccini's Daughter," have been discussed extensively in these terms. Another tradition generally ignored by scholars is the buried occultism of earlier times, which survived in American as in European folkways and occasionally surfaced in the "official" culture in the form of astrology or the material in almanacs, as well as in more bizarre superstitions or witchcraft beliefs.[6] Novelists like Hawthorne or Cooper, with an interest in history or with an eye on the market for popular historical romance of the kind popularized by Scott, did find their native materials predisposed in that direction—a point that the notable dearth of castles and monasteries has perhaps encouraged critics to miss. Recently it has been argued that writers of the nineteenth century, including Hawthorne, may have covertly expressed guilt over aboriginal genocide;[7] this too might be expected to return as an interest in the supernatural, as in Robert Montgomery Bird's *Nick O' The Woods* (1837), where the apparently supernatural is naturally (but also, as is usual in this period, psychologically) explained.

Further cause for the adoption of supernaturalist modes of fiction may be seen in the prevalent European aesthetics largely derived from Burke's ideas about the validity of strong emotion, whether pleasurable or not, in the reception of art. The graveyard school in poetry and the Gothic style in fiction are related to the theory of the sublime articulated by Burke and his followers, which provided a basis for the aesthetic education of American writers through the works of Archibald Allison and Lord Kames.[8] European romantics, especially Coleridge, had a more profound and also an earlier effect on the American literary scene than is sometimes supposed. Both Washington Allston and Richard Henry Dana, Sr., for example, in the 1810s and 1820s, followed the Coleridgean interest in depicting the effects of apparently supernatural phenomena on a mind that supposes them to be real, in *Monaldi* and "Paul Felton," respectively.

In attempting to understand the causes of this movement in European art, critics have proposed the importance of historical change, the overthrowing of the church and aristocracy, Protestant prejudice against Catholicism, and subsequent fictional representation of such institutions as oppressive.[9] If so, the American experience, although significantly different, can be seen to embody many of the same features. The effect of revolutionary violence in providing a model for social and personal chaos emerges in the work of Brockden Brown, which shows how the experience of the French Revolution might impinge upon interpretations of the less-complete American revolutionary war.[10] The legacy of regicide produces supernaturalism in Hawthorne's writing in "The Grey Champion," where there is perhaps an implication of antipatriarchal guilt, both historical and personal in origin. Another area to be considered is the Hofstadterian thesis of displacement in the personal experience of American writers like Hawthorne: as dispossessed bourgeoisie, they are obsessed by absences and the search for a lost, unspecified other, which for Poe and Hawthorne, at least—and the same may be true for Melville or, differently, Cooper—had direct familial origins, but which also relates to the larger political question of the displacement of one order by another. Here it is possible to extend the analysis by comparison with the earlier development of romance. In Fredric Jameson's view,

> the problem raised by the persistence of romance as a mode is that of substitutions, adaptations, and appropriations, and raises the question of what, under wholly altered historical circumstances, can have been found to replace the raw materials of magic and Otherness which medieval romance found ready to hand in its socioeconomic environment. A history of romance as a mode becomes possible, in other words, when we explore the substitute codes and raw materials, which, in the increasingly secularized and rationalized world that emerges from the collapse of feudalism, are pressed into service to replace the older magical categories of Otherness which have now become so many dead languages.[11]

The Gothic explores the chaos of deranged authority structures, whether microcosmic (familial or personal madness) or macrocosmic (religious, political, or institutional pathologies), and generally considers the fortunes of an unprotected figure, usually female and therefore represented in the Gothic period as in need of male protection. The utopian resolution of the project is found in a restoration of benign patriarchy or marriage. Unfathered American writers (Poe, Hawthorne, and Melville among them) entered a state of insurrection against the lost father in the very act of writing fiction, given the cultural opprobrium then attached to such unworldliness, which was redoubled through their adoption of gothicism, for the reasons given above. But in Hawthorne's Gothic tales there is a further turn of the screw, since so many of them concern the symbolic aspects of historical insurrection—becoming a political model of psychological rebellion against the father (of which regicide represents the most extreme instance).

In Hawthorne's hands, the Gothic is "performed": it is not allowed to direct the form of the narrative but is instead manipulated and distorted ironically for purposes that include a recognition of its origins in destabilized personal and political situations. The series of four "Tales of the Province House" (1838–39)—"Howe's Masquerade," "Edward Randolph's Portrait," "Lady Eleanore's Mantle," and "Old Esther Dudley"—are exemplary.[12] In these tales, Gothic elements such as ghostly prophecies, the speaking portrait, a magic shawl, a haunting old woman, are used emblematically to comment on the power struggle between the authority of the King's representatives and that of the democratic American colonists. The figure of the persecuted female victim is progressively replaced by that of a woman of dignity and power: initially the revolutionary Miss Joliffe; next the whimsical and artistic but ingeniously effective Alice Vane, who uses Italian arts in the service of American ideals; then the aristocratic and imperious beauty Eleanore Rochcliffe; and finally the sole remaining keeper of the monarchical faith, Esther Dudley.

Characteristically, Hawthorne chooses a signifying object that is heavily coded yet retains a certain inscrutability. The scarlet letter is, of course, the great paradigm of this embroidery of coding, but one can see even in the Province-House tales how the Gothic convention of the mysterious, unreadable object is adapted for thematic purposes. In "Howe's Masquerade," the face of the final masquer is concealed from the audience and from the reader (but not from Howe himself) by a cloak. His reaction suggests a more-than-human intervention in the masquerade. "Edward Randolph's Portrait" is itself a featureless darkness, blackened by time or the diabolism of the subject's expression until temporarily made visible by the Italian arts of Alice Vane. The speaking portrait of Radcliffean romance becomes itself a commentary on the revelation of a meaning that is hypothesized as too extreme for the framing of art and is only made available through occultist intervention. Thus the convention of explained supernaturalism becomes an illustration of the precariousness of resisted meaning; in the next two tales, it takes on the additional complexity of a meaning resisted by the author. The embroidered mantle in "Lady Eleanore's Mantle" is the cause of an epidemic among the Americans, metaphorically an indication of the pestilential effects of class in aristocratic isolation and of the arrogance of beauty. Reading the story in relation to the meanings of The Scarlet Letter, however, encourages a suspicion that the mantle metonymically refers to female sexuality itself:

> Whether or no the recollections of those who saw her that evening were influenced by the strange events with which she was subsequently connected, so it was, that her figure ever after recurred to them as marked by something wild and unnatural, although, at the time, the general whisper was of her exceeding beauty, and of the indescribable charm which her mantle threw around her. Some close observers, indeed, detected a feverish flush and alternate paleness of countenance, with a corresponding flow and revulsion of spirits, and once or twice a painful and helpless betrayal of lassitude, as if she were on the point of sinking to the ground. (IX, 278)

The characteristics of disease are described in terms close to those of sexual excitation, as the mantle—embroidered by a dying woman and perhaps "owing the fantastic grace of its conception to the delirium of approaching death," which was said to give its wearer a new and untried grace every time she put it on—weaves its spell.[13]

One of the complications of Hawthorne's positioning of himself as narrator can be seen by comparing his version of the Gothic with the conventional one. Leslie Fiedler remarks that "the guilt which underlies the gothic and motivates its plots is the guilt of the revolutionary haunted by the (paternal) past which he has been striving to destroy."[14] This, however, is only one part of Hawthorne's implication in these plots. Without real dignity or power, the weakest of Hawthorne's heroines in this series, Old Esther Dudley, has nevertheless force to express the narrator's perplexed situation. The narrator's sympathy with the authoritarian structures that have grown out of the "Revolution" is no greater than his sympathy with her, last representative of a vanished past that he—not one of John Hancock's "new race of men, living no longer in the past" but, rather, one of the "children of the past" conjured by Old Esther's stories—cannot but revere (IX, 301; IX, 197). Evan Carton's comment on this is perceptive: "For Hawthorne's narrator, then, British illusions and American realities (or vice versa) are dangerously conflated in the final legend, and he, in his post-revolutionary situation, is no less alienated from the authority of the revolution than from the authority of the crown."[15]

A certain blankness is willfully cultivated at such points of crisis in affiliation: Hawthorne's concluding gesture seems otherwise unwarranted by the material preceding it, which is, after all, a mild-enough anecdote of an old woman's deluded attachment to the old order. "I retired unbidden, and would advise Mr. Tiffany to lay hold of another auditor, being resolved not to show my face in the Province-

House for a good while hence—if ever" (IX, 303). As so often in reading Hawthorne, we are given the sense of something withheld, which might be simply an alienated writer's remark (the audience is instructed to expect no more Province-House tales, since their author is disgruntled by a lack of recognition) or a significant clue to his unresolved political and personal contradictions (the invoked specter of Esther as a woman, a loyalist, and a betrayed keeper of the faith touches some sensitive chords).[16]

In the concluding tale, the meaning of the key and the mirror is both vertiginously obvious and, finally, concealed from the reader. Esther Dudley is a faithful custodian of the key, which she eventually surrenders to the wrong governor (i.e., the revolutionary, Hancock). The mirror is her means of conjuring specters of the past and parallels her ability to conjure the past through stories told to the children ("she led them by the hand into the chambers of her own desolate heart, and made childhood's fancy discern the ghosts that haunted there" [IX, 297])—which parallels Hawthorne's narrator's ability to bring the past to life, which, in turn echoes Hawthorne's own. Key and mirror may well be sexual symbols of an obvious kind, yet their full meaning exceeds any such identification. Esther Dudley is a frustrated old maid, true; but she is frustrated by history, not by her personal circumstances.

Immediately after the Province-House tales in *Twice-told Tales*, Hawthorne placed "The Haunted Mind," which serves to psychologize some of the traditional Gothic motifs in the exploration of semiconscious or hypnagogic states of mind. The relation between the Gothic and what was later to be colonized as the Freudian unconscious is illuminated by Jameson's comment that "in the first great period of bourgeois hegemony, the reinvention of romance finds its strategy in the substitution of new positivities (theology, psychology, the dramatic metaphor) for the older magical content."[17] Hawthorne, as we have seen, resorts to all three of these "substitutions," but especially to the possibilities of psychology: "In the depths of every heart, there is a tomb and a dungeon, though the lights, the music, and the revelry above may cause us to forget their existence, and the buried ones, or prisoners, whom they hide. But sometimes, and oftenest at midnight, those dark receptacles are flung open" (IX, 306). In this sketch, feelings of guilt, sorrow, disappointment, fatality, and shame are represented as spectral beings beside the sleeper, in traditional Gothic figuration: "What if remorse should assume the features of an injured friend? What if the fiend should come in woman's garments, with a pale beauty amid sin and desolation, and lie down by your side? What if he should stand at your bed's foot, in the likeness of a corpse, with a bloody stain upon the shroud?" (IX, 307). What if, in other words, Young Goodman Brown were right? This conception is what the commonplace disparagement of fiction was intended to avert. Brown has no business looking for evil in his fellows, says one critic. "With a deeper sense of his own guilt he would not have gone into the forest, and instead of shrinking from his fellow men he would have discovered a parallel truth: the good that can be perceived in Salem village in the light of day" (this comment is not from 1850 but from 1982).[18] But Hawthorne's use of the Gothic to explore psychology necessarily resisted optimistic normalizing and relished a certain area of moral depravity located between the certainties allowed by his culture. His work is therefore resistant to the idea of right reading, which is often parodied and subverted by his mockingly inappropriate attached "morals."

The "dramatic metaphor" that Jameson identifies, along with theology and psychology, as one of the substitutions for older magic in the romance form, should properly extend to the whole idea of performance, including the visual arts. "The Prophetic Pictures" is a tale in which Hawthorne takes up the Gothic motif of the speaking picture and twists it to his own predilections. The story concerns a preternaturally acute artist who, foreseeing the fate of two young people through their expressions, paints portraits of them as they will become and makes a sketch of the murder or attempted murder he predicts. In time, the predictions are proved correct. Hawthorne concludes, "Is there not a deep moral in the tale? Could the result of one, or all our deeds, be shadowed forth and set before us—some would call it Fate and hurry onward—others be swept along by their passionate desires—and none be turned aside by the PROPHETIC PICTURES" (IX, 182). But this moral is characteristically obscured. Walter's attempt to murder his beloved Elinor is given no explanation and is prevented by the painter himself, who opportunely returns. On the other hand, the painter who prevents the evil deed may also be its instigator, as numerous remarks make clear: "Reading other bosoms, with an acuteness almost preternatural, the painter failed to see the disorder of his own"; and "Was not his own the form in which that Destiny had embodied itself, and he a chief agent of the coming evil which he had foreshadowed?" (IX, 189, 181). Measured against that touchstone of natural virtue, the American wilderness, he is found wanting—feeling that he could as soon paint the roar of Niagara as anything else that makes the cataract—and paints Indian chiefs and girls, fortresses and French partisans instead. Still, Hawthorne's own position regarding the wonders of American nature is also equivocal; he too achieves the picturesque rather than the sublime. The portraits haunt the artist, as they do their subjects, which makes the artist a victim of his own triumphant insight. So Hawthorne has created a closed circle in which the latent qualities of Walter and Elinor communicate themselves to the artist in a vision of murder.

But this vision, incorporated in the portraits' expressions and the action in his rough sketch (which Elinor sees and Walter may have seen), suggests back to them a fatal event, which in turn the artist forestalls. Art and life are brought face to face, but the result is a standoff between the natural guilt of Walter and the artificial guilt of the painter. The actual cause of either is left unwritten; a gap in the narrative allows slippage and the play of inference. Art and life are inimical, their union unholy, and their progeny demonic—that is all we are told.

In Hawthorne's Gothic, then, elaborate false mystifications point to the actual secret involving guilty voyeuristic eroticism, attacks on authority figures, fetishism, the abuse of images, the power of replication, and the uncanniness of repetition—and all of these attach to the idea of art and the artist-magus figure. "Drowne's Wooden Image," a tale of 1844, is a particularly vivid example. Drowne is portrayed as an Ur figure; the originator of art in primitive materials, thus a model of elemental powers, and therefore a model especially of the originary American artist. Hawthorne is concerned to show respect for this figure; but he also insists on showing how he overtakes this artist in sophistication, by stepping outside of him and drawing his frame. The revenge of the artist appears in Drowne's little image of his rival—a reduced Captain Hunnewell, with his diminished (phallic) telescope—which serves as a sign to a nautical instrument maker's shop. But it also appears in Hawthorne's own reduction of Drowne the artist to Deacon Drowne, the unfulfilled bachelor, with his progeny of "abortions" in wood.

Drowne was, I think, based on William Rush, doyen of the early American figurehead makers. Thomas Eakins's later reduction of the woodcarver Rush to a dimly lit clod, in his painting "William Rush Carving His Allegorical Figure of the Schuylkill River" (1876–77), stages the relationship between painter and sculptor in a curiously similar and revealing way.[19] The dimly lit woodcarver Rush is in the left background; his naked model, seen from the left side, her body brightly illuminated from the left, is at center right; her chaperone is on her right; and a chair, piled high with the model's clothes and brilliantly lit, stands in the center foreground. The figure that Rush carves, however, is clothed in classical drapery. There are hieroglyphic scrawls on the wall, wooden figureheads and carved scrolls of wood on the floor; the model holds a heavy book to produce the stresses required for the allegorical figure, who holds a bittern on her shoulder. The sculpture was famous in its day, and Rush (1756–1833) was celebrated as a ship's carver—probably America's most famous— before he became known for his other work. The relationship between Eakins and his subject seems to parallel rather exactly the stance adopted by Hawthorne toward his ship's carver and wood sculptor,

Drowne. Eakins's disparagement of Rush is as marked as the respect for him: Rush carves a crude wooden figure in a shadowed corner of the studio, whereas the painter controls the whole scene, possessing it in an incandescence of light that stresses the model's erotic nudity and the beautiful, sensuous textures of her discarded clothes. It is Eakins, not Rush, who has posed this naked model, set her clothes alight with the sun, and placed Rush in a craftsman's obscurity, portraying him as a blockhead who fails to catch the radiance of the real thing. Eakins possesses the model's beauty and the culture (signified by the model's clothes) to which we are invited to compare the clichéd draperies that Rush invents to dress *his* figure. And although Eakins's position mirrors Rush's, it is also our position as spectators and therefore is privileged; access to the nudity of the model is actually Eakins's/ours.

All this seems to reflect revealingly on Hawthorne's activity in "Drowne's Wooden Image," where the issue of clothing is similarly vexed. Drowne's model has a voluptuous mouth and bewitching coquetry; she is not naked, but erotically clothed in "foreign" South Seas dress—fantastic, yet "not too fantastic to be worn decorously in the street"—and with "strange, rich flowers of Eden" in her hat (X, 312,314). Hawthorne, in relation to Drowne, is in the place of Eakins in relation to Rush, which is also the place of the reader, who can be expected to suspend disbelief and pretend to be mystified along with the populace, but to whom the mystery of the statue's apparent coming to life is in fact transparent.

What this pictorial excursion enables us to appreciate is how relations of power are invoked within a simple positioning of the sort Hawthorne ingenuously proposes in so many of his Gothic tales. The artist figure—with which we may associate also the figure of the magus (Rappaccini), the philosopher (Ethan Brand), or the scientist (Alymer, in "The Birthmark")—exercises a power that extends into the sexual dimension but attracts, commensurately, a stricture of guilt that saturates the narrative and causes (or is made evident in) a redoubling complexity of structure and event. And this castigation of the artist-magus-scientist is once again a handing on of the cultural opprobrium attracted by the American writer, which the Gothic exacerbates by its excess and sensationalism but also evades by its qualities of disrecognition, disavowal, and stylized art performance.

Notes

1. Ken Russell's attempt at outrage in his film *Gothic* (1987) proves the point: it merely aligns itself with the established models of late eighteenth-century excess. In fact, the production is almost too tasteful.

2. See Michael Allen, *Poe and the British Magazine Tradition* (New York: Oxford

University Press, 1969) for evidence of the unfashionableness of Gothic sensationalism by this time. On the Common-Sense culture, Terence Martin's *The Instructed Vision: Scottish Common Sense Philosophy and The Origins of American Fiction* (Bloomington: Indiana University Press, 1961) is a useful source of information.

3. Donald Ringe, *American Gothic: Imagination and Reason in Nineteenth-Century Fiction* (Lexington: The University Press of Kentucky, 1982), 9. Figures given on pp. 13–17, based on the catalogs of libraries and booksellers in the late eighteenth century, indicate the great force of that popular demand.

4. Ringe, *American Gothic,* 8.

5. For example, Thomas Upham, *Elements of Mental Philosophy* (Boston: Wells, 1831), vol. 3.

6. On the Protestant tradition and gothicism, see Victor Sage, *Horror Fiction in the Protestant Tradition* (London: Macmillan, 1988). On persisting occultism, see Herbert Leventhal, *In the Shadow of the Enlightenment: Occultism and Renaissance Science in Eighteenth-Century America* (New York: New York University Press, 1976).

7. Robert Clark, *History, Ideology and Myth in American Fiction, 1823–1852* (London: Macmillan, 1984), 130 and passim.

8. See Samuel Holt Monk, *The Sublime* (Ann Arbor: University of Michigan Press, 1960); Patricia Meyer Spacks, *The Insistence of Horror* (Cambridge: Harvard University Press, 1962); A. G. Smith, *The Analysis of Motives* (Amsterdam: Rodopi, 1980), and Mary Arensberg, *The American Sublime* (New York: New York State University Press, 1986). On the common-sense tradition and its influence in America, see J. W. Fay, *American Psychology Before William James* (New York: Octagon Books, 1966).

9. David Punter, *The Literature of Terror* (London: Longman, 1980); Rosemary Jackson, *Fantasy* (London: Methuen, 1981), and Sage, *Horror Fiction.*

10. Shirley Samuels's article "Plague and Politics in 1793: Arthur Mervyn," 27 (Summer 1985); 225–46, weaves together the yellow fever, Jacobinism, supposedly loose French morals, and the Reign of Terror in Brockden Brown's fiction.

11. Frederic Jameson, "Magical Narratives," in *The Political Unconscious: Narrative as a Socially Symbolic Act* (London: Methuen, 1981), 131.

12. Nathaniel Hawthorne, *Twice-told Tales,* in *The Centenary Edition of the Works of Nathaniel Hawthorne* (Columbus: Ohio State University Press, 1974), vol. 9. Hereafter cited parenthetically.

13. On the intricate relationship between embroidery and female sexuality in Hawthorne's writing, see Allan Lloyd-Smith, *Eve Tempted* (London: Croom Helm, 1984).

14. Leslie Fiedler, *Love and Death in the American Novel,* rev. ed. (New York: Delta, 1966), 129.

15. Evan Carton, *The Rhetoric of American Romance* (Baltimore: The Johns Hopkins University Press, 1985), 188.

16. Consider Hawthorne's response to the death of his mother: he wrote *The Scarlet Letter.* Or the betrayal implicit in his reluctance to tell his family—his mother and sisters—about his engagement to Sophia Peabody.

17. Jameson, "Magical Narratives," 134.

18. Ringe, *American Gothic,* 161.

19. Michael Fried has explored some of the implications of this painting in *Realism, Writing, Disfiguration: On Thomas Eakins and Stephen Crane* (Chicago: University of Chicago Press, 1987). Fried's discussion of the painting raises some interesting questions about the relations between painting and writing. But Fried stresses the

competition between the pictorial form of representation and that of writing or drawing (which he approximates); the more elementary distinction, and surely the more powerful, is the dissonance between painting and sculpting (or, in Hawthorne's case, writing and sculpting).

CHRONOLOGY OF THE TALES

1830   "The Battle Omen" in the *Salem Gazette*, 2 November.
     "The Hollow of the Three Hills" in the *Salem Gazette*, 12 November, collected in *Twice-told Tales*, 1837.
     "An Old Woman's Tale" in the *Salem Gazette*, 21 December.
     "Sights from a Steeple" in the *Token* for 1831, collected in *Twice-told Tales*, 1837.
     "The Haunted Quack" in the *Token* for 1831.

1831   "The Wives of the Dead" in the *Token* for 1832, collected in *The Snow-Image*, 1852.
     "My Kinsman, Major Molineux" in the *Token* for 1832, collected in *The Snow-Image*, 1852.
     "Roger Malvin's Burial" in the *Token* for 1832, collected in *Mosses from an Old Manse*, 1846.
     "The Gentle Boy" in the *Token* for 1832, collected in *Twice-told Tales*, 1837.

1832   "The Seven Vagabonds" in the *Token* for 1833, collected in *Twice-told Tales*, 1842.
     "The Canterbury Pilgrims" in the *Token* for 1833, collected in *The Snow-Image*, 1852.

1834   "The Haunted Mind" in the *Token* for 1835, collected in *Twice-told Tales*, 1842.
     "Alice Doane's Appeal" in the *Token* for 1835.
     "The Village Uncle" in the *Token* for 1835, collected in *Twice-told Tales*, 1842.
     "Little Annie's Ramble" in *Youth's Keepsake* for 1835, collected in *Twice-told Tales*, 1837.

"Passages from a Relinquished Work" in the *New-England Magazine*, November-December, collected in *Mosses from an Old Manse*, 1846.

"Mr. Higginbotham's Catastrophe" in the *New-England Magazine*, December, collected in *Twice-told Tales*, 1837.

1835   "The Gray Champion" in the *New-England Magazine*, February, collected in *Twice-told Tales*, 1837.

"My Visit to Niagara" in the *New-England Magazine*, February.

"Old News I" in the *New-England Magazine*, February, collected in *The Snow-Image*, 1852.

"Old News II (The Old French War)" in the *New-England Magazine*, March, collected in *The Snow-Image*, 1852.

"Young Goodman Brown" in the *New-England Magazine*, April, collected in *Mosses from an Old Manse*, 1846.

"Old News III (The Old Tory)" in the *New-England Magazine*, May, collected in *The Snow-Image*, 1852.

"Wakefield" in the *New-England Magazine*, May, collected in *Twice-told Tales*, 1837.

"The Ambitious Guest" in the *New-England Magazine*, June, collected in *Twice-told Tales*, 1842.

"Graves and Goblins" in the *New-England Magazine*, June.

"A Rill from the Town-Pump" in the *New-England Magazine*, June, collected in *Twice-told Tales*, 1837.

"The White Old Maid" in the *New-England Magazine*, July, collected in *Twice-told Tales*, 1842.

"The Vision of the Fountain" in the *New-England Magazine*, August, collected in *Twice-told Tales*, 1837.

"The Devil in Manuscript" in the *New-England Magazine*, November, collected in *The Snow-Image*, 1852.

"Sketches from Memory. Nos. I and II" in the *New-England Magazine*, November and December, collected in *Mosses from an Old Manse*, 1854.

"The Wedding Knell" in the *Token* for 1836, collected in *Twice-told Tales*, 1837.

"The May-Pole of Merry Mount" in the *Token* for 1836, collected in *Twice-told Tales*, 1837.

"The Minister's Black Veil" in the *Token* for 1836, collected in *Twice-told Tales*, 1837.

1836   "Old Ticonderoga" in the *American Monthly Magazine*, February, collected in *The Snow-Image*, 1852.

"A Visit to the Clerk of the Weather" in the *American Monthly Magazine*, May.

"Monsieur du Miroir" in the *Token* for 1837, collected in *Mosses from an Old Manse*, 1846.

"Mrs. Bullfrog" in the *Token* for 1837, collected in *Mosses from an Old Manse*, 1846.

"Sunday at Home" in the *Token* for 1837, collected in *Twice-told Tales*, 1837.

"The Man of Adamant" in the *Token* for 1837, collected in *The Snow-Image*, 1852.

"David Swan" in the *Token* for 1837, collected in *Twice-told Tales*, 1837.

"The Great Carbuncle" in the *Token* for 1837, collected in *Twice-told Tales*, 1837.

"Fancy's Show Box" in the *Token* for 1837, collected in *Twice-told Tales*, 1837.

"The Prophetic Pictures" in the *Token* for 1837, collected in *Twice-told Tales*, 1837.

1837   "Dr. Heidegger's Experiment" in the *Knickerbocker*, January, collected in *Twice-told Tales*, 1837.

"A Bell's Biography," in the *Knickerbocker*, March, collected in *The Snow-Image*, 1852.

"Fragments from the Journal of a Solitary Man" in the *American Monthly Magazine*, July.

"Edward Fane's Rosebud" in the *Knickerbocker*, September, collected in *Twice-told Tales*, 1842.

"The Toll Gatherer's Day" in the *Democratic Review*, October, collected in *Twice-told Tales*, 1842.

"Sylph Etherege" in the *Token* for 1838, collected in *The Snow-Image*, 1852.

"Peter Goldthwaite's Treasure" in the *Token* for 1838, collected in *Twice-told Tales*, 1842.

"Endicott and the Red Cross" in the *Token* for 1838, collected in *Twice-told Tales*, 1842.

"Night Sketches" in the *Token* for 1838, collected in *Twice-told Tales*, 1842.

"The Shaker Bridal" in the *Token* for 1838, collected in *Twice-told Tales*, 1842.

1838   "Foot-prints on the Sea-shore" in the *Democratic Review*, January, collected in *Twice-told Tales*, 1842.

"Time's Portraiture," a *Salem Gazette* broadside issued
1 January.

"Snow-flakes" in the *Democratic Review*, February, collected in *Twice-told Tales*, 1842.

"The Three-fold Destiny" in the *American Monthly Magazine*, March, collected in *Twice-told Tales*, 1842.

"Tales of the Province-House. No. I. Howe's Masquerade" in the *Democratic Review*, May, collected in
Twice-told Tales, 1842.

"Tales of the Province-House. No. II. Edward Randolph's Portrait" in the *Democratic Review*, July,
collected in *Twice-told Tales*, 1842.

"Chippings With a Chisel" in the *Democratic Review*,
September, collected in *Twice-told Tales*, 1842.

"Tales of the Province-House. No. III. Lady Eleanor's
Mantle" in the *Democratic Review*, December, collected in *Twice-told Tales*, 1842.

1839   "Tales of the Province-House. No. IV. Old Esther Dudley" in the *Democratic Review*, January, collected
in *Twice-told Tales*, 1842.

"The Sister Years," a *Salem Gazette* pamphlet issued 1
January, collected in *Twice-told Tales*, 1842.

"The Lily's Quest" in the *Southern Rose*, 19 January,
collected in *Twice-told Tales*, 1842.

1840   "John Inglefield's Thanksgiving" in the *Democratic Review*, March, collected in *The Snow-Image*, 1852.

1842   "A Virtuoso's Collection" in the *Boston Miscellany*, May,
collected in *Mosses from an Old Manse*, 1846.

1843   "The Old Apple Dealer" in *Sargent's Magazine*, January,
collected in *Mosses from an Old Manse*, 1846.

"The Antique Ring" in *Sargent's Magazine*, February.

"The Hall of Fantasy" in the *Pioneer*, February, collected in *Mosses from an Old Manse*, 1846.

"The New Adam and Eve" in the *Democratic Review*,
February, collected in *Mosses from an Old Manse*,
1846.

"The Birth-mark" in the *Pioneer*, March, collected in
Mosses from an Old Manse, 1846.

"Egotism; or the Bosom-Serpent" in the *Democratic
Review*, March, collected in *Mosses from an Old
Manse*, 1846.

"The Procession of Life" in the *Democratic Review*, April, collected in *Mosses from an Old Manse*, 1846.

"The Celestial Rail-road" in the *Democratic Review*, May, collected in *Mosses from an Old Manse*, 1846.

"Buds and Bird-Voices" in the *Democratic Review*, June, collected in *Mosses from an Old Manse*, 1846.

"Little Daffydowndilly" in *Boys' and Girls' Magazine*, August, collected in *The Snow-Image*, 1852.

"Fire-Worship" in the *Democratic Review*, December, collected in *Mosses from an Old Manse*, 1846.

1844 "The Christmas Banquet" in the *Democratic Review*, January, collected in *Mosses from an Old Manse*, 1846.

"A Good Man's Miracle" in the *Child's Friend*, February.

"The Intelligence Office" in the *Democratic Review*, March, collected in *Mosses from an Old Manse*, 1846.

"Earth's Holocaust" in *Graham's Magazine*, May, collected in *Mosses from an Old Manse*, 1846.

"The Artist of the Beautiful" in the *Democratic Review*, June, collected in *Mosses from an Old Manse*, 1846.

"Drowne's Wooden Image" in *Godey's Lady's Magazine*, July, collected in *Mosses from an Old Manse*, 1846.

"A Select Party" in the *Democratic Review*, July, collected in *Mosses from an Old Manse*, 1846.

"A Book of Autographs" in the *Democratic Review*, November.

"Rappaccini's Daughter" in the *Democratic Review*, December, collected in *Mosses from an Old Manse*, 1846.

1845 "P.'s Correspondence" in the *Democratic Review*, April, collected in *Mosses from an Old Manse*, 1846.

1846 "The Old Manse" in *Mosses from an Old Manse*, 1846.

1849 "Main-street" in *Aesthetic Papers*, collected in *The Snow-Image*, 1852.

1850 "Ethan Brand" (under the title "The Unpardonable Sin") in the *Boston Weekly Museum*, 5 January, collected in *The Snow-Image*, 1852.

"The Great Stone Face" in the *National Era*, 24 January, collected in *The Snow-Image*, 1852.

"The Snow-Image" in the *International Miscellany*, November, collected in *The Snow-Image*, 1852.

1852   "Feathertop" in the *International Monthly Magazine*, February and March, collected in *Mosses from an Old Manse*, 1854.

INDEX